Preserving German
Texan Identity

Number 45

Elma Dill Russell Spencer Series
in the West and Southwest

Preserving German Texan Identity

Reminiscences of
William A. Trenckmann,
1859–1935

Edited by Walter L. Buenger and
Walter D. Kamphoefner

TEXAS A&M UNIVERSITY PRESS
COLLEGE STATION

This paper meets the requirements of ANSI/NISO Z39.48–1992
(Permanence of Paper).
Binding materials have been chosen for durability.
Manufactured in the United States of America

Library of Congress Cataloging-in-Publication Data

Names: Trenckmann, William A., 1859–1935, author. | Buenger, Walter L.,
    editor. | Kamphoefner, Walter D., editor.
Title: Preserving German Texan identity: reminiscences of William A.
    Trenckmann, 1859–1935 / edited by Walter L. Buenger and Walter D.
    Kamphoefner.
Other titles: Erlebtes und Beobachtetes. English
Description: First edition. | College Station: Texas A&M University Press,
    [2019] | Series: Number 45: Elma Dill Russell Spencer series in the West
    and Southwest | Includes bibliographical references and index. |
    Identifiers: LCCN 2018021209 (print) | LCCN 2018026359 (ebook) | ISBN
    9781623497149 (ebook) | ISBN 9781623497132 | ISBN 9781623497132 (printed
    case: alk. paper)
Subjects: LCSH: Trenckmann, William A., 1859–1935. | German American
    teachers—Texas—Biography. | Teachers—Texas—Biography. | German
    American journalists—Texas—Biography. | Journalists—Texas—Biography. |
    German American publishers—Texas—Biography. |
    Publishers—Texas—Biography. | German American
    legislators—Texas—Biography. | Legislators—Texas—Biography. |
    Agricultural and Mechanical College of Texas—Alumni and
    alumnae—Biography.
Classification: LCC F395.G3 (ebook) | LCC F395.G3 T7413 2019 (print) | DDC
    920.0092/310764—dc23
LC record available at https://lccn.loc.gov/2018021209

Cover photo courtesy of Bellville Historical Society.

Contents

Contents

Illustrations

Tables

Preface

William A. Trenckmann's memoir, titled *Erlebtes und Beobachtetes* (Experiences and Observations), was first published in his Austin, Texas, newspaper, *Das Wochenblatt*, beginning with its fortieth anniversary issue on September 17, 1931, and continuing intermittently until the last installment on February 16, 1933. Two appendixes previously authored by Trenckmann present alternative takes on material covered in the memoir—one of them dealing with his experiences at Texas A&M, originally written in English. These three documents, edited and annotated here, form the heart of Trenckmann's autobiographical work, his reminiscences of days gone by and of the people and major events in his life. They also provide a close look at Trenckmann himself, who, as a student in the first class of Texas A&M, a bilingual public schoolteacher, a German-language newspaper editor, and an office holder, served as a go-between who moved back and forth between the Anglo-dominated world of Texas and his culturally familiar German Texan world. As he says in his memoir, he was drawn in part to the newspaper business because he could better educate and inform his German readers about English-speaking Texas. Fluent in both languages, cautious, and even-tempered, he was in many ways an ideal person for this task. He sought to equip German Texans to operate as equal members in public life in Texas. Tellingly, however, he sought not to assimilate German Texans totally into the Anglo majority, but to preserve their distinctive identity.

As we wrote the introduction, prepared the annotation, and ensured we had the best possible translations of Trenckmann's autobiographical writings, the implications of our work for the history of German Texans became clear. Go-betweens such as Trenckmann helped German Texans adjust and even thrive in new surroundings and challenging times. Adjusting and thriving, however, did not mean total amalgamation into the Anglo world. As late as Trenckmann's death in 1935, German Texans remained separated by language and culture from Anglo Texans, and even the pressures of World War I had not erased the borders between the two groups. Anglos and German Texans, however, were not the only distinct groups in Texas, and Trenckmann also served as a go-between who helped negotiate German Texan attitudes and actions toward African American Texans. He proudly related how he encouraged German Texans to accept and support the exclusion of black voters from the political process. Take away then from Trenckmann's autobiographical writings an interesting and revealing story, but also remember the role of go-betweens, the persistence of a distinctive German Texan identity into the 1930s, and the reality that those German Texans grew closer to the dominant Anglo Texan model of white supremacy.

Trenckmann's revealing memoir was translated in the late 1950s by his children, retired lawyer William Trenckmann and German teacher Else Trenckmann. According to William's grandson, Stuart Strong, who witnessed their work while visiting on summer vacation, they sat around a table working together on a handwritten version that Else then typed. Given their contextual knowledge and language competence, the present editors have generally trusted the accuracy of their translation. But wherever a passage sounded unidiomatic or ambiguous, we have gone back to consult the original German. Even Trenckmann's wife reproved him for his "tapeworm sentences," and on rare occasions we split one that was too long and cumbersome. More frequently, we silently divided excessively long paragraphs at logical break points and modified punctuation to ease readability. Trenckmann started out providing section titles but omitted them in later segments, so we have adopted or adapted what his children provided. A couple of textual conventions should be noted: the German umlauts ä, ö, and ü have been rendered as ae, oe, and ue, respectively, as the translators did. Terms, often from English, that were in quotation marks in the original are rendered in quotation marks with the exception of *Texas A&M*. Instead of underlining or italics for emphasis, the German convention in Fraktur type was to print a word *g e s p e r r t*, or with a space between each letter; these occurrences are rendered in italics.

The two editors divided the work of drafting the introduction and annotations according to our respective areas of expertise: Kamphoefner for matters of immigration, ethnicity, and the German language; Buenger for matters of politics, race relations, and economics. But we have read and vetted one another's work and stand behind it all. The editors' introduction was designed to place Trenckmann's life and career in context, particularly with respect to the family and community in which he grew up and the communities in which he spent his adult life and political work. Annotations were added to clarify unfamiliar institutions and references and, with people of German ethnicity, to distinguish between the immigrant and American-born generations in order to gauge the speed of acculturation or the persistence of ethnic culture and language. On a few rare occasions erroneous assertions required correction. For Trenckmann and his immediate family, full citations of census information was provided, but this seemed excessive for other persons. However, absent other documentation, one can assume information was obtained from US Census manuscripts, immigrant passenger lists, and other associated material such as Texas Death Certificates and unofficial data on Find-a-Grave.com, indexed and made accessible through ancestry.com. Except for *Das Wochenblatt*, newspapers cited were accessed through the Portal to Texas History of the University of North Texas Libraries.

The editors would like to thank Dieter Lubinski and the Wesenslebener Heimatverein as well as Jürgen Trenkmann of Kamp-Lintfort and Carsten H. O. Tüngler for information on the German background of the Trenckmann family. Jonathan Sperber and Heinrich Best generously shared their insights on the 1848 Revolution. We are also indebted to James Hering of the Austin County Historical Commission and Paul P. Coan, John Grube, and fellow members of the Bellville Historical Society for information and material from the scenes of the first half of Trenckmann's life. Liz Hicks, the genealogy editor of the German Texan Heritage Society, also shared tips. We would especially like to thank Babette Hale and her fellow board members of the Friends of Winedale, along with Helen Trenckmann, for permission to reprint "Christmas in Troubled Times." We also thank Don Carleton, the Executive Director of the Dolph Briscoe Center for American History, University of Texas at Austin, where a typescript of the translated memoir is housed. Carleton generously provided us permission to use the translated memoir. Thanks also to Emily Nash, who entered that translation into Microsoft Word. Austin County native James Woodrick graciously allowed us to use his map of the Millheim community. James Kearney helpfully shared his draft translation of Trenckmann's roman à clef, *Die Lateiner am Possum Creek*. As usual, Bill Page proved to be an invaluable resource on the history of Bryan and Texas A&M University and called our attention to the material in the appendix "1907 *Long Horn*."

In the course of the project we made the acquaintance of three branches of the fifth generation of Trenckmanns in Texas, all now living in Austin, and we are grateful for the reminiscences and family material shared by Wood Bouldin Jr., Cynthia and Charles Trenckmann, and particularly Stuart Strong, who made available the papers of Clara Trenckmann Studer. They have all made the project stronger.

Last, but certainly not least, we would also like to thank our wives, Vickie Buenger and Anja Schwalen, for sharing their respective expertise in business and German and putting up with Trenckmann as an uninvited guest at various dinners. Above all, they reminded us now and then that there is more to life than this project.

Preserving German
Texan Identity

Introduction

What could be more mainstream than a Texas-German Aggie? William Andreas Trenckmann, born in 1859 of two immigrant parents on a farm near Cat Spring in Austin County, enrolled in the very first class at Texas A&M in 1876, finishing as valedictorian of its first graduating class in 1879. Of course, Texas A&M was not yet the academic powerhouse that it would later become. But valedictorian was only the first of Trenckmann's many achievements. He went back to his home county, and after a few years as a schoolteacher and principal, in 1891 he founded a weekly newspaper that he continued to publish for forty-two years. After the turn of the century he was elected to two terms in the Texas legislature and then continued his journalism career in Austin. He served his alma mater as a member and later president of the board of directors and was even offered the presidency of A&M. On the side he found time to author several works of literature and history. So at first glance, Trenckmann would seem to present an example of a second-generation German who was totally integrated into the Texas mainstream.

Mainstream, that is, until one encounters the name of Trenckmann's newspaper: *Das Bellville Wochenblatt*. Or his historical novel: *Die Lateiner am Possum Creek*. Or his play: *Der Schulmeister von Neu-Rostock*. Or his memoirs: *Erlebtes und Beobachtetes*, which is presented in translation here. There is little doubt that Trenckmann himself was fully at home in the English-speaking world, but he still chose to do the bulk of his writing and publishing in the German language. Well beyond the immigrant generation, there were German Texans—also outside the well-known areas of the Hill Country—who preferred or needed to remain German-language readers, speakers, and thinkers. Trenckmann had advantages of background and education that many of his neighbors and readers did not and was perfectly positioned to move between German and other Texans and in the process preserve German Texan identity.[1]

William Trenckmann exemplifies perfectly the old German proverb, "the apple doesn't fall far from the tree." His father, Andreas F. Trenckmann, was a fairly typical *Lateiner*, or Latin Farmer, a politically motivated immigrant with enough schooling to know Latin but who engaged in agricultural pursuits in America. The son of a middle-class farmer and carpenter from Wefensleben, a village in Prussian Saxony, Andreas had obtained an education and established himself as the founder and director of a private school, which reportedly enrolled as many as five hundred students, in the nearby provincial capital of Magdeburg. He came to own a home in a prime location just a stone's throw from city hall and the nearby open-air marketplace, with a number of merchants as neighbors. Although he married into the city's bourgeoisie, he had the misfortune of outliving three wives. His first wife, Sophie Dorothea Kreiss, died of a stroke (*Nervenschlag*) when just forty years old, leaving him with a daughter and four young sons below the age of fifteen. His second wife, Johanne Friederike Jockusch, the daughter of a prosperous stocking manufacturer, died two weeks after bearing their first child, Anna Friederike, in December 1850. Seven months later, he married

---

1. *Handbook of Texas Online*, Clara Trenckmann Studer, "Trenckmann, William Andreas," accessed June 18, 2016, http://www.tshaonline.org/handbook/online/articles/ftr08, uploaded on June 15, 2010, published by the Texas State Historical Association. A translated version, "The Schoolmaster of New Rostock," is available in *The Millheim and Cat Spring Pioneers: German Immigrants Building a New Life in Texas*, ed. James V. Woodrick and Stephen A. Engelking (CreateSpace Independent Publishing Platform, 2017). A translated and annotated version of the roman à clef, "The Latin Farmers of Possum Creek" was prepared by James Kearney of the University of Texas at Austin but as yet remains unpublished. The second appendix in this book, "Trenckmann's 1907 A&M Reminiscence," is an example of Trenckmann's original English. However, he does indicate in a letter of September 29, 1918, that he could not write in English that day because he was very much in a hurry, and unaccustomed work goes slowly. Trenckmann to "Liebe Tochter" [Clara], Clara Trenckmann papers, privately held by Stuart Strong.

Parental Family of William Andreas Trenckmann

Andreas Friedrich Trenckmann, b. 7/17/1809, Wefensleben, Prussia; d. 5/13/1883, Millheim, Texas

Marriage 1: 10/17/1833, Magdeburg, Prussia, to Sophie Dorothea Kreiss, b. 1808, Magdeburg; d. 8/10/1849, Magdeburg

Children:

1. Bertha Louise Auguste, b. 3/7/1834, Magdeburg; d. 1853, Galveston, Texas

2. Emil Julius Friedrich, b. 4/7/1835, Magdeburg; d. 3/6/1880, Shelby, Texas

3. Otto Alwin, b. 1/22/1837, Magdeburg; d. 11/22/1901, Millheim, Texas

4. Friedrich Adolph, b. 6/24/1839, Magdeburg; d. 9/17/1862, Battle of Antietam, Maryland

5. Albert Hugo, b. 2/20/1842, Magdeburg; d. 1866, Millheim, Texas

Marriage 2: 1/17/1850, Magdeburg, Prussia, to Johanne Friederike Jockusch,
b. 12/11/1822, Magdeburg; d. 12/19/1850, Magdeburg

Children:

6. Anna Friederike, b. 12/15/1850, Magdeburg; d. 12/11/1882, Shelby, Texas

Marriage 3: 7/28/1851, Magdeburg, Prussia, to Johanna Louise née Jockusch, widow Kopsel, b. 6/25/1817, Magdeburg; d. 1873, Millheim, Texas

Children:

7. Louise Helene, b. 5/2/1852, Magdeburg; d. ca. 5/5/1873, Austin, Texas

8. Paul, b. 1857, Colorado County, Texas; d. ca. 1861–63, Millheim, Texas

9. William Andreas, b. 8/23/1859, Millheim, Texas; d. 3/22/1935, Austin, Texas

her cousin, Johanne Louise Kopsel née Jockusch, a childless widow from a well-established family of brewers.[2]

Andreas Trenckmann was active in the Lichtfreunde (Friends of Light), a rationalist Protestant movement that combined religious, political, and social protest. Not surprisingly, he was in sympathy with the 1848 Revolution and was part of a delegation sent to Berlin, probably from the provincial assembly, to deliver a petition to the Prussian king. Emigrating "because he wanted to live under a democratic form of government and wanted to get away from Prussian militarism," he, his wife, and six children arrived in New Orleans on May 12, 1853, stating his occupation as farmer and their destination as Texas. Their middle-class status is confirmed by the fact that they traveled cabin class; they were the very first passengers listed on the manifest. Brother-in-law J. W. Jockusch already had come to the United States in 1846 and by 1850 was a prosperous merchant in Galveston, so he may well have attracted the Trenckmanns to Texas. But if so, they did not remain long in the port city.[3]

2. The city directories, *Magdeburger Staats-und Gewerbs-Adreß-Buch* (1840–53), consistently list Andreas Trenckmann as a private school director at the address Warthe 4, and from about 1846 on as a proprietor there. Besides Trenckmann's house on this small cul-de-sac, three of the other four multifamily houses were home to a total of five merchants and one rentier. Two teachers, probably his employees, resided in Trenckmann's house in 1852, along with a rentier and a widow.

The prominence of the Jockusch family is confirmed by the fact that they were among just a dozen of the city's leading families featured in a recent illustrated volume, Günter Hammerschmidt, *Magdeburger Familien in Handel, Gewerbe, Industrie, Wissenschaft, und Verwaltung: Ein historischer Streifzug in Wort und Bild* (Magdeburg, 2008), 269–93.

3. Cat Spring Agricultural Society, *The Cat Spring Story* (San Antonio: Lone Star Print Co. [1956]), 84–85 (hereafter cited as *Cat Spring Story*). The Trenckmanns applied for an emigration permit on December 23, 1852; their official release was granted on January 4, 1853. "Auswanderungsgesuche aus dem Kreis Magdeburg, 1852 bis 1853," C 28 I f Nr. 76 Bd. 1, Landesarchiv Sachsen-Anhalt, Magdeburg. Ship *Auguste* passenger list, arriving from Bremen May 12, 1853, New Orleans Passenger Lists, series M432, National Archives, accessed via ancestry.com. The eldest son, Emil, was not noted on the application and did not accompany them. He signed on as a crew member of the Bremen ship *Wilhelmina* on May 9, 1854, bound for New York. Jokusch's record is in *Empressario* passenger list, arriving from Havana March 9, 1846, New Orleans Passenger Lists, series M432, National Archives, accessed via ancestry.com. Jockusch had also traveled from Havana to New York the previous year, arriving on the ship *Normal* on September 3, 1845; in both cases he was listed as a merchant. The 1850 census also lists him as a merchant, owning real estate worth five thousand dollars. 1850 US Census, Galveston, Galveston County, Texas, population schedule, NARA microfilm M432, roll 910, p. 241B, image 473, accessed via ancestry.com.

Barely two months later, the Trenckmanns purchased a farm from a fellow German on the south bank of the San Bernard River some seventy miles west of Houston, paying $1,100 for two hundred acres.[4] In 1858 they moved a few miles north across the river and the county line, settling at Millheim in Austin County near Cat Spring, one of the oldest German settlements in the state, established before the Texas Revolution. It was there that William Andreas Trenckmann was born on August 23, 1859, the youngest of his father's nine children.

From all indications, William Trenckmann grew up in a prosperous farming household, as is reflected in both deed records and the observations of contemporaries. In 1858 his father paid four thousand dollars for three plots totaling 140 acres, a price reflecting considerable improvements. Two years earlier he had acquired 1,000 acres in the vicinity, probably grazing land, for a mere six hundred dollars. A neighbor who arrived about the same time remarked, "In 1856 the hardships of pioneer life had gone. . . . The farmers of Millheim lived in frame dwelling houses." Another former neighbor ranked Andreas Trenckmann as the fourth most influential member of the community, the "proud proprietor of a grain mill, and the customary farm," outranked only by two graduates of German universities and one of the community's earliest pioneers.[5]

In 1860 the elder Trenckmann's real estate was valued at $3,500, with another $5,000 worth of personal property, a net worth exceeding $200,000 in 2015 purchasing power. In the 1860 agricultural

4. Purchased on July 13, 1853, Colorado County Deed Records, Book 8, p. 540.

5. The purchases were made on April 9, 1858, from J. A. Wilm and wife Amalie; the same day Trenckmann purchased another eight acres for thirty dollars from John F. Hollien. The parcels were south of Mill Creek, originally part of the Louis Kleberg grant and Cummins Hacienda. Previously on December 18, 1856, he had bought the Mexican equivalent of one thousand acres nearby for six hundred dollars. Austin County Deed Records, Book G, pp. 321–26; Book I–J, pp. 682–83. The farm lies in the northeastern corner of the intersection of present-day FM 949 and Trenckmann Road about two miles east of Millheim. Quotes from Adalbert Regenbrecht, "The German Settlers of Millheim before the Civil War," *Southwestern Historical Quarterly* 20 (1917): 28–34, here 29, and Charles Nagel, *A Boy's Civil War Story* (Saint Louis: Eden Seminary Press, 1935), 40–41. The Regenbrecht account is based on a letter Trenckmann wrote in German on February 18, 1916, sketching his family's history for Regenbrecht (Clara Trenckmann papers, privately held by Stuart Strong). Regenbrecht was listed immediately after Trenckmann in the 1870 census, indicating close proximity. In 1850 Nagel was just two entries up from the Rombauer family, from whom the Trenckmanns bought their original farm, and both moved to Millheim about the same time.

census he reported 240 acres of land, eighteen horses, and 550 head of cattle. Although concentrating on grazing, he had produced six bales of cotton and also owned a cotton gin. With four sons between ages eighteen and twenty-five, he was well supplied with family labor. However, despite adding 85 acres in the next decade, his real estate had not appreciated by 1870, and his personal property had declined to $2,000 in value, since he was down to only six horses and 315 cattle.[6] The Civil War cast a long shadow over the Trenckmann household during William's childhood.

The memoir relates the family's wartime experiences but needs to be placed in a broader context. The secession movement and the Civil War posed a serious dilemma for most German Texans. Few of them owned slaves, whether for economic or ideological reasons, and many of them who had arrived after 1845 had sworn allegiance to the United States upon naturalization. Political refugees such as Andreas Trenckmann and many of his Millheim neighbors were more strongly opposed than others to secession. In the February 1861 secession referendum there were only 8 votes in favor out of 107 total votes cast in the Cat Spring–Millheim precinct, a rejection nearly as extreme as that in frontier Fredericksburg. According to one of the Trenckmanns' closest neighbors, Adelbert Regenbrecht, "Many Union men of our neighborhood enlisted in the Confederate Army because they believed it to be their duty." As he related, William's father had voted against secession but "did not object to the enlistment of two sons in the Confederate Army at the beginning of the war." Apparently there were some differences within the Trenckmann family on this issue, as the memoir reflects. Two other sons of military age enlisted later and much more reluctantly. William showed no regrets for the Lost Cause in his 1899 county

6. 1860 US Census, Cat Spring, New Ulm, and Industry, Austin County, Texas, population schedule, NARA microfilm M653, roll 1287, p. 202, Image 413; 1870 US Census, Cat Spring, Austin County, Texas, population schedule, NARA microfilm M593, roll 1574, p. 342A, Image 91813; 1860 US Census, Cat Spring Precinct, Austin County, Texas, manuscript agricultural schedule, p. 43, line 11; 1870 US Census, Precinct 4, Austin County, Texas, manuscript agricultural schedule, p. 9, line 22; all accessed via ancestry.com. The value of $8,500 in 1860 was the equivalent of $231,850 in 2015, based on Bureau of Labor Statistics Consumer Price Index from 1913 on and data from 1865 to 1912 from a study by political science professor Robert Sahr at Oregon State University.

history published in German: "There can in the end no longer be any doubt that abolition was a blessing for the whole South and especially for the immigrants from the Old World."[7]

Trenckmann's father had taken the lead in an important community institution quite soon after his arrival. In 1856 he was one of the three founders and was elected as the first president of the Cat Spring Agricultural Society, the oldest society of its kind in Texas. Here, "the book farmers of Millheim and the practical farmers of Catspring [sic] exchanged their knowledge," as Regenbrecht, one of the book farmers, related. He was one of six Millheim settlers educated at German universities, and he mentions another half-dozen "highly educated Germans," including the elder Trenckmann, who had graduated from a "normal school." The editor who published Regenbrecht's reminiscences characterized the educated Germans as the "*Lateiner*, those cultured, genial spirits who found it much easier to cultivate music and song and literature than corn and cotton."[8]

Millheim had a singing society before the Civil War, and Cat Spring had a *Turnverein*, or athletic club, as early as 1869. Millheim, however, was never home to a German church, and Cat Spring only intermittently. The Latin Farmers tended to be freethinkers, many of them more radical than Trenckmann's father. The Cat Spring centennial book made no attempt to disguise this, even in the conservative atmosphere of 1956. Its chapter on churches is one of the shortest in the book: "The German settlers at Cat Spring who were so greatly interested in agriculture, education, literature, music, and art, manifested little interest in religion." It goes on to note that the

7. Walter L. Buenger, *Secession and the Union in Texas* (Austin: University of Texas Press, 1984); Walter D. Kamphoefner, "New Americans or New Southerners? Unionist German Texans," in *Lone Star Unionism, Dissent, and Resistance: Other Sides of Civil War Texas*, ed. J. F. de la Teja (Norman: University of Oklahoma Press, 2016), 101–22, here Table 1; Regenbrecht, "German Settlers of Millheim," 30, 32; William Trenckmann, "History of Austin County," 32; translation of 1899 supplement to *Das Bellville Wochenblatt*, William A. Trenckmann Papers, 1931–33, Dolph Briscoe Center for American History, University of Texas at Austin.

8. Cat Spring Agricultural Society, *A Century of Agricultural Progress, 1856–1956: Minutes of the Cat Spring Agricultural Society* (Cat Spring, Texas, 1956; hereafter cited as Cat Spring, *Minutes*), 1–6. Trenckmann held the presidency of the society for nine of the fourteen annual terms between 1856 and 1873; the office was vacant for three years during the Civil War. *Cat Spring Story*, 20, 99–100; Regenbrecht, "German Settlers of Millheim," 30–32, 28.

constitution for the first public school of the community excluded religious instruction from its curriculum, concluding in summary: "The German settlers . . . worshipped free land, free air and sunshine and freedom to work out their own social and economic problems." One early settler complained in a critical article published in a Berlin newspaper in 1858, "To confess Christ is a crime, only to divine [that is, discern] God in the Nature [*sic*] is permissible." The Reverend Louis Ervendberg did organize a German Evangelical church at Cat Spring in 1840, but he soon departed for greener fields in New Braunfels. Czech Protestant Josef Bergmann arrived in 1850 and preached in German at Cat Spring for two decades. Although he was "very active in the Cat Spring Agricultural Society and his opinion seems to have been highly respected," he needed to supplement his ministerial income with farming and teaching, and by the 1870 census he simply called himself a farmer. Not until 1927 was there another church in Cat Spring. Since Bergmann's parish records have not survived, it is impossible to say to what extent, if at all, the Trenckmanns were involved in his congregation, but it seems unlikely that they were.[9]

It is apparent that William Trenckmann, perhaps even more than his father, shared the (ir)religious outlook of his community. His only "confirmation" that he mentions in his memoir was of his fears. The word *God* occurs only once there, merely a parenthetical *Gottseidank* (thank God), without any theological implications. Jesus and Christ are never mentioned, and Christian only obliquely, praising a teacher who despite being "a minister of one of the strictest Protestant churches, did not condemn the geologists as being unchristian for their estimation of the age of the earth." The dozen or so references Trenckmann makes to churches are often pejorative, associating them with prohibition and the Ku Klux Klan.

9. *Cat Spring Story*, 20, 23–24, 99–100; Cat Spring, *Minutes*, 29. Bergmann was a founder of the Agricultural Society and its first vice president. He solemnized 108 marriages during his time in Austin County, or about 5 per year. According to David Z. Chroust, "Jozef Ernst Bergmann: 'Father' of the Czech-Speaking Immigration in Texas?" *Kosmas: Czechoslovak and Central European Journal* 20 (Fall 2006): 48–64, "Bergmann was committed to . . . theological rationalism," and his starting salary as pastor was only one hundred dollars annually, not even one-fifth of what Ernst Maetze earned from his subscription school.

If there was one thing the Latin Farmers of Millheim did worship, it was education, and in that respect they were extremely fortunate. In fact, they probably had the most highly educated elementary schoolteacher in the state at the time. As Trenckmann writes, "Absolute sovereign in Millheim was only one man, and that man was our teacher E. G. Maetze, who reigned supreme in his own kingdom—the school." A graduate of the University of Breslau, Ernst Gustav Maetze had been headmaster of an intermediate school in Silesia until he was elected to the Prussian *Landtag* (parliament) in Berlin as a supporter of the democratic 1848 Revolution and debated the conservative future chancellor Otto von Bismarck. After the collapse of the Revolution he took refuge in Texas and was initially engaged as a tutor for the Engelking family in Millheim. The demand was so great that he soon opened a school and then needed a larger building. When arsonists destroyed that building during the Civil War, Maetze resumed teaching on his porch until Trenckmann's father led a campaign to build a new school, where his youngest son would soon be enrolled. In all, Maetze taught for twenty-seven years, supported only by subscriptions, until public schools were introduced during Reconstruction.[10]

All the eyewitness accounts confirm Trenckmann's testimony to the quality of the school. Regenbrecht calls it "one of the best elementary schools in Texas." According to Trenckmann, "it was the real heart and also the pride of the settlement." Charles Nagel, who left the community at age fourteen, fleeing the Confederacy with his father, devotes an entire chapter of his memoir to Maetze's school. Although he continued his studies all the way to the University of Berlin, Nagel states that "Gustav Maetze was probably as great a teacher as I ever had." This was not merely ethnic pride; the English-language paper in the county seat of Bellville announced in 1860: "Mr. Maetze will commence his school in Millheim on the 1st Monday in September. This is one of the best schools in the country. Let those Americans who wish their children to learn to read, write and speak the German language fluently and grammatically send their children to Mr. Maetze. He is a gentleman every way fully competent for his position." He certainly equipped William Trenckmann

---

10. *Cat Spring Story*, 61–62, 95–96.

for the next stage of his education, which followed after a hiatus of more than three years.[11]

The year 1873, when he turned fourteen, saw two momentous changes in Trenckmann's life. That spring he finished his schooling under teacher Maetze, and that fall his mother's death left him and his father alone on the farm. From then on he carried on the dual role of farmhand and household help. Not surprisingly, it was Maetze who informed the Trenckmanns of the educational possibilities that had opened up at the newly established Agricultural and Mechanical College of Texas in 1876. But despite the challenges it entailed for him back on the farm, William's father was fully supportive when he learned of the opportunity.

In Texas and elsewhere in the South, land-grant colleges labored under the handicap of being regarded as Yankee institutions, having their origins in Republican legislation passed during the Civil War. Ultimately, federal largesse proved irresistible, although, as Trenckmann relates, "the chief consideration in the selection of the faculty had been that only Southerners free from every influence of the hated Yankees" were hired. In fact, the Agricultural and Mechanical College's supporters initially offered the presidency to Jefferson Davis in a vain effort to counteract the Yankee taint. As a historical sketch repeated in several of the school's annual catalogs relates, "A hostile spirit was developed in the legislature and in the newspapers. The college was named a nursery of military aristocracy. The farmers looked coldly upon it or pronounced it a 'humbug.' Students began to return to their homes." Not until Confederate general and two-term governor Lawrence Sullivan Ross took over the presidency in 1891 did A&M really attain stability and acceptance. But since the Trenckmanns were neither fire-eaters nor Lost Cause devotees, they had no reservations because of the Yankee associations of the college.[12]

The new institution got off to a slow start, with only 6 students enrolling during the first few days. When Trenckmann arrived, he

11. Regenbrecht, "German Settlers of Millheim," 30; Nagel, *Civil War Story*, 101–13, quote on 108; *Bellville Countryman*, August 25, 1860.

12. Henry C. Dethloff, *A Centennial History of Texas A&M University, 1876–1976* (College Station: Texas A&M University Press, 1975), 1:9–16; *Eighth Annual Catalogue of the Agricultural and Mechanical College of Texas* (1883–84), 3–4.

was the twentieth. The count was up to 48 by the end of the fall term, and by the end of the school year it had reached a respectable tally of 106. When he graduated two years later it was up to 248. The scene that greeted Trenckmann on arrival could not have looked promising. The school was situated out on the open prairie, five miles from the young town of Bryan, which itself had become the county seat only in 1866 and was reached by the railroad only a year later.[13]

The morning after he arrived at college, Trenckmann was confronted by a fellow student who "wanted to deride the young German as a 'Dutchman,'" but Trenckmann more than held his own. While he was one of the very few ethnics in the original student body, it is apparent that such prejudices were not very deep or widespread. Among just a handful of fellow Germans in the initial class was one whose parents reportedly spoke no English but who still attained the highest rank a student could hold, that of adjutant. There were at least two other German classmates, and the following year saw two more. But Trenckmann was the only one whose father was not a merchant or grocer, and all the others had grown up in county seats: two from San Antonio, one from Gonzales, another from Bellville, and one from Corsicana, the last Jewish. The year Trenckmann graduated, immigrant George Pfeuffer of New Braunfels joined the board of directors of the college and served as board president from 1883 until his death in 1886.[14]

Despite its name, the Agricultural and Mechanical College in its initial years "made little or no effort to teach either practical agricul-

13. Dethloff, *Centennial History*, 1:16, 25–43.

14. Charles August Burchard was the only student from Gonzales listed in the first *Catalogue of the Agricultural and Mechanical College of Texas* (1876–77); he is described but not named by Thomas Gathright, first president of Texas A&M, writing a pseudonymic "Letter from William," September 6, 1877, in the *Weekly Clarion* (Jackson, Mississippi), Gathright's former home. Further verification is provided by the graduation report in *Galveston Daily News*, June 27, 1877. Burchardt attended only one year; he was born in Texas of German parents who had arrived by 1852. The other German Texans in the first year were Meyer Cohen of Corsicana and Martin Joseph Muench of San Antonio. The second year they were joined by Louis Dietrich Stumberg of San Antonio and Charles Stonewall Miller of Bellville. Like Burchard, all of them were born in Texas of German parents. All their fathers were listed as merchants or grocers in the 1870 and 1880 censuses. On Pfeuffer, see *Handbook of Texas Online*, Robert Lee Williamson, "Pfeuffer, George," accessed July 10, 2016, http://www.tshaonline.org/handbook/online/articles/fpf01, uploaded on June 15, 2010, modified on May 2, 2016, published by the Texas State Historical Association.

ture or mechanics"; instead, "course offerings . . . remained intrinsically literary and classic in orientation." This is apparent from the subjects in which Trenckmann graduated in 1879: German, French, Spanish, English, mental and moral science, chemistry, and natural science—in fact, all the subjects the school offered except for Latin, Greek, and mathematics. As his career developed, he was probably better served by this curriculum than by the agricultural and mechanical focus that developed later.[15]

Having graduated in three years, and prodded by financial need, Trenckmann followed in his father's footsteps and took up teaching. He spent more than a decade working in three heavily German towns within thirty miles of his birthplace: first Frelsburg, then Shelby (also known as Roedersmuehle), and finally the Austin County seat of Bellville, where he rose to principal of the public schools.

Despite the best efforts of Republicans, and particularly the Germans among them, the quality of Texas schools progressed rather haltingly during Reconstruction. The state required only a four-month school term and provided a modest per-pupil subsidy of $4.50. In rescinding most of the Republican educational reforms, including a provision for up to two hours per day of German, French, or Spanish instruction, Redeemer Democrats left school policy mostly to the locally elected county judge, the chief administrative and judicial officer of each county. Ironically, this allowed more ethnic influence in school policy in communities they dominated. Trenckmann reported in 1888 to the state superintendent on the Bellville school he oversaw: "German is taught in all the grades. Though instruction in the language is optional, 55 percent of the pupils pursued this study. The work of the teachers is materially increased by the addition of German . . . but the interest manifested by the pupils in this study demands its continuance."[16]

From the time Trenckmann took over, Bellville school enrollment saw a steady increase almost every year, growing from 138 pupils in 1883 all the way to 182 in 1888. Thereafter it experienced a slight downturn (if official statistics are to be trusted), which became

15. Dethloff, *Centennial History*, 1:47, 49; *Fourteenth Annual Catalogue of the Agricultural and Mechanical College of Texas* (1889–90), 68–69.

16. Carlos Kevin Blanton, *The Strange Career of Bilingual Education in Texas* (College Station: Texas A&M University Press, 2003), 18–22, 34.

much more serious the year after Trenckmann left. Bellville school's students were all white, and African American students evidently went to schools outside of town. According to the statistics gathered by the state, the county's schools were strictly segregated throughout the time Trenckmann taught in Austin County, and white schools and students outnumbered African American schools and students by about two to one. Black families were slightly larger than those of other groups, and African Americans were roughly 30 percent of the school age population in the 1880 US census. Thus, Austin County's African American children attended schools at about the same rate as other population groups, but they did so in segregated schools in which black teachers were paid substantially less than white teachers.[17]

Trenckmann repeatedly criticized the state for insufficient financial support of public schools, but no evidence remains to answer the question whether Trenckmann favored equal funding of all schools. His experiences with overt segregation and discrimination and his frustrations with state government, however, may have laid the groundwork for his later acceptance of the exclusion of African Americans from politics and his decision to run for the state legislature. Segregation and discrimination were habits of mind for Trenckmann, and the striving and achievement of blacks were outside his purview. State government's failures in education, on the other hand, were a daily fact of life.[18]

Despite frustrations with poor state funding, Bellville offered Trenckmann a much fuller life. Besides a more rewarding employment, with more students and a higher salary, the county seat of Bellville also provided more opportunities for social life than did the two smaller towns where Trenckmann had previously taught. It was there that he courted his wife, Mathilda "Tillie" Miller, the daughter of a prosperous town merchant, seven years his junior, whom he

17. State Superintendent of Education, *Biennial Reports of the State Superintendent of Public Instruction for Texas, 1882–1892* (Austin: State Department of Education, 1882–92). See in particular the tables for Austin County and Bellville schools and students. Also see L. L. Foster, *Forgotten Texas Census: First Annual Report of the Agricultural Bureau of the Department of Agriculture, Insurance, Statistics, and History*, introduction by Barbara J. Rozek (Austin: Texas State Historical Society, 2001), 5–7.

18. For example, see State Superintendent of Education, *Sixth Biennial Report Ending in 1887 and 1888*, 284–85.

married in 1886. Their acquaintance was hardly coincidental: two of her brothers had been younger classmates of Trenckmann at Texas A&M, and her eldest sister had married a son of William's revered teacher Maetze. The families had similar educational and political views; the eldest Miller son had been sent to Germany for four years of education, and according to him, both his father's and his mother's families had emigrated in the wake of the 1848 Revolution.[19]

Tillie Miller had also been sent away to school by her parents and spent time in Austin at the Alta Vista Institute. While there, as part of a school assignment she kept a journal that reveals an energetic and independent spirit with a good sense of humor. Like her husband, Tillie spoke and wrote excellent English and made friends beyond her German Texan world. She and her husband would enjoy many

Conjugal Family of William Andreas Trenckmann

William Andreas Trenckmann, b. 8/23/1859, Millheim, Austin County, Texas; d. 3/22/1935, Austin, Texas

Marriage: 4/20/1886, Bellville, Texas, to Mathilde Miller, b. 11/3/1866, Galveston, Texas; d. 3/11/1946, Austin, Texas

Children:

1. Robert Trenckmann, b. 2/2/1887, Bellville, Texas; d. 2/2/1950, Shelton, Washington

2. William Trenckmann, b. 2/17/1890, Bellville, Texas; d. 12/25/1964, Austin, Texas

3. Else Trenckmann, b. 7/6/1893, Bellville, Texas; d. 7/3/1969, Austin, Texas

4. Clara Trenckmann, b. 7/31/1897, Bellville, Texas; d. 6/19/1979, Austin, Texas

19. Charles Stonewall Miller of Bellville first appears in the second *Catalogue of the Agricultural and Mechanical College of Texas* (1877–78) and his brother Herman Julius in the *Fourth Catalogue of the Agricultural and Mechanical College of Texas* (1879–80). William Johann Miller, "The Story of My Life, by a Born Texan," as told to his daughter, Emy Applegate, http://www.rootsweb.ancestry.com/~txaustin/Pioneers/Miller.htm.

years of marriage in which they respected and relied on each other. William repeatedly referred to his wife as "the editress," an equal partner in the newspaper enterprise, and they shared in all major decisions.[20]

This acceptance of greater equality and the move beyond a world that relegated men and women to separate spheres of activity may have owed something to Tillie Trenckmann's mother, a strong and decisive woman who, according to William Trenckmann in his auto-biography, often weighed in on family matters. It may also have been connected to his freethinking religious background. While tra-ditional German women were often confined to *Kinder, Küche, Kirche* (children, cooking, and church), those outside the hierarchies of faith probably rested more comfortably outside the domains of male dominance in public life. In addition, free thinking about religion

Portrait of the Trenckmann family, Sealy, Texas, about 1903. Photo courtesy of Thomas Trenckmann, D-31171 Schellerten, Germany.

20. Tillie Miller, "Excerpts from the Journal of Tillie Marie (Miller) Trenckmann, Alta Vista Institute, Austin, 1882–1883," and Tillie Miller Trenckmann, "Scrapbook, 1883," both in Austin History Center, Austin Public Library.

probably encouraged free thinking about other social institutions, including gender roles. In later years, certainly, the Trenckmann daughters acquired university educations and pursued their own paths with the encouragement of their parents.[21]

Before the birth of their daughters, however, in September 1891 Tillie and William Trenckmann began a new phase of their life together. Having just turned thirty-two years old, and now the father of two young sons, with the full support of his wife William Trenckmann switched professions. The need for additional income to support his growing family obviously played a role in this decision, but his writings suggested other factors that moved him to enter the field of German-language publishing. He commented in his autobiography about earlier times when wanderlust seized him, so he was clearly drawn to new challenges. He also often displayed what he termed an aversion for "idleness." He did not run from work as a teacher, but toward work as a newspaper editor and public figure. He gravitated toward a larger public role in which he shaped German public opinion and the reputation of Germans in the wider community. As his daughter Clara later put it, he sought to be an interpreter of "American institutions" for the German community.[22]

Trenckmann entered the publishing field at a propitious time, just as the German press was reaching its apex in the United States. His *Bellville Wochenblatt* was one of some 763 periodicals published in that language nationwide in 1891. Two years later the German periodical count reached its all-time high with almost 800 publications, including nearly 100 dailies, with a weekly circulation high enough to supply every second German immigrant with a copy, or one for every five German Americans if the second generation is taken into account. Two-thirds of all foreign-language publications at the time

---

21. On the connection between religious affiliation and gender roles, see Jon Gjerde, *The Minds of the West: Ethnocultural Evolution in the Rural Middle West, 1830–1917* (Chapel Hill: University of North Carolina Press, 1997), 1–24, 135–224.

22. *Handbook of Texas Online*, Clara Trenckmann Studer, "Trenckmann, William Andreas," accessed July 18, 2016, http://www.tshaonline.org/handbook/online/articles/ftr08, uploaded on June 15, 2010, published by the Texas State Historical Association.

were German. In 1880 Texas was supporting 13 German papers, 2 of them dailies. Twelve new German papers were founded in the state in the decade before 1889, and by 1904, Texas could count 30 German periodicals of various kinds.[23]

Trenckmann proudly states, "My *Wochenblatt* retained the record of being published in the smallest town in which a German newspaper could exist." Indeed, Bellville numbered only 807 inhabitants in 1890; Fredericksburg, New Braunfels, Bastrop, and Seguin, the next smallest towns with viable German weeklies, were all about twice as large, and more heavily German to boot.[24] But town size is perhaps not the most telling indicator for a paper's viability. Austin County had the fifth largest German population of any county in Texas, surpassed only by urban Bexar and Galveston and bordering Washington and Fayette counties. It was home to over twenty-five hundred German immigrants, whereas New Braunfels, Giddings, and Fredericksburg supported German papers in counties with ethnic populations below fifteen hundred, and in the last case barely over one thousand. Moreover, because of its earlier settlement, Austin County had a larger second generation than counties farther west.

As he openly acknowledged, Trenckmann changed course at the peak of German immigration to Texas. By the late 1880s over 40 percent of the citizens of Austin County and half the citizens of Bellville were German. In contrast, Anglo Americans made up about 25 percent of the county's population, and African Americans made up slightly less. Most of the rest were Czechs or some other Slavic group. In that multilingual time and place, others—African Americans, Anglos, Czechs, and Poles—also spoke and read German.

23. The exact numbers were 796 publications, including 97 daily papers. Robert E. Park, *The Immigrant Press and Its Control* (New York: Harper and Brothers, 1922), 309–20; Carl Wittke, *The German-Language Press in America* (Lexington: University Press of Kentucky, 1957), 205.

24. Karl J. R. Arndt and May E. Olson, *German-American Newspapers and Periodicals, 1732–1955* (Heidelberg, Germany: Quelle & Meyer, 1961). Boerne, a town of only 433 inhabitants, is listed with two struggling German papers between 1882 and 1888 but none thereafter. There is also an entry for a *Wochenblatt* in Franklin in 1876 that is almost certainly erroneous. All the larger Texas cities with populations upwards of fourteen thousand—Dallas, San Antonio, Galveston, Houston, Fort Worth, Austin, and Waco—had German newspapers by 1891.

Trenckmann caught the wave of popular interest in carving out a place for Germans in Texas and rode that wave the rest of his life.[25]

In some respects ethnic weeklies such as *Das Wochenblatt* played a role little different from that of their English-language counterparts. One page of the four or eight was usually devoted to serial fiction of varying quality, and a few lame jokes often served as filler. The majority of papers were closely identified with and sometimes subsidized by one political party, and beyond local politics they provided at least cursory coverage at the state and national level. They reported on other local news, weather, and crops and often covered market prices and carried ads for local businesses. Patent medicines and dubious cures were standard fare regardless of language. But ethnic papers also helped immigrants adjust to a new economic and legal system and came to the defense of ethnic interests by instructing their readers in the political process, urging them to become citizens and voters, and educating them on the issues.

From the outset Trenckmann's ambitions were larger:

> I had not planned to found a local paper, although . . . the majority of my readers were living or had lived in Austin County. I always tried to extend my fields to the happenings which were important to the Germans of the entire state. I have as far as possible in an eight-page paper reported all outstanding achievements of Germans in our country as well as matters of importance in regard to national and state laws, politics, and the most important world news, so that even those who have access to no other newspaper might be fairly well informed on current events.

Trenckmann provided his readers with a broader literary offering than the standard fare. Although some of the fiction set in the Old Country consisted of potboilers by deservedly forgotten authors, Trenckmann himself penned a good deal of content, be it news, opin-

25. For an overview of German immigration to Texas, see Terry G. Jordan, *German Seed in Texas Soil: Immigrant Farmers in Nineteenth-Century Texas* (Austin: University of Texas Press, 1966); Rudolph Leopold Biesele, *The History of German Settlements in Texas* (Austin: Press of Von Boeckman-Jones, 1931). On the demographics of Austin County, see William A. Trenckmann, "Austin County" *Das Bellville Wochenblatt*, 1899, translation in William A. Trenckmann Papers, Briscoe Center; Foster, *Forgotten Texas Census*, 5–7.

ion, history, belles lettres, or humor, the last under the pseudonym Tante Lotte (Aunt Lotte). He also had regular contributors, some writing dialect humor under names such as H. W. Schnüffelmeyer and others reporting news from their local communities. Although he promoted cultural preservation, Trenckmann was at home in the modern world, not bound by conservative convention. In the 1920s, under the headline "The Sexual Education of the Youth," he editorialized that this was "absolutely appropriate," though he preferred that it be done by parents rather than in schools. In the wake of America's first Red Scare, he reminded readers of "how much we have stolen from the Socialists, and what hearty thanks we actually owe them."[26] Moreover, he promoted a local Bellville author who was anything but conventional: poet and novelist Clara Matthaei. This strong-willed daughter of a prominent Bellville family (her brother had attended Harvard) rejected more socially appropriate suitors and married a Mexican refugee of revolution, and later after their divorce she married another Mexican friend of the family.

Early on, Trenckmann had begun publishing Matthaei's poetry under the pseudonym Gertrud Hoff, and in the 1920s he serialized in *Das Wochenblatt* two of her autobiographical novels, published under the name Walther Gray. Set in a thinly disguised Bellville, they presented "the paradox of a strict localism of setting combined with an exceptional broadness and nonconformity of outlook." As late as 1931 Trenckmann published under her real married name, Clara Reyes, an expansive letter reporting on her life in Mexico and at least one of her poems. Her death in 1934 was memorialized by a full-column obituary.[27]

26. *Das Wochenblatt*, February 24, 1921, p. 2; September 23, 1920, p. 8.

27. The two families were acquainted early on; Trenckmann's father had purchased a plot of land from Matthaei's father in 1871. Austin County Deed Records, Book P, p. 369; Selma Metzenthin-Raunick and Nolan Schulze, "The Tragedy of Clara Matthaei," *Southwest Review* 21 (1935), 52–64, quote on 60–61; *Handbook of Texas Online*, Charles E. Patrick, "Matthaei, Clara," accessed August 15, 2016, http://www.tshaonline.org/handbook/online/articles/fmabp, uploaded on June 15, 2010, published by the Texas State Historical Association. In 1997 Patrick also translated and published bilingual editions of the two novels under the titles *A Man So Quiet: A Story of Death and Resurrection*, and *The Compadre: The Story of Two Hearts* (both Manor, Texas: Bois d'Arc Press, 1997). See also *Das Wochenblatt*, September 17, 1931; September 24, 1931; November 16, 1934, the last apparently the source of much of the background information on Matthaei.

While many weekly newspapers were primarily one-person operations, in some cases with even longer tenure than Trenckmann's
four decades, he and his newspaper became so fused in identity that
both he and his readers often dubbed him simply the Wochenblattmann. Over time his paper developed into an organ for German Texas as a whole. This was especially true once he made the move to
Austin in 1909, but by then his paper already had sprung the bounds
of Austin County. For example, the *Seguiner Zeitung* praised Trenckmann's bipartisanship and also quoted one of his articles on soil
erosion and a second noting that prohibition had not stemmed the
rising divorce rates.[28] His last issue published in Bellville included
correspondence not only from neighboring Colorado County, but
also from Thorndale, ninety miles away, and even Ballinger, a distance of three hundred miles, where a brother-in-law had settled in
1889.

The *Wochenblatt* agents listed just before the move encompassed
seventy-five communities in twenty-five different counties, although
Austin County and the three adjacent "German counties" accounted
for thirty-six of them. The paper's circulation was just short of twelve
hundred in 1895, the only figure available from the Bellville location.
The first year in Austin, 1910, it was double that, and during the
1920s the paper routinely if erroneously claimed to have the largest
circulation of any German-language newspaper in the South. Circulation rose to 2,851 by the time Trenckmann retired in 1935. By
then the number of communities with *Wochenblatt* agents remained
constant at seventy-five, but coverage had expanded to thirty-two
counties, some as distant as Runnels in the West and Refugio and
Jim Wells in South Texas. But it was above all a paper for rural
and small-town Germans; the largest towns with agents were New
Braunfels and Brenham.[29]

Trenckmann began *Das Bellville Wochenblatt* as Austin County and
Texas entered a momentous and tumultuous two decades that buf-

28. *Seguiner Zeitung*, June 17, September 9, December 23, 1909, accessed through
The Portal to Texas History, https://texashistory.unt.edu/.

29. Arndt and Olson, *German-American Newspapers*, 616–17, 628–30. The *New
Braunfelser Zeitung* had a circulation of four thousand in 1925 and the San Antonio *Freie
Presse für Texas* as high as twelve thousand. See agent lists in *Das Bellville Wochenblatt*,
July 29, 1909; *Das Wochenblatt*, April 28, 1932. See also *Das Wochenblatt*, June 12, 1924.

feted Germans as much as any other Texans. Between 1891 and 1909, when Trenckmann moved from Austin County, four key questions roiled politics and society. What was the status of the Democratic Party in the political process? What role should government play in promoting the economy and regulating business? Would prohibition become the law of the land? What was the place of African Americans in politics and in society? By 1909 Trenckmann and many of the Germans of Austin County moved from ambivalence toward if not opposition to the Democratic Party to active support of the party. They came to accept that party's growing insistence that well-constructed government programs and policy were essential to modern life. Prohibition continued to galvanize the German community like no other issue, and on that issue and the related Sunday Laws Germans resisted an activist government. At the same time they acquiesced to and in some cases actively supported the exclusion and segregation of African Americans, among their strongest allies in the struggle against prohibition. Trenckmann, who was elected to the state House of Representatives as a Democrat in 1906, found himself in the middle of this transformation.[30]

In the 1880s Austin County voters often gave the majority of their votes, or at least a significant minority, to Republican and third-party candidates. That pattern changed by 1890 when James S. Hogg, a young and energetic reform Democrat, captured a sizable percentage of the vote in the gubernatorial election. In 1892 when Hogg ran for reelection, however, county voters gave a large majority to his leading opponent, George Clark, and almost no votes to the other major candidate, the Populist Thomas L. Nugent. Clark combined the support of conservative Democrats outraged by Hogg's successful passage of laws regulating railroads with that of Republicans, especially African American Republicans. Thus, Clark's success indicated the lingering presence of African American voters in meaningful elections and the unwillingness of some Germans and Anglos to accept a larger role for state government. Germans and Czechs, according to Trenckmann, were particularly irritated by Hogg's insistence on the enforcement of Sunday Laws, which limited business activity and alcohol consumption on Sunday. In Bellville, Sundays were treated

---

30. On Trenckmann's election, see *Das Bellville Wochenblatt*, November 15, 1906.

as they were in Europe, with all businesses, including saloons, open before and after church. Most festivals were also held on Sunday.

Resistance to supporting reform Democrats like Hogg continued on in subsequent elections in the mid-1890s with one major alteration—by 1896 populist candidates, who advocated a far more active state and federal government than did reform Democrats and reached out to gain the support of African Americans, almost carried the county. Perhaps it was due to the sharp downturn in cotton prices, but it could also have sprung from the long-standing presence in the county of the Farmer's Alliance, a precursor of the Populist Party. Voter turnout remained high through the decade, and the pages of *Das Wochenblatt* and Trenckmann's autobiography attest to an intense level of interest in politics. Partisan loyalty and willingness to accept regulation by government seemed in flux, probably because of the economic recession and deflation of the currency that continued until late in the decade. Through the 1890s prohibition, like Sunday Laws a challenge to German culture and customs, remained an issue, and African Americans continued to participate meaningfully in the electoral process.[31]

Although—devoted Democrat that he was—Trenckmann seldom mentioned it, through the 1890s German Texans also often voted alongside African Americans for Republican candidates. In both 1896 and 1898, for example, the voters of the Tenth Congressional District of Texas, which included Austin County, elected Robert B. Hawley, a Republican. Newspaper accounts cite German and African American support as key to Hawley's victory, but he also benefited from running in a field of multiple candidates. Populist candidates appear to have drawn support from the Democrats and allowed Hawley to win with a plurality of the vote.[32]

31. Mike Kingston, Sam Attlesey, and Mary G. Crawford, *The Texas Almanac's Political History of Texas* (Austin: Eakin Press, 1992), 58–69. On the Farmer's Alliance in Austin County, see Cat Spring, *Minutes*, 142, 180, 183, 189, 191, 194–98.

32. *Handbook of Texas Online*, Anne W. Hooker, "Hawley, Robert Bradley," accessed November 13, 2017, http://www.tshaonline.org/handbook/online/articles/fhabd, uploaded on June 15, 2010, published by the Texas State Historical Association. Also see *Galveston Daily News*, October 17, 22, 1896; Our Campaigns, "TX District 10," 1896, https://www.ourcampaigns.com/RaceDetail.html?RaceID=376356 and 1898, https://www.ourcampaigns.com/RaceDetail.html?RaceID=376368.

Both opposition to prohibition and a greater tendency to vote for Republicans marked German Texans as distinct from most Anglos. Between 1898 and 1909, however, Trenckmann and many of his fellow Germans in Austin County, while greatly agitated by the increasing prominence of prohibition in state politics, seemingly grew comfortable with becoming Democrats. They also accepted a more active government and helped exclude and segregate African Americans. Perhaps they were influenced by the return of good economic conditions and then the sharp and frightening recession of 1907. More likely the issues were linked. Sacrificing greater African American equality was the price for membership in the reform Democratic coalition and a chance to block or curtail attempts at enacting statewide prohibition. Perhaps they were concerned with social order and sought to put both "raggedy" Anglos and African Americans in their place. Perhaps Democrats seeking to end the chances that a Republican such as Hawley might win with a plurality convinced or intimidated enough voters, German Texans included, to back changes in the political rules or to drop out of the political process. Perhaps as Democrats strove to make their party all white, German Texans wanted to belong to the dominant group. Whatever the cause, the political world changed dramatically in Texas and in Austin County from 1898 to 1909.[33]

The 1902 vote on a poll tax amendment to the state constitution offered the clearest window to what happened and when it happened. That year the Democrats, who controlled the state legislature, put an amendment before voters that created a tax to be paid by all who sought to vote. It hit the poor hard, both black and white, and its many elaborate requirements for when and where it was to be paid, as well as keeping up with the tax receipt to show poll watchers, discouraged voting by the less well educated and well established. Voter participation had already begun to decline, perhaps because of physical intimidation of some voters, and the 1902 total vote was particularly low. Almost four thousand Austin County voters cast

33. The term *raggedy* was used among Seguin-area German Texans as a derogatory term for non-Germans. See Wolfgang W. E. Samuel, *In Defense of Freedom: Stories of Courage and Sacrifice of World War II Army Air Forces Flyers* (Jackson: University Press of Mississippi, 2015), 256–62.

ballots in the 1896 gubernatorial election, but only twenty-six hundred voted in 1902. Those voters supported the poll tax by a higher
percentage than did voters statewide. This fit a trend among the ten
counties identified by Seth Shepard McKay as German dominated,
where most of those counties went for the poll tax by a higher percentage than did voters in Austin County. To be clear, voters realized
the poll tax would suppress the African American vote and under-
mine the political power of poorer rural Anglos who had often supported the Populist Party. Somewhat counterintuitively, these were
voter groups who also opposed statewide prohibition in 1887. Now
Germans abandoned their allies in the cultural and political wars
over prohibition.[34]

What the poll tax began, the Terrell Election Laws and the white
primary system completed. Between 1903 and 1906 Democrats in
the state legislature pushed through new laws named for their chief
sponsor, Alexander W. Terrell. These laws replaced the long-in-place
convention system of selecting a party nominee with the primary
system that has been in use ever since. The primary system, billed as
a way to clean up the political process and prevent back-room deals
and rigged conventions, called for a primary election to select the
nominee of the party in cases where a party received over one hundred thousand votes in the previous general election. It also allowed
the party to set the rules determining who could vote in that primary, and the state Democratic Party and most counties required
a test oath saying that the applicant was white and had voted for
the nominee of the party in the last election. These requirements,
combined with the primary system itself, meant the end of viable
third-party candidates, black influence in most meaningful elections

34. For the vote, see Kingston, Attlesey, and Crawford, *Political History of Texas*, 66,
and Texas Secretary of State, Elections Division, Election Returns for 1902, Texas State
Archives and Library, Austin. On violence and the expulsion of black voters from the
political process, see Alwyn Barr, *Reconstruction to Reform: Texas Politics, 1876–1906*
(Austin: University of Texas Press, 1971), 193–208; Walter L. Buenger, *The Path to a
Modern South: Northeast Texas between Reconstruction and the Great Depression* (Austin:
University of Texas Press, 2001), 75–103. For events in Grimes County, next door to
Austin County, see Lawrence C. Goodwin, "Populist Dreams and Negro Rights: East
Texas as a Case Study," *American Historical Review* 76 (December 1971): 1435–56.

(except municipal elections and congressional elections in some urban areas), and compromise candidates who appealed across party and racial lines.[35]

Trenckmann supported this new system, and combined with the poll tax and intimidation of black voters, it ensured the dominance of the Democratic Party in all elections from the county level on up. The test oath recommended by the state party in 1904 read in part: "We recommend that the party authorities in all primaries permit all white Democrats to participate in said primaries who will be qualified voters under the law at the succeeding general election and who will pledge themselves to support the entire Democratic ticket at the succeeding election, and that the chairman in calling the State convention, prescribe this test. The term white includes all races except negroes." Austin County does not appear to have put in place a White Man's primary in 1906, as did neighboring Colorado County, but a White Man's Union similar to those in neighboring counties was formed in Austin County in 1900. The White Man's Union tried to mobilize all white voters to get to the polls, and it tried to suppress African American voters often by violent methods. In Colorado County as late as 1906 one of these methods was to have an elimination primary in advance of the Democratic primary that narrowed the field of candidates in the Democratic primary to one acceptable white man, usually the candidate of the local white elite. Despite the absence of such an elimination primary, Trenckmann faced no opposition in the Democratic primary of 1906 and won the general election that November by a vote of 1,267 to 975. The main issues in the election seem to have been the new primary system and the exclusion of African American voters from meaningful elections. Trenckmann commented after his victory that he would "make an effort to fulfill the expressed expectations in every way," and those expectations certainly included entrenched and institutionalized discrimination against African Americans. From that point forward lower voter turnout became the norm for elections in Austin County,

35. Barr, *Reconstruction to Reform*, 200–236; Buenger, *Path to a Modern South*, 75–103. Whites constituted 72 percent of the adult males in Austin County in 1900, but there were enough blacks to influence elections if they voted as a bloc.

and soon the Democratic primary, limited to whites, was the only election that mattered in Austin County and in most of the state.[36]

Trenckmann offered a few clues about the reasons for this baffling transformation. He passed on to his readers the standard Southern white condemnation of Reconstruction, suggesting that his family had not been enthusiastic supporters of the Republican coalition that controlled Texas from 1869 to 1873. Indeed, he expressed lifelong allegiance to the Democratic Party, and the repeated linkage of white supremacy with their party by prominent Democrats did not appear to trouble him.[37] In his autobiography he occasionally made the same racist comments about African Americans commonly shared with Anglos: African Americans smelled. They sweated profusely. They were easily duped at the polls and could be voted like sheep by political bosses. African Americans were corrupt. Cleaning up the political process and allowing reforms to ensue required removing African Americans. Directly or by inference Trenckmann wrote all those things.

These clues suggest that being a go-between linking the Anglo and the German worlds led to accepting white supremacy and South-ern mythology about Reconstruction. Thus, defending and enabling the preservation of German Texan identity encouraged adapting to white supremacy and the exclusion of African Americans from pol-itics in the early twentieth century. Trenckmann's tone was always more measured. He never challenged the basic humanity of Afri-can Americans. He went out of his way to praise Governor Hogg for listening to African Americans in 1892. In 1893 he strongly con-demned the brutal lynching in Paris, Texas, of Henry Smith, an Afri-can American accused but never convicted of the murder of a young white girl. While reporting on the incident Trenckmann observed, "Henry Smith was executed in a manner which will remain for a

36. *Texas Almanac and State Industrial Guide, 1904* (Galveston: A. H. Belo & Co., 1904), 37; *Das Bellville Wochenblatt*, November 15, 1906. Also see Barr, *Reconstruction to Reform*, 206, 235–36; *Das Bellville Wochenblatt*, November 8, 15, 1900; May 3, 10, 17; July 19, 26; November 8, 1906.

37. For example, Trenckmann reported approvingly on the violent ouster of the Grimes County sheriff by the White Man's Union (cf. Goodwin, "Populist Dreams"). *Das Bellville Wochenblatt*, November 15, 1900.

long time as a shameful blemish on the state, and which almost overshadows his inhuman crime by the brutality with which it was punished."[38]

Still, like so many paternalistic Democrats, after 1900 he insisted that pushing African Americans out of the political process would be good for them and good for the political process. He acquiesced in and supported more complete relegation of African Americans to an inferior status, and he benefited from that acquiescence and support by gaining a seat in the state legislature. Power, influence, and good connections to the elite class came with that seat in the House. Perhaps in a sense German Texan support for such things as the poll tax and the white primary sprang from Germans' antipathy toward those perceived as incapable or unwilling to strive for upward mobility. It came from their own cultural bias. It also came, however, from those like Trenckmann who served as a go-between who expounded on the place of African Americans in Texas and justified and helped embed Anglo racism in law and public policy.[39]

Such cultural bias and self-motivated reasoning led Trenckmann and (if voting returns are any clue) other German Texans in Austin County and elsewhere to accept a more moderate version of the dominant Anglo culture's insistence on white supremacy. In a nearby county some European ethic groups may have gone so far as to accept lynching. In any case, while German Texans moved toward the Anglo majority in politics and in support of segregation, continued vigorous resistance to prohibition still separated them from that majority community. In 1909, when Trenckmann completed his second term as a member of the state legislature, they remained German Texans, not Anglo Texans.[40]

Reflecting this distinctiveness, not all German Texans moved comfortably into the Democratic Party and supported segregation and disenfranchisement. Most notably Harry M. Wurzbach, a Republican

38. Ibid., February 9, 1893.

39. Ibid., July 12, 1906.

40. Cynthia Skove Nevels, *Lynching to Belong: Claiming Whiteness through Racial Violence* (College Station, Texas A&M University Press, 2007); Ruby Grote Ratliff, "A History of Austin County Texas in the World War," MA thesis, University of Texas, 1931.

congressman from the Seguin and San Antonio area, remained an ally of African Americans and a champion of their civil and political rights. Like the Democrats, after 1900 Texas Republicans, led by the so-called Lily White faction, moved to exclude blacks from positions of power and influence in their party and indeed to exclude them from the political arena. Elected to congress from 1920 to 1930, Wurzbach led the opponents of the Lily Whites and enjoyed a close alliance with African American political leaders in San Antonio. He also enjoyed strong support in counties in his district with a large German Texan population. Wurzbach courageously voted for the Dyer antilynching bill in 1922 and was the only member of the Texas delegation to vote to end that brutal practice. Despite continuous efforts by Democrats and Lily Whites to oust him, Wurzbach still won reelection, and he always asserted he did so in part with the votes of Democrats. Given the usual splits in the German Texan community, some of those Democrats were probably Germans who were willing to back their popular congressman despite his support of the Dyer bill. Thus, by 1909 German Texans clearly had moved decisively toward Anglos in matters of politics and race, but as late as the 1930s important distinctions remained.[41]

Meanwhile, in 1909 Trenckmann moved his family to the city of Austin and changed his newspaper into a more statewide vehicle for connecting German readers. He had spent much of the time he had served in the legislature in Austin, and when he completed his second term it probably seemed a natural progression to move his base to that city. His family by that point had grown to four children: two sons, Robert and William, and two daughters, Clara and Else. His older son had recently graduated from A&M College and moved out of state. His second son was attending the University of Texas, and his daughters were approaching college age. He hoped they, too, would attend the University of Texas. As his

41. *Handbook of Texas Online*, Jeanette H. Flachmeier, "Wurzbach, Harry McLeary," accessed November 1, 2017, http://www.tshaonline.org/handbook/online/articles/fwu04, uploaded on June 15, 2010, published by the Texas State Historical Association; *Dallas Morning News*, December 21, 1920; January 27, 1922; November 7, 8, 1931; *Brownwood (Texas) Bulletin*, April 17, 1922; *New York Times*, July 17, 1928; November 7, 9, 1931; *San Antonio Register*, November 13, 1931.

son William and others who knew the family recalled, furthering their daughters' education heavily influenced his parents' decision to move to Austin. Trenckmann and his wife faced the choice of staying in Bellville or moving to Austin to be nearer their children. He also hoped to expand his influence in the German community of Texas. Wanderlust may again have played a role in the move, as did the chance to take advantage of the political friendships and connections he had developed while in the legislature.[42]

Once in Austin, Trenckmann assumed a leadership role among all German Texans and continued to interpret and explain the swirl of events in the world beyond their communities to his readers. The political role of *Das Wochenblatt* was apparent just from its Austin addresses. It was initially published from 404 Congress Avenue, sharing a building with the law office of his son William, but sometime between 1918 and 1922 it moved to the prestigious corner of Congress and Tenth Street, just a block away from the capitol grounds.[43] In all his Austin locations Trenckmann served for twenty-five years as a mediator between multiple worlds. He tried to slow the drive for universal prohibition, keep the United States neutral in World War I, preserve the German language and culture, help a desolate Germany after the war, and fend off the attacks of the 1920s Ku Klux Klan. Of all these endeavors perhaps prohibition requires the most explanation.

What Trenckmann wrote in his 1899 pamphlet on the history of Austin County still applied to German Texans in 1909 and later as they vigorously fought attempts at prohibition: "Cheerful enjoyment of life after honest labor is the guiding principle followed by the people of our county." That cheerful enjoyment of their singing societies, athletic clubs, Maifest and Oktoberfest celebrations, and most special occasions customarily involved the consumption of alcohol. Not surprisingly, in the 1887 vote on statewide prohibition Austin County voters rejected statewide prohibition 2,987 to 325. In the heavily German Cat Spring and Millheim precincts the

---

42. *Austin American Statesman*, March 22, 1935; Interview with Hubert Heinen, by Walter D. Kamphoefner, November 21, 2015; W. Trenckmann Jr., "Wilhelm Andreas Trenckmann," *Das Wochenblatt*, March 29, 1935.
43. *Polk's Morrison & Fourmy Austin City Directory*, 1918, 485; 1922, 101.

vote was 238 to 0. Not even the passage of nationwide prohibition after World War I kept German Texans from drinking beer. The Cat Spring Agricultural Society, for example, kept serving beer as part of their activities into the 1920s and even recording their keg orders in their German-language minutes, despite prohibition laws outlawing the practice. Except for the views expressed by some German Methodists, an attack waged against drinking wine, beer, whiskey, and other spirits was deemed a general assault on German culture. For most German Texans such attacks were blatant forms of discrimination, eliciting fierce and mostly uniform responses as witnessed in the 1887 statewide prohibition campaign and subsequent elections during the next four decades. Besides, making and selling beer and wine were an important part of the local economy, and many families had past or present ties to the industry. Trenckmann's mother's family, for example, had owned a brewery in Magdeburg, and German Texans like Trenckmann whose income or family history linked them to the production and sale of wine and beer had added incentive to resist prohibition.[44]

In 1911 Texans again voted on an amendment to the state constitution that would have mandated statewide prohibition. Since 1887 when Texans decisively defeated such an option, numerous counties and parts of counties had gone dry as a result of local-option elections. Local-option elections never had a chance of passing in German-dominated counties, but the patchwork system led to complaints among the advocates of prohibition that easy access to alcohol remained for those willing to cross county and precinct lines. Prohibitionists also charged that alcohol corrupted politics because breweries financed much of the antiprohibition cause. The 1911 vote proved especially close, but the antis again prevailed by about 6,000 votes. In Austin County, as in other German counties, the vote was overwhelmingly against prohibition, with 2,657 votes against and only 275 votes for prohibition. This time Millheim and Cat Spring

44. Trenckmann, "Austin County," 13; Cat Spring Agricultural Society, *Century of Progress*, 293–333; *Texas Almanac and State Industrial Guide, 1912*, 42–45; Walter D. Kamphoefner, "The Handwriting on the Wall: The Klan, Language Issues, and Prohibition in the German Settlements of Eastern Texas," *Southwestern Historical Quarterly* 111 (2008): 60–61.

did scrape up 4 votes in favor of prohibition, barely 1 percent of the 378 cast. Trenckmann enthusiastically exclaimed in *Das Wochenblatt*, "Bravo!—Austin County has done its part, as in 1887." Without a similar lopsided vote in the other German-dominated counties, statewide prohibition would have carried. Ironically, however, the close vote probably resulted from the new political order supported by Trenckmann and other German Texans. That new order discouraged voting among groups such as poorer rural whites and blacks who had opposed statewide prohibition in 1887.[45]

Despite political storms (such as the 1911 prohibition election) life in Austin soon settled down into a comfortable routine for the Trenckmann family, but the start of World War I in Europe in 1914 and the eventual entry of the United States into the war in 1917 brought distress and disruption to all German Texans. While proclaiming their loyalty to the United States, in the first years of the war German Texans strongly supported American neutrality, and in 1916 they backed Woodrow Wilson for president and endorsed his campaign slogan, "He kept us out of war." Up to that point many German Texans also hoped for a victory by Germany or a negotiated peace without losers. Not surprisingly, they bitterly resented Wilson's support of a declaration of war against Germany the following year. Yet most German Texans tried to balance loyalty to the United States with concern for the start of war with their ancestral homeland. In Dallas the local *Turnverein*, about one-third of whose four hundred members had been born in Germany, announced its support for the war effort and President Wilson. In a resolution published in the *Dallas Morning News* they declared, "When our common country is forced to engage in a great struggle to enforce its rights as a nation and defend itself against foreign aggression" we are with "our beloved President and our fellow-citizens in prosecuting to a successful termination the present war."[46]

In that same issue of the *Dallas Morning News* the editorial writers for the paper castigated Jeff McLemore, the sole member of the Texas

45. *Das Wochenblatt*, July 27, 1911. Also see Texas *Almanac and State Industrial Guide, 1912*, 42–45; McKay, *Texas Politics*, 24–43; Buenger, *Path to a Modern South*, 104–31.
46. *Dallas Morning News*, April 7, 1917.

delegation to Congress to vote against entry into the war. After saying that McLemore's views did not fit those of citizens of the nation or the state, the editorial board added, "save for a few communities where Germans are in the majority."[47]

Not surprisingly, given this predisposition, despite their declarations of loyalty to the United States, the war brought varying degrees of discrimination against most German Texans, including the Trenckmanns. Like the Dallas *Turnverein*, the Wochenblattmann openly declared his loyalty to the United States, and he worked to remain an interpreter of American ways to German Texans. Albert Sydney Burleson, whom Trenckmann had known since his days at A&M, served as Wilson's postmaster general and gave *Das Wochenblatt* the very first certification issued in the country exempting it from the requirement to file English translations of all articles dealing with the war. Politics played a large role in such exemptions; the *Seguiner Zeitung* never received one before the end of the war, although it published a special twenty-two-page Liberty Loan edition on April 18, 1918, and in August even published the letters of two local doughboys writing home from France in the German language. At the same time, however,the state government, and especially Governor William P. Hobby, moved aggressively against the use of the German language in public and the teaching of German in public schools and universities. Germans were routinely demonized as warmongers and barbarians, and German Americans were forced repeatedly to demonstrate their loyalty to the United States by volunteering to serve in the US army or buying Liberty Bonds.[48]

The end of the war brought heartache to German Texans as they watched the US government and their allies ignore the plight of many citizens of Germany who were left destitute and starving by the last days of the war. Trenckmann took the lead in organizing relief efforts and watched with dismay as anti-German sentiment and suspicion continued.

47. Ibid.

48. *Seguiner Zeitung*, April 18, August 15, 1918, p. 1. A normal issue of the paper consisted of eight pages. Both of the soldiers writing in German, as well as the two named recipients, were of the third generation. Lewis L. Gould, *Progressives and Prohibitionists: Texas Democrats in the Wilson Era* (Austin: University of Texas Press, 1973), 150–248.

Worse was to come as the rebirth of the Ku Klux Klan and enforcement of nationwide prohibition during the early 1920s brought violent intimidation and coercion to German Texans. Austin, Fayette, Washington, and Williamson counties all witnessed violent encounters with Klansmen determined to enforce English-only and self-defined Protestant morality. The worst incident of Klan violence directed at Germans in Texas, and possibly nationwide, struck rather close to Trenckmann personally, although he only mentions it peripherally in his memoir. It started at the Cat Spring Agricultural Society, which his father had helped to found and presided over, which admitted him to membership by unanimous vote in 1906, and where he was invited frequently to deliver addresses in German, even after his move to Austin.[49] At the anniversary fest and barbecue hosted by the Agricultural Society in June 1922 there were, as usual, speakers in German as well as English. When a young lady remarked to Robert Schaffner that the man speaking in German ought to be tarred and feathered, Schaffner replied that the people who were doing the tarring and feathering around there ought to be the ones tarred and feathered. Klansman Thompson Bell, who was with the young woman and may have been the target of the remarks, reacted by threatening Schaffner, and the two would have come to blows had not the sheriff and one of his deputies intervened. Both sides promised that there would be more later, and there was.

On the morning of September 5, Thompson Bell attacked Robert Schaffner with a knife on the streets of Sealy. Schaffner ran into a nearby store, grabbed a baseball bat, and managed to fend off Bell with a glancing blow. Both sides apparently gathered reinforcements. That evening on a corner of Main Street in Sealy, it came to a showdown. A crowd of eight or nine men, including Bell and two of his brothers, attacked Fritz Schaffner, Robert's father and a prominent Sealy real estate agent. The elder Schaffner was not armed, but his son, who came to his aid, was. It is unclear who fired the first shot, but at least fifteen rounds were counted in the aftermath. Fritz Schaffner died of four bullet wounds, a four-inch stab wound, and a fractured skull from brass knuckles; his son Robert died of five bullet wounds to the back and head. His younger brother Ernest survived

49. Cat Spring, *Minutes*, 209, 235, 244, 248, 253, 257, 259, 261, 266, 274, 278.

a three-and-one-half-inch stab wound that put him in the hospital for six weeks. But the attackers paid dearly: Thompson Bell and his brother Luther both died of bullets probably fired by Schaffner, and another brother, Austin Bell, was charged with murder. Despite a change of venue to Austin, he was convicted and sentenced to five years in prison.[50]

The elder Schaffner had grown up in the Cat Spring community, where his father was a member of the Agricultural Society; Trenckmann described him as a "fine friend." The Wochenblatt-mann had various other acquaintances in Sealy, a larger town only twelve miles from Bellville. His newspaper reports on the incident were based on telephone conversations with people at or near the scene.[51]

Trenckmann and other German Texans fought back on multiple levels: with hot lead as well as cold type, and not least at the ballot box. Although a Klansman presided as Washington County sheriff until his defeat in 1924, his German counterparts in neighboring counties were particularly tough on the hooded empire. Austin County sheriff A. J. Remmert, notoriously lax in enforcing Prohibition, refused to allow masked parading in his jurisdiction. He was reelected the entire decade, and his next three successors through 1953 all had German names. Colorado County sheriff John Wegenhoft defied Klan threats on his life if he refused to resign, equipping each of his sons with a rifle, a revolver, and the name of a likely suspect should he be assassinated. If anything, the close of the 1920s left German Texans more united and more determined to preserve their distinctive culture than at the close of World War I.[52]

50. Ibid., 294–95. Additional background and details are provided by Kamphoefner, "The Handwriting on the Wall," 52–66.

51. Trenckmann provided detailed accounts of the incident in *Das Wochenblatt* of September 7 (p. 5), September 14 (pp. 4, 8), and September 21, 1922 (p. 5). The *Dallas Morning News* also gave extensive coverage to the story and trial; the most detailed account was given on September 16, 1922 (p. 2). See also the issues of April 13; July 11, 13, 15, and 16; and November 20, 21, 22, and 23, 1923.

52. "KKK Parade at Sealy Fails to Materialize," *Houston Post*, September 27, 1921 (p. 1); James C. Kearney, *Nassau Plantation: The Evolution of a Texas-German Slave Plantation* (Denton: University of North Texas Press, 2010), 226; Walter L. Buenger, "Memory and the 1920s Ku Klux Klan in Texas," in *Myth, Memory, and Historical Meaning*

In 1924 Klan membership in Texas reached perhaps as high as 170,000 men (official membership was limited to white Protestant males). Together with Klan sympathizers such as the Klan's women's auxiliaries, they made up almost twice that many voters, and in the 1924 Democratic runoff primary Felix D. Robertson, who was backed by the Klan, received 316,000 votes. Robertson lost by almost 100,000 votes, however, to Miriam Ferguson, the first woman elected governor of Texas. German Texans had long supported her husband, James E. Ferguson, because he opposed prohibition and the Ku Klux Klan, and they struck a blow against the Klan and prohibitionists by voting overwhelmingly for Miriam Ferguson. Trenckmann, always the loyal Democrat, had grown disenchanted with Jim Ferguson, who had run for president on the antiwar American Party ticket in 1920, and he hoped that another anti-Klan candidate besides Miriam Ferguson would win the first primary. Yet once Miriam Ferguson garnered enough votes to make it into the runoff, he supported her as did most German Texans. Austin County, for example, voted for her 3,520 to 568, indicating that turnout was reaching toward 1890s levels in elections that mattered to German Texans. German Texans also supported Ferguson in the general election against her Republican opponent with all ten of the most German counties overwhelmingly supporting her successful candidacy.[53]

In the days after Miriam Ferguson's victory, Trenckmann seemed genuinely optimistic about the future of Texas politics and the place of German Texans in the state. He was cheered by efforts to exclude known Klansmen from leadership roles in the state Democratic Party but also to extend an olive branch to former Klansman. He hoped that if approached in the right manner they would renounce their Klan membership and resume a more inclusive approach to civic life. Such tranquility would benefit everyone, including German

---

in Texas, ed. Elizabeth Hayes Turner and Gregg Cantrell (College Station: Texas A&M University Press, 2007): 119–42. Wegenhoft did leave office in 1922 but continued on as a deputy; his successor, Adam Burttschell, was not only German but Catholic besides, even worse from a Klan standpoint.

53. Norman D. Brown, *Hood, Bonnet, and Little Brown Jug: Texas Politics, 1921–1928* (College Station: Texas A&M University Press, 1984), 49–252; McKay, *Texas Politics,* 103–58.

Texans. With the help of Jim Ferguson, Trenckmann also expected Miriam Ferguson to provide "a good and moderate leadership of the government." The future looked bright immediately after that momentous election.[54]

After 1924 Trenckmann and German Texans did seemingly settle into more peaceful times. Of course, they too experienced a volatile economy and the pending approach of the Great Depression, but if anything those years saw a flowering of Trenckmann's life's ambitions and German Texans' cohesiveness. Taking advantage of smoother sailing, Trenckmann continued to highlight locally produced German literature and creative endeavors, and he participated fully in life in Austin. Trenckmann's newspaper featured the efforts of Austin area writers as well, and he built close ties with those connected to the University of Texas. In 1931, for example, he published "The Functions of a University Outside Its Walls," written by one of his neighbors, prominent University of Texas professor Roy Bedichek. Trenckmann also followed and reported state, national, and international news to his readers, including Adolf Hitler's rise to power in Germany. In February 1933, when Hitler assumed power, Trenckmann noted: "The boundary beyond which the constitutional government in Germany totally ceases, is thus crossed. The Wochenblattmann will spare himself saying more about this today; it is too painful for him and many others."[55]

As long as he lived, he happily worked on *Das Wochenblatt*, but on April 7, 1933, shortly after finishing his serialized memoir and commenting on Hitler, he sold ownership of the paper to National Weeklies of Minnesota, though he still edited the local news page until shortly before his death.

When his children were away from Austin he kept up a steady stream of correspondence with them. In one letter of December 20, 1934, to daughter Clara he noted: "You know I used to boast a little

54. *Das Wochenblatt*, September 4, 1924.

55. Ibid., February 2, 1933. Also see ibid., September 17, 1931. Of all the Texas German newspapers, Trenckmann's was the one most strongly opposed to Nazism. As early as May 1932, before Hitler had taken power, Trenckmann took a "resolute stand" against antisemitism. Dwayne E. May, "Changing Attitudes of the German-Americans in Texas towards *Deutschtum* and the Fatherland," MA thesis, Sam Houston State University, 1973, 59–65.

about the fact that I always have written to my children, who are of the third generation in this country, in German. And was indecently proud that the three youngest at least could themselves write German for publication. So I'll stick to the system and wish you "Froeliche Weinachten," which of course included your Alfredo."[56]

All of the Trenckmann children reflected their father's influence, if in rather different ways. William Jr. became a lawyer and deputy county clerk in Austin. Daughter Else, who never married, also remained in town, teaching high school German and directing German plays, some of them authored by her father, on the side. Son Robert followed his bride to Washington State, became a well-established farmer, and by 1940 became a Mason County, Washington, commissioner. Daughter Clara was the most venturesome, seemingly reflecting the family's freethinking tradition and less rigid adherence to traditional gender roles. In 1918 she enlisted in the US Navy and "fought Germany with her trusty Underwood on Capitol Hill," as she put it. She traveled widely in Europe and the Americas, both before and after marrying an Italian immigrant in New York, and occasionally recounted her adventures in *Das Wochenblatt*. She followed her father into journalism, if of a different kind, working under Amelia Earhart at the publicity division of Curtiss-Wright Aircraft and later writing a biography of Glenn Curtiss and leading the effort promoting a commemorative postage stamp for Earhart. Shortly before her seventy-fifth birthday she was arrested along with eighteen others for blocking the railroad tracks to a New Jersey naval ammunition depot in protest of the Vietnam War.[57]

William Trenckmann did not live many months after his loving letter to Clara. He died at his home, 704 East 23rd Street, on March 22, 1935. His wife, Tillie, and children and grandchildren survived him. On his death the Texas legislature passed a resolution honoring him that declared: "In the passing of this distinguished gentleman his community and his State have lost a scholar, a man of honor

56. William A. Trenckmann to Liebes Klaerchen, originally German letter translated by Clara, in Clara Trenckmann papers, privately held by Stuart Strong.

57. *From an Oblique Angle*, blog, "Clara and Alfredo Studer as Forteans," August 23, 2016, http://www.joshualublubuhs.com/blog/clara-and-alfredo-studer-as-forteans; "Aviation Pioneer Dies," *The 99 News*, September 1979, 6.

and integrity and a loyal citizen." The resolution also noted his being valedictorian of the first graduating class at Texas A&M, his contin- ued contributions to the leadership of the college, his work as an edu- cator and newspaperman, and his role in the legislature. Trenckmann deserves to be remembered not only for these accomplishments and his other contributions to life in Texas, but also for his efforts to hold together the Texas German community. His success in that endeavor tells us much about the nature of German immigration and German immigrants, a group who over at least three generations remained distinctive and preserved their culture, language, and identity. His children translated this autobiography, indicating that they, too, retained an interest in preserving the German language and the his- tory and culture of their people.[58]

Even more than that, however, Trenckmann deserves to be remem- bered for what he stood for and his very human failure to always live up to his ideals. In his autobiography he wrote of his college expe- rience at A&M: "The fact that I had two years of French and three years of Spanish, graduating in both, probably did not enable me to instruct Mexicans in chopping cordwood, nor would my French have been understood in Paris; but my reading knowledge of both these languages did preserve me from the assumption that only the English and German-speaking peoples are fitted to be the bearers of culture and that other peoples are inferior." Education opened doors and opened minds for Trenckmann and the people he touched as a schoolteacher and newspaper editor. He never seemed to realize that African Americans deserved the same understanding that he demon- strated with French and Spanish speakers, or that this blind spot con- tradicted his basic philosophy. In that, however, he demonstrated the essential reality of German Texans. They adapted and compromised with the people around them, especially the Anglo elite. Yet they also resisted the larger culture and through 1935, a century after the first Germans arrived in Texas, still maintained an identity somewhat apart from that of other Texans and other Americans.

58. *Austin American Statesman*, March 22, 1935; *Das Wochenblatt*, March 29, 1935; Legislative Library of Texas, "William Andreas Trenckmann," 44th Legislature, April 10, 1935, 1274, http://www.lrl.state.tx.us/legeleaders/members/member display.cfm?memberID=3052, accessed on October 12, 2016.

Erlebtes und Beobachtetes
(Experiences and Observations)

W. A. TRENCKMANN

In the heading of the *Wochenblatt*, the years of service are calculated from October 1, 1891. The first two issues of my paper I sent out as sample copies, as I had only two subscribers, and both of these had paid in advance and both were living in Austin. Actually, the first weekly issue was ready for printing on September 17 of that year, and today, again on September 17, the *Wochenblatt* completes forty years of membership among the German publications in America.

Since I had been in public service as a schoolteacher for twelve years, and since I have slipped into the seventies in the meantime, it would be expecting too much to postpone the Jubilee issue of my paper to the fiftieth anniversary of its founding. Besides, it would be inadvisable, as the young people of this day and time think more in terms of the present and a hopefully brighter future than of the past. So what I would have to tell in a commemorative issue, believing a backward glance toward that which formerly existed can be valuable, might lose even more in interest after ten additional years. In

This autobiography of William Andreas Trenckmann appeared in issues of *Das Wochenblatt* from September 17, 1931, to February 16, 1933. It was translated by his children, William Trenckmann and Elise Trenckmann, and the translated manuscript is in the Dolph Briscoe Center for American History, University of Texas at Austin (hereafter cited as Briscoe Center).

the meantime, many a one who belongs to the first or second generation of Germans in Texas will have departed from my circle of readers and from life, even if the editing of the *Wochenblatt* should at that time still be in my hands.[1]

If I as one who never attained any kind of fame am telling a lot about my life history and the history of the *Wochenblatt*, it is for two reasons: first, because I firmly believe that many of my readers of long standing are kindly disposed to me and might like to know me better, even though it is only by means of a newspaper report; second, because the story of my life, even a humble one like mine that has never climbed the highest peaks nor fallen to the lowest depths might still hold valuable lessons. These can be culled only from an autobiography written by one whose purpose is not the glorification of self and who does not hide his own weaknesses. The older one gets, the more each one of us who loves humanity wishes that the lessons of his fate might be of use to others. If what I tell here accomplishes that in a few families of my circle of readers, then my purpose in telling it will be attained.

Suitable to the times, this edition does not appear in an astonishingly great number of pages. In the past I have had financial losses on almost every expensive special edition due to the fact that although in my opinion I am a passable newspaper editor, I have always been a poor solicitor of advertising. I am not able to stand financial losses today; for when his readers are hard up, the newspaper publisher who does not have his chief income from advertising is doubly so.[2]

---

1. Texas stands out for the persistence of the use of the German language. The 1940 census shows some seventy thousand third-generation Texans with German mother tongue, the only state in the union where third-generation speakers outnumbered those in the second generation.

2. By 1931 when Trenckmann began publishing his memoirs, major daily newspapers were growing in importance, but papers such as *Das Wochenblatt* that circulated in multiple counties could still compete even though the Depression lowered spending on advertising. See Patrick Cox, *The First News Barons* (Austin: University of Texas Press, 2005). On the distribution of Trenckmann's paper, see the list of agents and their cities in *Das Wochenblatt*, September 17, 1931.

Millheim and Its School

For long years the conviction has been growing in me that the region in which a person grows up influences him both physically and mentally. I have had this conviction confirmed in my present surroundings as well as in the past when I compared the "Sandhasen" (sand hares) of the Bernard Prairie with their kinsmen who grew up on the black hilly land around Shelby or between Mill Creek and the Brazos. I noted differences between those who grew up on the "Hog Wallow Prairie" and those of the Brazos Bottom. That difference did not consist only in the fact that the inhabitants of the sandy prairie averaged a few inches taller in height than the others. Later in Travis County I found similar differences between the hill folks from our cedar brakes and the folks from Pflugerville, Dessau, and Richland. Therefore I believe that I should tell something about Millheim, where my cradle stood, if I ever had a cradle. If I had one, it was soon given away, because I was the youngest in my family. Cradles were in great demand in Old Millheim, where a dozen children per family were no rare exception.

Originally published in *Das Wochenblatt*, September 17, 1931.

Millheim was the third oldest of the solid German settlements in Austin County.[1] Even before the first German settler, Louis Kleberg, settled there at the beginning of the 1840s, Anglo-American squatters, who came there because things were getting too crowded for them on the other side of the Mississippi, had settled north of Millheim in the extensive forest on the southwest side of Mill Creek. They had built log cabins in a clearing, had probably planted a small patch of corn for bread, and had lived chiefly on a great abundance of game. One of them, more industrious than the rest, is even said to have planted fruit trees.

When the Germans arrived, these squatters had already moved on. San Felipe, which was supposed to become the capital of Texas, was too near to suit them. A few years before Kleberg, two Anglo-American farmers—Swearingen and Clark—who really liked hunting better than farming, had settled near the edge of the flat prairie. They soon became good friends of the Germans, whose language the young Swearingens learned, even the Low German and Swiss German dialects. Then, according to the report of our neighbor's son Sigismund Engelking, came Kleberg's brother-in-law, F. Engelking, who was married to a daughter of the von Roeder family, which had settled near Cat Spring in 1834; Karl Wenmohs; the Swiss brothers, Marcus and Fritz Amsler; Vornkahl; H. Bolten; the actor Louis Constant, who, according to reports, attempted to make Mill Creek navigable and who did other things that caused the neighbors to shake their heads in disapproval; Carpenter W. Mersmann; A. Hagemann, the inventor of tomato wine; F. Langhammer, who set up a tannery; the musically gifted Emil Kloss—it is said that he taught even his

---

1. Germans settled in Austin County as early as 1831, and the county continued to draw German immigrants through about 1890. Industry and Cat Spring were the two all-German towns in Austin County founded before Millheim. Trenckmann assembled a history of the county: William A. Trenckmann, "Austin County: A Supplement to the *Bellville Wochenblatt*, Issued June 16, 1899," English translation available in the William A. Trenckmann Papers, 1859–1833, Briscoe Center. Also see Terry G. Jordan, *German Seed in Texas Soil: Immigrant Farmers in Nineteenth-Century Texas* (Austin: University of Texas Press, 1966); Rudolph Leopold Biesele, *The History of the German Settlements in Texas, 1831–1861* (Austin: Von Boeckmann-Jones, 1930).

dogs to howl musically, and I can testify that they howled differently from any other dogs that I ever heard when they answered the wolves; his brother, the goldsmith, Robert Kloss; J. A. Wilm, who erected a gin driven by horses and mules; J. H. Krancher; Rudolph Goebel; the brothers Wilhelm and Carl Schneider from Palatinate; August Goebel, who attained the age of ninety in good health and clarity of mind (his widow, Mrs. Helene Goebel, née Roggemann, is still alive to tell of olden times in Millheim); Otto Goebel; F. Buntzel; Theodor Brosig; Dr. Carl Nagel; the teacher, E. G. Maetze; B. Siegert; A. F. Trenckmann; F. Heinecks; H. Kluever; if I am not mistaken, Millheim's first tailor, Riniker, from Switzerland; and the skilled shoemaker Necker, who provided the neighborhood with shoes from leather tanned in Texas.

For the most part they were young life-loving and enterprising people, and the bachelors among them were soon married. They learned to love their new home in spite of a meager income. There was little that could be sold for money. With the exception of a few like Emil Kloss, who became a wealthy man and spent the last half of his life on Lake Garda in Italy with his wife; Wennmohs; Dr. Nagel, and Constant, they remained in Millheim and found their last resting places in its sandy soil. Most of their descendants live in Millheim or in its vicinity today. I know of no other settlement in that part of the state from which so few have moved away.[2]

My old friend and first teacher, Mrs. Ida Schulze née Maetze of Hempstead, recently told me that during the Millheim festivities to honor the visiting Carl Nagel from Saint Louis, who had served as secretary of commerce under Taft—the highest post attained by a Millheimer—that Adalbert Regenbrecht, then high in his seventies, had said to her, "In all the world there can't be a prettier place than

2. Emil Kloss, a highly educated refugee of revolution from the city of Rostock, was by 1860 living as a farmer in Burnet County, Texas, and apparently returned to Europe with his wife the next year, but their stepdaughter stayed behind. Adolph Wennmohs arrived in 1846 and died in Flatonia in 1921, but his older brother Charles and wife Theodosia appear along with him only in the 1850 census in Millheim. Louis Constant, a native of France who had lived in Germany, immigrated in 1848, was a postmaster and merchant in Millheim, and returned sometime after 1867. *Cat Spring Story*, 55, 29. On Nagel, see below.

Millheim." And Regenbrecht should know, as he hailed from the fine old city of Breslau.[3]

Certainly the old settlers had a discriminating eye for natural beauty and also for the practical values of a new place to locate. Millheim offered one advantage over the nearby Cat Spring. It was crossed by two clear, steadily flowing creeks, each bordered at the lower end by forests. In the pamphlet Austin County, which I published in 1899 and which furnished many accounts of Austin County and of the early days in Texas,[4] Sigismund Engelking tells that in Clear Creek there was one deep swimming hole after another. Over this clear, never failing brook, "wild peach" [Wildlorbeer, wild laurel] trees made a leafy canopy to shut out every ray of the sun. When I was old enough to find the paradise of my childhood in the creek, it was not so beautiful any more. The wild peach trees, which cannot bear to have the hooves of cattle cutting into their fine roots, had almost disappeared, and the sand that had washed down from the cow trails on the hills and from the much traveled Houston road had filled up the water holes. Sometimes floods washed out these water holes, but they soon sanded up again. There I could build dams of sand for a shallow bathing pool that would fill up gradually and wash away with the first rain; but it was fun, and building them over and over was a good lesson in perseverance. Similar conditions must have prevailed at Constant Creek farther to the west. But in nearby Mill Creek there was one water hole after another in which the youth of Millheim could learn to swim and dive under the direction of the teacher and from which the anglers rarely returned without a rich haul of fish.

3. Charles Nagel fled Texas with his father during the Civil War and settled in Saint Louis. After his appointment to Taft's cabinet, he visited his birthplace and was given a parade and reception at the Colorado County Fair in Columbus on November 1, 1909. *Houston Post*, October 24, 1909, 45. Ida Schulze née Maetze was the schoolmaster's daughter. Both she and Regenbrecht were from Silesia. *Cat Spring Story*, 61–62, 65, 69–70.

4. This pamphlet was edited by Trenckmann and contained contributions from several educated German speakers. It was part of Trenckmann's efforts to promote literature and a sense of belonging among German Texans. See Trenckmann, "Austin County."

The upper part of Millheim had hilly, black land, the center mixed soil, and the lower edge deep sand. Here began the great wide, gradually descending Gulf Prairie, on which until the 1870s one could have ridden to the Gulf on horseback without encountering a house or a fence. At that time it was assumed that this prairie with its fine stand of grass would always provide free grazing for cattle, but this hope soon faded when the useful but hated freedom-restricting barbed wire made its appearance. Mill Creek Bottom provided much good wood and was only a short distance away. Most valuable of all were the splendid white oaks, which furnished sturdy steps and shingles; the Spanish oaks, which were also suitable for shingles; the wild mulberries, which can be split so easily into durable fence posts, and the ash trees for wagon building. The post oaks on the higher sandy soil furnished good fence rails; and the wood from the hickory was used for yokes for oxen, ax handles, implement handles, and bows and crossbows for the boys. Half a dozen varieties of dewberries and blackberries furnished fruit from May until midsummer. Mustang grapes were made into wine, and wild plums in great abundance into delicious preserves. Ice cold springs burst forth on the hills in a number of places. Even the steep hill on the east side of Constant Creek, where the brakes always had to be used on the thrilling but scary downgrade, was valued by the settlers because in one of its steep slopes a hard, cross-grained sandstone jutted out, which could be used for many purposes. Dr. Nagel built the first and the only remaining stone house in Millheim.[5]

In his account of the baptism of the settlement, Sigismund Engelking, the jovial, phlegmatic humorist, who could see the funny side of just about anything, tells how merrily, even boisterously, things went on among the old—at that time almost all fairly young—Millheimers. He writes, "In the fifties a meeting was held in my father's first store, which he conducted in partnership with Nolte, for the purpose of giving our settlement a name, naturally I was a spectator, but I can't recall all the details. I do remember, however, that toward evening the meeting became very jolly. Barrels of tar were

---

5. This house survived into the twenty-first century.

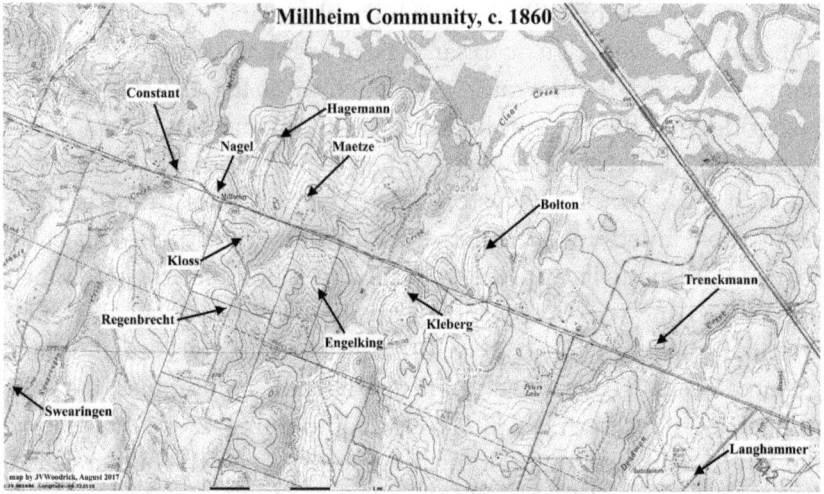

Map of the Millheim community about 1860, showing the location of farms.
Map created and supplied by James Woodrick, Austin, Texas.

lighted and bets for wine and other drinks were made as to who could jump through the flames. A certain Quensel, also known as the Ranger, didn't jump high enough and fell into a burning barrel, searing his legs badly before the others could pull him out. Dr. Nagel smeared oil on his burns, and the drinking and merriment, as well as the wrestling and racing, went right on into the night. Dr. Nagel was the best jumper, and I always envied him for his achievements in this art. Such were the Swabian capers in which the old Texans delighted."[6]

During this hilarious meeting the name Muehlheim was chosen at the suggestion of Wilhelm Schneider, who came from the Rhine-Palatinate, but it wasn't long before the Anglo-Americans had botched it up into Millheim.

Naturally life in Millheim did not always run such a merry course, but on the whole the settlers were a jolly folk, among whom a singing society soon came into being under the direction of schoolmaster Maetze, and many happy singing festivals were held. In origin the

6. Sigismund Engelking (1843–1905), son of a Heidelberg University graduate, was born and died in Millheim. A Swabian caper, in German, *Schwabenstreich*, is a foolishly audacious undertaking—a regional putdown playing on the Swabian reputation for awkwardness.

settlers were a motley company. The majority had originally been artisans; there was probably not one among them who had engaged in farming in Europe.[7] They came from all German lands: the Amsler brothers, the dyer Hillboldt, and the mason Hiltpold from the Canton Aargau; the tailor Riniker also from Switzerland. Except in the school, where the teacher firmly insisted on High German, all sorts of dialects were common. Louis Kleberg, who died at an early age, Dr. Nagel, Regenbrecht, my father, and surely Hagemann too had received a higher education; the brothers Kloss and J. H. Krancher had attended good city schools.

Most of these educated men were somewhat better situated financially than their neighbors, but they were not in full command in Millheim. Genuine democracy prevailed. Just about everyone voiced and fought for his own opinion, and in the meetings where important matters were discussed my old friend Krancher, who though not highly schooled, was skilled in the use of tongue and pen, or the equally glib-tongued Carl Schneider, with his innate motherwit, carried their opinion just as often as did the Lateiners.[8] And it turned out that the artisans, to whom farming was an unknown calling too, got ahead faster than did the scholars, who tried to farm according to books published in Germany and England. Absolute sovereign in Millheim was only one man, and

7. The 1829 travel report of Gottfried Duden, based on his sojourn in Missouri, attracted a number of German political refugees, both from the 1830s and from 1848, to become "Latin Farmers" who knew more about the former than the latter. They congregated in settlements such as Dutzow, Missouri, and Belleville, Illinois, similar to Millheim. The father of Texas immigration, Friedrich Ernst, was bound for Missouri attracted by Duden when he diverted to Texas. James W. Goodrich, "Duden, Gottfried (1789–1856)," *Dictionary of Missouri Biography* (Columbia: University of Missouri Press, 1999), 262–63; Detlef Dunt, *Journey to Texas, 1833*, trans. Anders Saustrop, ed. James C. Kearney and Geir Bentzen (Austin: University of Texas Press, 2015), 59, 175.

8. Lateiners, or "Latin ones," was the name given to German settlers with a high level of education, as indicated by their knowledge of Latin. Millheim, Latium, Bettina, Sisterdale, and Tusculum were usually considered Latin settlements because a high percentage of their original settlers were educated enough to have some knowledge of Latin. See *Handbook of Texas Online*, Rudolph L. Biesele, "Latin Settlements of Texas," accessed July 28, 2016, http://www.tshaonline.org/handbook/online/articles/ue103, uploaded on June 15, 2010, published by the Texas State Historical Association.

that man was our teacher, E. G. Maetze, who reigned supreme in his own kingdom—the school.

I shall have to devote separate space to this school, because it was the real heart and also the pride of the settlement. Old Millheim never had a church, and most of the Lateiners, my father being an exception, were even opposed to churches, as were the majority of the intellectuals of Germany of that time. When as chairman of the school board my father wanted to permit a wandering preacher to hold services in the schoolhouse, he was outvoted by his two colleagues, who insisted that a sermon would only create dissension in the otherwise so beautifully harmonious settlement. I was present at this meeting and heard the decision with my own ears. Millheim now has its fourth schoolhouse; with its school it has been moving slowly westward. The first schoolhouse had originally been the home of the Engelking family. It stood on their big farm and was well built. A part of it had been used in the erection of a new home, the largest in the community, for the rapidly growing Engelking family.

Ernst Gustav Maetze was the first teacher. He held his position for more than twenty-five years. A graduate in Protestant theology of the University of Breslau, he is supposed to have preached only one sermon. Then he became principal of the public school, Bürgerschule, in Bernstadt, Silesia. He played a leading part in the movement of 1848. After Bismarck had become the forger of the German Reich, Maetze liked to recall the fact that in 1848 in the National Assembly in Berlin he had crossed verbal swords with the "mad Junker." When reaction prevailed, Maetze had to flee. Coming to Texas, he earned his living for a while in New Ulm as a day laborer, but ill-fitted for plowing and rail splitting, he gladly accepted Mr. Engelking's invitation to come to Millheim and teach the latter's two elder sons and the sons of a few neighbors. His pupils increased fast in numbers. It did not take long for the news to spread that Millheim had an excellent teacher. Pupils came from great distances; for example, Rudolph Kleberg, who was later elected to Congress; his brother Marcellus, who became a prominent attorney; and W. D. Cleveland, the son of a wealthy planter, who was for a long time one of the leading merchants in South Texas and who attributed much of his success to the knowledge of the German language that he had acquired in Millheim.[9] Maetze impressed the Anglo-Americans too, who could not fail to respect the iron zeal that enabled his quick mastery of the English language. They called on him as a political speaker, and in time he was elected to the Senate of the State of Texas, where he was able to play an important role.

In a very few years the schoolhouse had become too small. Later it was used as a home for colored tenants. A new one was built between the Engelking and Kloss places. This burned down during the last half of the Civil War—the common theory being that it was set on fire as an act of vengeance by a passing soldier, an ex-pupil who, like so many other young Texans, had been unable to adjust himself to school discipline and had resented the rod. It was a different time in Texas. Most of the young men were either in the army or they were hauling cotton to Mexico for the government. Some were in hiding to evade the army service. Most of the fields lay uncultivated, and what little was grown was unsalable.[10] The Confederate paper money had become worthless, and the few who were somewhat better off had sacrificed their cash money to save ardent

9. The Kleberg family originally lived in Austin County, where Rudolph Kleberg was born in 1847. They soon moved to DeWitt County, where Rudolph later practiced law. He served as a member of the US Congress from 1896 to 1903, and he died in Austin in 1924. William D. Cleveland was a prominent Houston cotton merchant, wholesale grocer, and banker. His firm, Wm. D. Cleveland & Co., was among the largest in Texas during the late nineteenth century. See *Handbook of Texas Online*, Craig H. Roell, "Kleberg, Rudolph," accessed July 28, 2016, http://www.tshaonline.org/handbook/online/articles/fk107, uploaded on June 15, 2010, published by the Texas State Historical Association; Max H. Jacobs and H. Dick Golding, *Houston and Cotton: Commemorating Seventy-five Years of Leadership and Progress as a Cotton Market* (Houston: Houston Cotton Exchange and Board of Trade, 1949), 15–28.

10. German Texans' attitudes toward secession and the Confederate cause ranged from strong opposition to grudging support of the inevitable. Few were enthusiastic supporters. The war left many, even those whose family members fought for the Confederacy, bitter because of loss of life and property and the general suspicion that Anglos held for Germans. Attitudes forged in the Civil War era persisted for decades even among post-1865 German immigrants, and Trenckmann saw himself as a bridge between Anglos and Germans. On later German immigration, see Terry G. Jordan, "The German Settlement of Texas after 1865," *Southwestern Historical Quarterly* 73 (October 1969): 193–212. On Germans in western Texas, see Gilbert Giddings Benjamin, *The Germans of Texas* (New York: D. Appleton & Company, 1910), 90–110.

Unionists from being shot.[11] At that time a new school building was not to be thought of. So school was held on the porch of the teacher's home, and on very cold days in his parlor. But as soon as peace reigned again and the few bales of cotton raised were for a short time bringing an excellent price—my father's gin book showed that in nine years the biggest yield of any one farm was three bales and most farms had produced only one—the word was, "We must build a real schoolhouse." Money was still scarce, but at a meeting that was held on the porch of my parents, I heard each man offer his contributions: one promised cash, another lumber hauled from Spring Creek, most offered their services in constructing the building.

On my first school day immediately after Easter in 1867, the schoolhouse, which afforded room for at least sixty children, had been in use for quite a while. Somewhat airy, since it had only been weatherboarded, it was certainly no palace, but we did not freeze because the nearby woods protected us from the north wind, and the iron stove gave off excellent heat.[12] After a short time an inside wall and a small roof over the entrance were added and—a rare thing in those days—it was provided with wall maps and a blackboard. An excellent practice introduced into this school as soon as circumstances permitted was that the tuition was paid on the first school day, if possible with a twenty-dollar gold piece. If I am not mistaken, another fine custom provided that the fourth child of a family of children attending school at the same time was given free tuition. Probably not one defaulted in paying the school money, since after twenty-seven years of teaching Maetze was able to retire in comfortable circumstances. In this respect Millheim was a model settlement. Today, forty years after his death, the memory of this teacher is honored by his pupils, even by those who felt his punishing hand.

11. Nagel relates that several of the Germans who started for Mexico with them gave up and returned home. At least one, Meissner, was tried and sentenced to death but was pardoned on the morning of his execution because many neighbors had taken gold out of their hiding places to ransom him. Nagel, *Civil War Story*, 254. This was probably Carl Meissner, a charter member of the Cat Spring Society.

12. Weatherboards were overlapping horizontal slats nailed onto the studs as siding, so there was no plastering or insulation.

Childhood and Youth

In another place in this issue my good friend Henry Westermann has revealed the fact that I was born on the twenty-third of August 1859. But for that fact I might have kept my birthday a secret, not for reasons of vanity but for business considerations, for there are people who think that if a man amounts to anything, he should be able to retire at the age of sixty; and at seventy he should certainly be in a home for the aged, where he would not be telling younger people what to do or entering into competition with them. I cannot retire, even if I wanted to. If I could I would not want to. My father, Andreas Friedrich Trenckmann, was fifty years old when I was born, my mother forty-two. I have observed that children of older parents often differ in several respects from other children. For one thing they are of a less happy temperament than those of younger parents. They are less quick at decisions and not impulsive enough to enjoy the pleasures of the moment. I have known sons of quite old parents who already in their childhood showed characteristics of old age.

My father's childhood—he was born in 1809—came at a time when foreign armies often trampled the crops of Germany underfoot and practiced incendiarism on Prussian territory. He was baptized Andreas after the noble Tyrolese hero whose resistance and

Originally published in *Das Wochenblatt*, September 17, 1931.

heroic death were the first signal for the War of Nations that ended with the burning out of Napoleon's star at Waterloo.[1] He remembered the Russian Cossacks who gave him his first horseback ride.[2] His birthplace was the village of Wefensleben—a five hours' walk from Magdeburg. As a child and as a youth he had to walk this distance twice a week to get clean laundry from home. On one such occasion he was found in the deep snow almost frozen to death. His childhood was gloomy. His mother died early, and his stepmother, who resented the presence of two sons by the first wife in the home, was the kind that is often described in Grimm's fairy tales. My father was not a complainer and did not often mention her, but our Cousin Tramm, the great hunter who had married my father's youngest half-sister, did the talking. Cousin Tramm lived with us for a time to satisfy his great love for hunting. He declared that his mother-in-law had driven him and his wife first to Hungary and then him, without his wife, to Texas.

After a hard period of school—he had to spend all his spare time tutoring at the seminar in order to have enough money to eat—my father became a successful teacher. For a long time he was owner and director of a private school in Magdeburg. Much sorrow was his lot. His first wife died young, leaving four sons and a daughter; his second died soon after the birth of a baby girl. His oldest daughter became the victim of yellow fever soon after their arrival in Galveston, and when he died alone in his home at the age of seventy-three, only two sons out of his nine children survived him. No wonder he was a serious man who seldom laughed and who was seldom able to abandon his reserve. He had a good voice and loved to sing,

1. Andreas Hofer was a Tyrolean folk hero who led the resistance to Bavarian and French occupation of that Austrian province but was defeated, betrayed, captured, and executed, reportedly on Napoleon's orders. That a family in a distant German province was inspired by Hofer demonstrates their political and national consciousness that was awakened by resistance to Napoleon.

2. After Napoleon's disastrous Russian campaign in the winter of 1812–13, the Prussians joined Russia in the coalition against him. Russian Cossacks were involved in the battle of Möckern on the outskirts of Magdeburg on April 5, 1813. This campaign culminated in Napoleon's defeat at the Battle of the Nations near Leipzig, October 16–19, 1813, by a combined army of Prussians, Russians, Austrians, and Swedes.

but I never heard him sing except when he took me on fishing trips into the depths of the Mill Creek virgin forest. His guiding principle in life was Kant's teaching of the compulsion of duty. The reaction that set in after 1848 made Germany unbearable to him, although he stood in the good graces of the Prussian government, which gave him a recommendation when he emigrated, stating that he was a well-meaning democrat. This was probably given him because he had prevented the hated governor, Count Haack, from being strung up on a lamppost during a bloody street battle in Magdeburg. As chief of that civil guard, my father had done this by means of a carefully chosen warning to avoid a stain on the cause of freedom.

In later years when I read in Fritz Reuter's *Ut mine Festungstid* how heartlessly the count had mistreated the students who were imprisoned in the fort, I regretted my father's having taken this step.[3] One of his happiest memories was of a kiss given him by the aged poet of liberty, Ernst Moritz Arndt, after my father, as a member of a delegation from Magdeburg, had made a speech during a meeting of friends of freedom in Berlin.[4] The son of a farmer, my father's innate love of country life, from which he was banned at such an early age, had evidently influenced his choice in coming to Texas.

My mother, born Johanne Jockusch, was the eldest daughter of a long established Magdeburg family, owners of a brewery that produced a light, agreeable white beer. Opposition to prohibition I have thus probably inherited from my ancestors. She had received as good an education as was available to the girls of Magdeburg in those days. In her girlhood she had been vivacious, sentimental, and somewhat overly emotional, and from early youth on often plagued

3. The governor in question was probably a Graf von Hacke, from a prominent Prussian military family, but not the same man who had tyrannized Fritz Reuter (1810–74). A law student in Jena, Reuter was arrested in 1833 for his membership in a democratic revolutionary student organization and sentenced to death, which was commuted to a thirty-year prison term, seven years of which he served, partially in Magdeburg, before being pardoned in 1840. His prison memoir, written in the Low German language, which was closer to Dutch than to High German, was published in 1862. It is indicative of an international, democratic consciousness that Trenckmann would have read it in America.

4. Ernst Moritz Arndt (1769–1860) was a German romantic nationalist, author, and poet who had agitated against Napoleon and for German unification.

with a nervous ailment. After a childless marriage she had been a widow for quite a while before marrying my father. She too had lost her mother early.[5] Her only brother, Julius Willhelm Jockusch, who was several years younger than her, had been educated to be a merchant and had attained a respected position in Galveston as a businessman.[6] Hence she too was drawn to Texas. My parents emigrated in the spring of 1853 and bought an established farm from the poet Johannes Romberg in the wooded Bernard Valley in Colorado County. Five years later they moved to Millheim on a larger farm, on which the former owner Wilm had erected a horse-and-mule-drawn gristmill and gin. I have never learned the reason for their move. They left behind them on the Bernard many dear, congenial neighbors in the families Himly, Reichardt, Litzmann and others who remained lifelong friends.[7]

My childhood memories do not reach very far back.[8] The first, a very dim one, is of a song that I begged my mother to sing over and over for me as she rocked me to sleep in her lap on the old porch rocking chair. Another is of *iron drops*. These I liked, and I got them regularly because I was anemic. My brother Paul, who was two years older than I, had died of this disease.[9] I can also remember that

5. Parish records show Johanna Louise Jockusch as the daughter of a distillery and brewery owner, born on June 25, 1817, in Magdeburg. Her mother died in childbirth before she was two years old, and seven months later her father married a sister of his first wife. At age twenty-two Johanne married her uncle, a fifty-six-year-old wine merchant, who died five years later in 1844. *Stamm-Register und Geschichte der Familie Bonte* (Magdeburg, 1844), 162–63,

6. Johann Wilhelm Jockusch, born in 1819, had trained with merchants in his home town and in Hamburg and by 1844 was working for a German merchant in Havana. *Stamm-Register der Familie Bonte*, 163. He immigrated via New Orleans in 1846 and appears in the 1850 census as a merchant with five thousand dollars in real estate. He served as Galveston consul for several German states and for the North German Confederation in the 1870s.

7. Although on the opposite side of the small river that forms the Colorado County line, the San Bernard community was in close communication with Cat Spring, only a half-dozen miles away. A. Himly, C. Reichardt, and Ledwig (*sic*) Litzmann were all charter members of the Agricultural Society. *Cat Spring Story*, 110–11.

8. Trenckmann's other reminisces of his childhood during the Civil War were published four decades earlier in *Das Bellville Wochenblatt* and are included in this book as the appendix "Christmas in Troubled Times."

9. It remains unclear just when brother Paul died. He is enumerated in the 1860 census, age three, but he is not mentioned in Trenckmann's account of Christmas 1863.

often the wide passageway between the two parts of our house was crowded with Confederate soldiers, who, seeking shelter there from blizzards, had leaned their guns against the wall. I can remember how I was often deprived of the buttermilk I loved so well because my mother had emptied the churn to refresh these thirsty and hungry soldiers with buttermilk and butter bread. I can also remember how busily leafy tobacco was pressed into rolls with ropes to be sent with butter, ham, and sausages to my brothers in the army. I can remember the anxious faces of my parents when with our meager mail service they had been waiting in vain for months for word from them, and their grief when after a long period of wavering between hope and sorrow, it became certain that my dashing, gay brother Adolph, whose daguerreotype I later found in the photograph albums of so many charming ladies, had escaped from the hospital in Virginia in order to take part in the expedition into Maryland and must have fallen along with a great part of his regiment at the battle of Sharpsburg in Yankee-land. In the casualty list his name appeared as A. Frenchman.[10]

One occurrence with its results remains unforgettable to me. I was standing at the gate of the fence around our gin and stables, which was the exit of the tree-lined road leading to the house. I had been sent to call my father. Suddenly about a dozen well-armed horsemen stopped at the gate, which had probably been locked against plunderers. They had come to recruit my brother Hugo, youngest of the sons of my father from his first marriage. Hugo, who had just reached recruitment age, was opposed to Secession and did not want to fight against the Union. Since ginners were not required to fight,

10. One of Adolph's letters home, written June 17, was reported in the *Bellville Countryman* of August 9, 1862, reflecting the slowness of postal service. Adolph was a private in Company B of the First Texas Infantry, organized at Livingston, Texas, and mustered in at New Orleans on May 16, 1861. The distance from home and the early date of enlistment indicate strong dedication to the Confederate cause, as does his battle record, which is confirmed by muster rolls. They indicate Adolph was hospitalized in Richmond in April and May 1862 before being wounded in the foot at Malvern Hill on July 1, 1862, and then killed on September 17, 1862, at Sharpsburg/Antietam after his term of service had actually expired. The First Texas Infantry suffered a casualty rate of 82 percent, the second highest of any unit on either side in any Civil War battle. Nicholas Roland, "Texans at Antietam: 150 Years Ago Today," Not Even Past, September 17, 2012, https://notevenpast.org/texans-antietam-150-years-ago-today/.

my father had installed him as manager of the gin. The leader of the party cursed, threatened, and waved his sword. My father raised his big whip, which was weighted with lead, to defend himself. I, a sickly child weakened by illness, closed my eyes and could not utter a sound. No shot fell. The recruiters finally rode off jeering. My father seemed to be his usual calm self. What I had witnessed during those dreadful moments caused me to have nightmares of bloodshed for many nights afterwards. When I awoke the morning after one of these, my first glance fell on the bed of my father, which stood opposite mine. I saw a big red spot beside his bed and assumed that he had been murdered. I could not scream for fright. When it grew lighter in the room, I heard my father's voice and realized that the spot of blood was his red house slippers.

I had practically no contact with other children, because the beautiful harmony that had previously reigned among the Millheimers had been disrupted by the war. Our nearest neighbors, the families of Engelking and Kleberg-Langhammer, had already at the beginning of the Secession movement been placed in a position of sharp disagreement with the other *Lateiners*, especially with Dr. Nagel and Mr. Regenbrecht, who enthusiastically supported the freeing of the slaves. The men who disagreed with the latter had been in the country so long that to them as to almost all Anglo-Americans slavery in the South seemed unavoidable and therefore justified. They themselves kept a few slaves. The fact that probably all the other Millheimers were against Secession seemed to strengthen the pro-slavery leaders, intelligent men who knew how to defend their views in the violent battle of mind against the "abolitionists" whom they sharply denounced. Teacher Maetze and my father, both against Secession and both expecting nothing but harm and certain defeat against superior power, regarded it as proper in a democracy to comply with the decision of the majority.

Two of my father's sons promptly volunteered for army service. Otto participated in the daring expedition into New Mexico and returned sound and unwounded.[11] Adolph was killed. Emil, who

---

11. Otto Trenckmann and his cousin Hermann enrolled on September 5, 1861, in the heavily German Company G of the Fourth Texas Cavalry and participated in the Sibley Campaign into New Mexico, which won a tactical battle but failed its strategic

went unwillingly, as he was leaving wife and child, became a prisoner at Vicksburg.[12] Hugo, who was drafted shortly before the end of the war, died about a year after the war's end of malarial poisoning, which he had contracted in the slimy ditches near Velasco at the mouth of the Brazos.[13]

Gustav Maetze participated in the last war years, and his father, the teacher, served obediently as major of the Home Guard. Dr. Nagel, however, fled with his son Carl to prevent his having to serve the Confederacy.[14] Regenbrecht, who did not want to fight against the Union nor to desert his family, finally let himself be persuaded to join the Confederate Army after he had been pursued for a long time and in danger of being shot. He once told me with great glee how he had helped other heads of families who had been conscripted to escape

---

objective at Val Verde, was repulsed at Glorieta Pass, and limped back to Texas without its supply train by July 1862. Otto was fortunate; of the 810 men in his regiment who left San Antonio in October 1861, 47 were killed or mortally wounded, 28 died of disease, 92 were wounded, and 194 were taken prisoner in the campaign. Otto advanced from the rank of private to sergeant. *Handbook of Texas Online*, Thomas W. Cutrer, "Fourth Texas Cavalry," http://www.tshaonline.org/handbook/online/articles/qkf18, and Don E. Alberts, "Sibley Campaign," http://www.tshaonline.org/handbook/online/articles/qds03, published by the Texas State Historical Association.

12. Emil Trenckmann (only listed once as Emil [www.fold3.com/image/15069993]), usually as Ernst or E. or F. E. in muster rolls, but with same rank and correct age and marital status) had married Johanne Dorothea Witte on November 28, 1861, and enlisted on June 20, 1862, in Wickland's Company of Waul's Texas Legion, where he was elected junior second lieutenant. The letters of a German captain from Austin County in Waul's Legion are published in Walter D. Kamphoefner and Wolfgang Helbich, eds., *Germans in the Civil War: The Letters they Wrote Home* (Chapel Hill: University of North Carolina Press, 2006), 403–26. There is only an incidental mention of Trenckmann on p. 409. After Vicksburg his unit was consolidated into Company B, Timmons's Regiment, and served at Galveston and Mud Island.

13. Hugo, who turned eighteen in 1860, was inducted into the Fourth Texas State Troops for a six-month term in January 1864, with the notation, "Claims exempt as a miller" and current station at Cedar Lake; www.fold3.com/image/10919874. A German stationed at Velasco wrote a month earlier, "The weather has been very fine up to now, and nobody in our mess (thirteen men) has been sick—The Americans have been sick more often and try to shirk whenever they get a chance." Kamphoefner and Helbich, *Germans in the Civil War*, 461.

14. The translated letters of Dr. Hermann Nagel are published in Kamphoefner and Helbich, *Germans in the Civil War*, 394–403. For a more detailed account, see Nagel, *Civil War Story*.

when he was on duty at night. I do not know how many Millheimers were killed in the war, but I do know that many a one returned sick and miserable from the battlefield to find his unprotected wife and children in great distress. Many died because the most necessary medicines could not be obtained. Many heads of families dodged army service by remaining hidden and used bright moonlight nights when no conscriptors were near to do the hardest and most urgent work on their little farms. One of them, Fritz Amsler, committed suicide when he was caught. His brave fourteen-year-old daughter and Ernst Gross, who as an orphan had found a home with the Amslers, succeeded in keeping the family fed.[15]

Women rendered truly superhuman services in order to supply the necessities of life for their children, to keep them clothed in a time when only very rarely a chest of colored dress material could be smuggled in from Mexico. Few could produce money for the high-priced goods. The rest supplied themselves as best they could with used and made-over garments to cover their own and their children's nakedness. All of this created bitterness, which in some instances led to the planning of acts of vengeance against the Secessionists. My father, who possessed the confidence of his neighbors, learned of one of these plans in time to prevent its execution.

The war over, everything slowly slipped back into the good old order of the past. Old friends were reunited. The first regular task came to me when whist was played at our house. It was to take a newspaper—there was a greater supply again—to fold it to make fidibi, paper pipe lighters, until I had filled a cup with them, to light these on a homemade tallow candle, and in turn to light the long pipes of the whist players, one after another. At the whist table at our house, men who had been fiery opponents during the war found each other again in their old friendship; and in the case of the Engelking and Regenbrecht families a closer relationship later developed out of this friendship.

15. The Amslers immigrated from Switzerland in the 1830s. The Gross adoption is verified in *Cat Spring Story*, 41. Two older Amsler brothers, but not Fritz, are profiled on 21–22, where it also mentions that Carl Conrad's first three slaves were bought in New Orleans. According to his tombstone, Friedrich Amsler died on June 14, 1863, at the age of forty-six; his daughter was actually fourteen in 1860, as was Gross.

Christmas 1866 when many toys were to be bought in the store again, and I received a Noah's Ark as my chief gift, I heard them say in our best room—it even had white clay walls—that little Willie would soon have to start school. The news sent no small shock through my system because I had tremendous respect for Mr. Maetze, whose hair was now snowy white, and for his commanding voice. Former pupils and already grown men had told me—a child who had never received even so much as a slap from my parents—of Maetze's powerful wielding of the switch. My fears gradually diminished as I realized that my sisters liked to go to school and when my mother told me that I would learn to read letters like those she read to me from Germany and books from distant lands like the stories by Christoph Schmid. Tante Maetze, my mother's cousin, had been commissioned to bring these from Europe for me in nine beautiful red-bound volumes.[16]

On the Tuesday after Easter—in Millheim, as in Germany, the school year began after Easter—I marched to school with my brother Otto, who carried the rawhide chair for me; school satchel containing slate, slate pencils, and primer hanging around my neck. Every child had to furnish their own seating facilities. Every vestige of fear that I probably felt as we approached the schoolhouse was gone when I was given my place at a long table near the teacher of the ABC pupils. She was the friend of my sister, Mr. Maetz's daughter Ida, whom I liked as much then as I do today. Under her gentle direction I mastered the Reffelt reader in a few months to the degree that long before vacation time I was permitted to read short tales from Schmidt, alternating at reading with my dear mother. We even got as far as one of his long, pious, sentimental stories.[17] When my mother was unable to continue our reading hours, probably because we had important guests for the week, I couldn't wait for her. In my eagerness to learn what became of the devout model hero of the story, I finished by myself, and when

16. Widower Ernst Gustav Maetze had married Emma Elizabeth W. Baum on May 27, 1860.

17. German immigrant Hermann Reffelt (1811–89), a teacher in Hoboken, New Jersey, published a number of school books in German and English. Bavarian Catholic priest Christoph Schmid was a prolific author of children's literature, mostly with religious overtones.

she was ready to resume our reading hour, I was engrossed in a new story.

From that time on I have been a bookworm. I read everything in our home library in the way of lighter reading, then stories in newspapers, taking particular interest in the day's news, Schiller's works—some of them over and over—the Bible, Wolff's *Hausschatz*, the big Brockhaus books about rearing children, doctor books, finally in my reading hunger, even books on agriculture—whole volumes from the Department of Agriculture, later serialized novels in magazines and newspaper, even by bright moonlight in the cow pen to beat my sisters to them.[18] Once, after I had been a teacher for quite a while and should have had more sense, I read the three-volume novel *Kampf um Rom* by Ebers in an uninterrupted twenty-five-hour stretch.[19] It is a miracle that my eyes have lasted as long as they have.

One vivid memory of my first school is of an almost daily "fight," instigated by the older pupils, that I had with Joseph Willrodt, who like me was at that time small and pale cheeked. That didn't hurt either of us; on the contrary, I learned to defend myself. I saw him again, a vigorous giant of a man at the centennial celebration in honor of Father Maetze. I went through a second fighting period a few years later and was finally cured of my excessive love of fighting by Theodor Brosig, who was much stronger, after he had sat on me so long that I was finally forced to say, "I give up."[20]

Learning was easy for me. In my second school year Mr. Maetze, observing that I followed geography lessons with rapt attention, took

18. Friedrich Schiller (1759–1805) was known as the "poet of freedom" for his dramas such as *William Tell*. The *Grosse Brockhaus* was the standard multivolume German encyclopedia, which went through dozens of editions between the early nineteenth and twenty-first centuries. Oskar Ludwig Bernhard Wolff (1799–1851) was the editor of several popular anthologies; Trenckmann probably means his *Poetische Hausschatz des deutschen Volkes* (1839, with fifteen editions by 1851 and many more thereafter), or possibly his prose *Hausschatz deutscher Prosa* (1845, with five editions by 1851).

19. Trenckmann has either the wrong author or the wrong title. He is probably referring to Felix Dahn, *Ein Kampf um Rom* (1876), which ran over twelve hundred pages, or possibly Georg Ebers, *Eine ägyptische Königstochter* (1864), both popular three-volume works by university professors of antiquity.

20. Joseph Willrodt, who later lived in Colorado County, was only a few months older than Trenckmann, but Brosig, born at Millheim in October 1856, was almost three years older.

me into a class where geography was taught entirely by means of maps and oral explanation. Geography books were not available until later. Arithmetic was easy for me too, but I did not become a good mathematician. When I hear teachers complaining today that they have so much to do, I think back of all the things that our teacher accomplished and that I as a country schoolteacher did later using him as my model.

The instruction in English began early. We were made to translate most of our English reading selections into German—sometimes orally, sometimes on the blackboard. Then we had to make a corrected copy of what we had translated and our teacher had to correct all the copybooks. He wrote the models for penmanship into our writing books, which he had ruled himself, and the translations of English words that we did not understand into smaller notebooks, which we exchanged in order to save him a little work, as he had the only dictionary. So he also wrote for us the names of oceans, rivers, mountains, etc., which we had to locate on the maps. At that time I was able to find them with the pointer as fast as they were called out. In penmanship alone I reflected discredit on my teacher, for my hand was not sure and has remained illegible to the sorrow of my typesetters. But my dear friend Willie Keuffel, a model pupil in every respect, even today writes the beautiful, uniform handwriting of his teacher—a fact that may have contributed to his rapid success in life. Keuffel never had an ink spot in his book, whereas an attempt to ink over one brought me my first school punishment. We received instruction six days a week for ten full months except that on Wednesdays and Saturdays we were excused at one o'clock, on other days at four.

Our school grounds were unsurpassed and incomparable. Directly in front of the schoolhouse a big space for playing ball, to the south a small oak grove in which we played "conscripting." After they had escaped from imprisonment in the bullpen, the pursued could swing up on the mustang grapevines out of reach of the long switches of the pursuers. Later they could make their real escape in the wide prairie. And what wonderful children's games we played! Besides running games and "townball"—football and baseball were unheard of—the even more delightful "hotball" and "rolly holy," at which one was bombarded with heavy rubber balls, and "cotton ball," which was almost as dangerous as football.[21] Everyone played; there were no onlookers and "rooters." The girls had their games for themselves in front of and around the schoolhouse.

As I have previously related in the *Wochenblatt*, I was made girl-shy by the teasing of my older brothers and sisters. In school I had little to do with any girls except Sissy and Linchen Langhammer, neighbor's children, whom I regarded as harmless because they, like me and their brother "Jungschen," roasted their bare feet in the hot sand and even went on snake hunts with us.[22] The other girls I admired at a distance, especially two who by my standards were real beauties.

The little shack out back was something that caused a lot of aggravation for the teacher and the neighborhood, but the woods behind the schoolhouse provided a substitute. Sometimes Mr. Maetze's well gave out in the summer, or the ants got into it. Then drinking water had to be carried nearly a mile in buckets. Since two boys were ordered to attend to this job and we were no different from other boys, we often returned with half empty buckets. More serious was the fact that some pupils were sent by their parents from neighboring towns and cities to study German or to get acquainted with stricter discipline. From these boys we learned all sorts of mischief, e.g., vigorous cursing and other things that were not to our benefit. (I never had much use for sex education in the schools, but I am for the father and mother giving their children the necessary clarification early on.) Another peculiarity of the Millheim school was the fact that the boys considered it a disgrace to wear shoes except when there was thick ice on the water; and even then, I regularly left my shoes under the schoolhouse when I left for home—fortunately

21. Townball was a precursor of modern baseball in which the batter stood between first and fourth bases. Batters were out if fielders caught the ball on the fly or the first bounce. Base runners were often put out by being hit with the thrown ball, but rules and the number of people on a team varied. The other games mentioned were all variants of modern ball games such as dodgeball. See David Vaught, *The Farmers' Game: Baseball in Rural America* (Baltimore: Johns Hopkins University Press, 2013).

22. Caroliana "Linchen" Langhammer was just Trenckmann's age; her brother Ernst was a year older, and her sister Marie about three years older. Their mother was a Kleberg. They and the Trenckmanns were nine families apart in the 1860 census.

stealing was unknown in Millheim at that time. Not to be omitted was the festival of gorging on fruit indulged in by the boys on the last days before the summer vacation.

I must add that to my great joy many of the boys and girls I went to school with back then are still wandering about in the sunshine. Theodor Brosig is still lively and full of enterprise. Karl Hillboldt is said to be a lively dancer. And this in spite of the fact that we youngsters lived chiefly on bacon, cornbread, and molasses and drank highly doubtful water. We had no good wells. No one had ever heard of "calories." Malaria was still prevalent. Even a few of our highly respected seniors like Ulrich Kloss and Wm. Reichardt are still quite vigorous.

At Easter 1873 my school days came to an end. I had completed Ray's *Arithmetic* as a final achievement. Now a difficult time began for me. I had never known really hard work. Hunting eggs, chopping wood and bringing it in, the delightful hauling of barrels of water with horse and sled, driving in the calves early in the morning and in the evening the cows when the grass still tasted too good for them to come home, roping off the calves while my sisters milked, feeding the hogs, laying cornstalks in the furrows before the plow, leading the oxen before the iron plow for deep plowing—that was about all I had ever done. It left me ample time for self-invented war games, for which my study of United States history stimulated me, also for hunting nuts, berries, fruits provided by nature and for picking strawberries, grapes and other fruit in our big garden, for lying for hours under a tree in the woods to think out my own fairy tales and the almost unending stories in which I was always the hero and for fishing and hunting with my single-barreled, light shotgun—a Christmas present. In the year 1872 my sisters married—Helene in the spring, and later in the fall Anna, my half-sister—but I never knew the word: all the children of my father were real brothers and sisters to me. In December my brother Otto, considered a confirmed bachelor, married Marie Himly, whom I soon regarded as a sister.[23]

23. Louise Helene Trenckmann married Saxon immigrant Carl August Hermann Bendrat on June 4, 1872. The city directory of that year shows him a lumber merchant in Austin in partnership with Cat Spring native S. G. Amsler. They resided on Congress Avenue, but she died the next year in childbirth along with her infant and

In that period, so rich in family happenings, the nervous ailment of my mother, which she had apparently conquered, reappeared in a more severe form, so severe that she who had until now been carrying the heavy burden of housewifely duties in a big household, besides sewing all our clothes—even my father's and mine—could no longer attend to her duties but needed much attention herself. My father, who had over-exerted himself in trying to keep up the field work, was often hindered in his activities by severe attacks of rheumatism in addition to suffering with a hernia. The house and kitchen work as well as much of the care of my mother usually fell on my young shoulders. Field work was a pleasure to me, even though the splitting of rails to replace those that had rotted in the fences proved rather arduous at first, or hurriedly bringing in the fodder when thunderstorms were threatening on sultry days. In fact, I believe I would not have made a bad farmer because I developed many ideas about farming at that time which were commonly accepted later; for example, the selection of the best cotton seed pods of our Meyer's cotton for planting, protection but also thinning of our young pecan trees, and prevention of erosion by hemming the flow of water in the small tributaries leading to our big branch.

In the kitchen too I was able to find my way around because I had often watched my mother in her happier days and my sisters at work when there seemed to be an opportunity for licking the pans. I'm sure, however, that my dishwashing left much to be desired. Finally I not only managed to concoct a usually quite edible cornbread in the bread pot on our open hearth, but also a real pudding and even molasses cakes.[24] I tried myself at washing, ironing, sewing on but-

---

was buried in the city's Oakwood Cemetery on July 5, 1873. "Oakwood Cemetery Database," Austin History Center, http://www.austinlibrary.com/oakwood/index.cfm?option=individual&record=1117. Anna Frederica Trenckmann married Fritz Engelking on December 4, 1872. Otto Trenckmann was married to Mary Himly on November 17, 1872, by a justice of the peace.

24. A bread pot was a cooking utensil similar to a Dutch oven used in the Americas and in Europe for baking and roasting often in an open fireplace. It was typically cast iron and had feet that allowed the pot to be placed over the coals. Some had a lip around the edge of the lid to contain coals placed on top of the oven. Cookstoves did not become common until later in the nineteenth century.

tons and darning when no female help was to be had or when in the case of hired colored help too many linen napkins, tablecloths, and too much good porcelain began to vanish. In the late fall of 1873 my beloved mother was released from a life that had become a torture for her. Now my father and I lived alone in the old home. We took turns with the outside work, but I usually did the cooking. In old age it is hard to acquire new tricks. This practice period certainly did me no harm. In the case of all marriages except the very wealthy ones, circumstances occur when it is exceedingly advantageous if the husband can occasionally take the place of the wife.

Not often has a son revered his father more than I did mine, a father who was never able to show his love for me by means of a single caress or expression of affection, and yet he loved me dearly and made sacrifices for me that were far greater than I suspected at the time he made them. It did hurt me that in the time when I was cut off from all association with young people because of home conditions and was doing my utmost to accomplish unaccustomed tasks, he never gave me a single word of praise. His position—one that was held by many German fathers of that day—was that praise makes children vain, and vanity he despised. One evening Brother Emil and Mr. Surmann from Rockhouse came to visit us. I was happy because I had cleaned the house particularly well that day, even to changing the bed linens. I spared no effort to put on a good evening meal on the only still clean tablecloth we had. When I had gone to the kitchen to fetch a missing article, I heard through the thin door that my father was talking about me. Stopping to listen, I heard him say that I was accomplishing wonders, that he was proud of me and that I was the greatest joy of his old age. I never forgot that, and I did my work with much greater zest from then on. But right then I resolved that if I should ever have children, I would praise them freely when they deserved it.

For that matter, at that time, I never really thought that I would ever be a father because I was well convinced that I would die young of tuberculosis. That was because I had read about this disease in a book of home remedies and believed to have found every symptom in myself. In Hofstetter's Almanac, which I usually read just for the sake of the jokes, I found confirmation of my fears. At the same time, thanks to my physical labors, I was fast growing stronger. At seventeen I was full grown and weighed more than I weigh today—a proof that my cooking agreed with me, and that I ate well and sufficiently.

Once—it must have been in the spring of '76—after the most pressing field work had been completed for a while, my father said that I most certainly had to visit the Himly family, as they had invited me. Having become shy, I did not want to go. In my youthful vanity I thought that my country-store-bought clothes, from which the buttons were constantly popping, left much to be desired. But an obedient son, I rode forth with carefully shined shoes on my feet. When I was approaching one of the two creeks between Cat Spring and the Bernard, I saw some young fellows lying on the ground on one side of the road beside their horses, whose bridles they were holding. I rode on. Soon I heard loud yelling behind me. Looking around, I saw that they were chasing me, and suspecting evil, I gave my horse the whip. By the time I had crossed the creek bed at full gallop, I had made the firm resolution that let come what might, I would flee no farther. I brought my horse to a walk and raised my whip in defense but the riders slowed up too. They may have thought that I was armed, trotted their horses peacefully by me. That taught me a lesson: he who runs away will be bitten by the dogs. I decided, not out of courage but out of prudence, to leave running away to others.

The visit to the Himlys' with the kind, highly educated housewife, whose house and yard fairly shone with cleanliness, who was able to question me without embarrassing me about my knowledge of German literature, who aroused my eagerness to read Jean Paul, at that time the idol of many (later I acquired his works for myself, but he did not appeal to me); the delicious roast mutton she put on the table; the motherly instructions she so gently imparted to me; her husband, who was an authority on agriculture and sheep raising and who was constantly plying me with his mustang wine—the whole family remains unforgettable to me![25]

25. Alexander and Clothilda Himley and their children settled at Bernardo in 1848, after he had studied agriculture in Germany. He continued to experiment in horticulture and introduced an improved breed of sheep from Kentucky. *Cat Spring Story*, 45. Jean Paul (1763–1825) was an early German romantic writer whose works were particularly admired by women and members of the radical German student movement.

Encouraging for me too was the interest that Wm. Regenbrecht showed in me. He brought me several books suitable for a youngster in my years, also more recent German historical works, which taught me to value the new Germany that developed after Sedan more highly than the divided, ever self-destroying Germany of which I had read up to this time, and thus strengthened my pride in my race. Later I developed the deepest respect for this man whose long, cadaverous figure was often ridiculed in the community on account of his stammering and his superlative feats in absentmindedness and who exposed his own weakness so that others could laugh. In Millheim he will long be remembered on account of his forgetfulness, and yet he was a model official who accomplished much. For more than a quarter of a century he was the most conscientious and most successful agent for a large fire insurance company. I have never known a more truly noble and at the same time a more highly cultured man than this descendant of an old family of scholars, a man who never harbored any hatred of those who hounded and ridiculed him, and who was constantly striving to give pleasure to every child and to be a friend to every sufferer.[26]

One evening in July 1876 I returned from a short hunting expedition in the course of which I had encountered a terrible storm that had flooded my campsite. I brought no game, since I was never a good marksman. Suddenly my father told me that Mr. Maetze had been there and had advised him to send me to A&M College, which was opening in September. He had left me a geometry book in which I was to do some preparatory studying. My heart beat for joy at this prospect for further study, but then I realized that I should not leave my aged parent alone. He insisted, however, that he could make out and that I should not let the opportunity slip by. He would take a tenant family or a suitable single person into the house. This thought consoled me. I worked hard on geometry, brought in the corn and all the cotton except a few remnants. In the hope of securing a scholarship, I rode to Bellville in order to have myself examined. In my whole life I have never been so embarrassed as I was when I rode into Bellville and noticed that my new

26. Regenbrecht was clearly the prototype for "Winzig" (Tiny), in Trenckmann's Civil War novel, *Die Lateiner am Possum Creek* (1907), originally serialized in *Das Wochenblatt*.

pants had slipped almost up to my knees. In Bellville I was directed to Brenham. My trip to Brenham was also embarrassing. A big boil under my arm made it necessary for me to guide my horse with my left hand. I could not sleep for pain at night in the big hall over Giesecke's brewery, in which I had taken lodging because Superintendent Rote could not be seen that day. He examined me the next day and recommended me for a scholarship after he was convinced that I knew my multiplication tables and the capital cities of Texas and New York. Supremely happy, I returned home with the good news and a boil that had finally begun to drain.

Thus far my writing has often been interrupted, and I have probably spun out the thread in regard to Old Millheim and my growing up at too great length. I must hasten and condense.

In college I was lucky.[27] On parting from me in Hempstead my brother Otto, an old soldier and cattleman, had given me this advice from his own experiences: "Don't let anybody impose on you." When I finally arrived at dusk at the first of the two lovely college buildings in the midst of the prairie, which was covered with grasshoppers, I was hazed in the empty dark main building by nineteen earlier arrivals under the leadership of a young Austin man who owned a uniform from T. M. I. and had possessed himself of a sword and the sash of the commandant.[28] I was taken to the unlighted building and ordered to stop anyone who sought to pass without the countersign. Then in a very few minutes ghosts went flitting by in the long, dark hall and earthly sounds could be heard. Resolved to do my duty or die, I caught one of the supposed thieves of college property, and he kindly informed me that the boys were just hazing me. I had never heard of hazing before, so I held tight; and since I had handled the ax a good deal, a sore shoulder was the reward of his kindness. The next morning another wanted to deride the young

27. For another account of Trenckmann's years at A&M, originally written in English, see the appendix "1907 *Long Horn*."

28. Texas Military Institute, founded in Bastrop before the Civil War, relocated to Austin in 1870 and by 1873 enrolled 150 students. Its faculty was absorbed by Texas A&M in 1879 when its president, John G. James, was hired as A&M's president. *Handbook of Texas Online*, Nancy Beck Young, "Texas Military Institute, Austin," accessed July 13, 2016, http://www.tshaonline.org/handbook/online/articles/kbt17, uploaded on June 15, 2010, published by the Texas State Historical Association.

German as a "Dutchman." He found me just incensed enough after a sleepless night for a slugging match. He excused himself, and from then on I was accepted as an equal in spite of my little tin trunk and my Millheim garments in a fairly wild pioneering time when droves of deer sometimes ran across the drill grounds and at night a Mexican lion after game wandered around our student home.[29]

I am grateful for the military drill that I received at this institution, which, under the first commandant, was very sharply executed. After I had had my heels stepped on often enough by the men behind me, I not only learned to keep step but also to stand erect—a good thing for my health. I am also particularly grateful for my two roommates, who gave me what I had lacked in the past—intimate association with gifted young men of my own age. Basically different as we were in appearance, in ancestry, and in temperament, there soon existed full understanding, which rapidly developed into lasting friendship. One, of Irish descent and our most brilliant orator, was later made a bishop of the Baptist church and head of a leading Baptist theological school. He died two years ago. The other, of Scotch descent, which he showed plainly, became a prominent lawyer, and I hope he will last it out with me.[30]

29. Until late in the nineteenth century colleges and universities tended to stress character building and providing a classical education befitting a member of the elite instead of more pragmatic and career advancing skills. All-male colleges with a military bent also emphasized honor and discipline. A culture of hypermasculinity often prevailed in which hazing, fighting, and heavy drinking were the norm. Trenckmann's brother Otto probably was expressing this military tradition when he advised resisting slights and impositions. For general background, see Rod Andrew Jr., *Long Gray Lines: The Southern Military School Tradition, 1839–1915* (Chapel Hill: University of North Carolina Press, 2001).

30. His children/translators noted "Mullins," that is, Edgar Young Mullins (1860–1928), who became president of the Southern Baptist Theological Seminary in Louisville, Kentucky. However, the Baptist Church has no bishops. *Twenty-sixth Annual Catalogue of the Agricultural and Mechanical College of Texas* (1901–2). The other classmate is probably Charles Rogan (a name of Gaelic origins), who rivaled Trenckmann in his academic record and had a distinguished career in law and government. He was one of only two classmates mentioned by name in Trenckmann's reminiscence of his college years (see appendix "1907 *Long Horn*). *Handbook of Texas Online*, William N. Todd IV and Gerald Knape, "Rogan, Charles," accessed July 24, 2016, http://www.tshaonline.org/handbook/online/articles/fr057, uploaded on June 15, 2010, published by the Texas State Historical Association. Rogan died in 1932, the year after this was written.

I committed great follies in my student days and ruined my chance to graduate by dropping math courses. At the end of the first semester I was one among practically the entire corps to suffer with an attack of roseola. At the same time I must have had an attack of pleurisy too, but it was not recognized by our school physician, whose chief claim to fame lay in the fact that he brought cadets who hated studies and guard duty back to life quickly with drastic doses of pills.[31] I could not seem to get well again, and the doctor decided that I had to go home. When I had traveled a few miles, I noticed to my horror that I had left my purse in my room. The friendly conductor agreed to take me to Hempstead without pay. When I returned on his train two weeks later, he did not recognize me, for I had filled out so much in the meantime. He said he had not expected to see me or the ticket money again. During that interval I had missed the beginning of the algebra course. Our Professor Hogg was a fairly thorough mathematician but a confusing one who could not explain anything, and as I was foolishly ashamed to ask my more advanced roommates for help, I foundered and dropped the course.[32] As a result, I could not cope with applied mathematics. All this I never made up until I had to teach such subjects. Latin, in which my father had given me a good foundation, I dropped because our dear kind professor had almost regularly fallen asleep before he had a chance to call on me. He took us in alphabetical order, and "T" was too near the end of the alphabet.

I must confess that in my last year I was one day relieved of my rank of quartermaster and expelled from the school. For once, contrary to my general habit, I had attended chapel. On account of my rank I was excused from chapel and had therefore gotten accustomed to sleeping longer without having to respond to the customary awakening cannon shot.[33] Somehow, though, I never failed to

31. Roseola is a mild viral infection accompanied by fever and followed by a red rash, hence the name. It usually occurs in very young children but is rare among teens. Pleurisy is a painful inflammation of the lung linings that can be caused by a viral infection, so perhaps the two were related.

32. This was essentially the same charge against Hogg raised by student J. C. Crisp that led to the deadlock among the faculty and their wholesale replacement; see below.

33. The first *Catalogue of the Agricultural and Mechanical College of Texas* (1876–77),

hear the breakfast bell. After the morning prayer President Gathright, a highly gifted but very hot-headed man, was thundering out against the negligence of the officers and among other things he said that the quartermaster had failed to provide a late-arriving newcomer of good family with a bed. Having never had an explanation of my duties, I considered this an unwarranted accusation. I promptly wrote out my resignation as quartermaster, sent it to the president by a sergeant, and before breakfast I received a message in writing stating that I had been relieved of my office. With equal promptness I demanded an honorable discharge from the school, and before the whole corps in military formation an order was read which banned me from the school for insubordination. I arrived at a decision at once: "I shall not face my father's eyes as an expelled cadet. I am going to Austin before the governor and the directors who are living there." Still without breakfast, I packed my trunk and went to the Main Building to bid my most intimate friends goodbye. On the steps of the first door the president met me. After we had exchanged a few words, he was fair enough to admit that not I but he was wrong. At noon, an order was read that restored me to all the honors of my rank.[34]

I will add that I owe to my revered teacher in Millheim the fact that I always headed the class in English during the three years, and in my second year I was accorded the honor of contributing the essay for the commencement exercises.[35] In the third year I was

---

23, stated that students were required to attend chapel every morning, a stipulation repeated in subsequent catalogs.

34. President Thomas S. Gathright was born in Georgia in 1829. He headed up schools in Alabama and Mississippi before being recommended to head Texas A&M by Jefferson Davis, the former president of the Confederacy. Ironically, Gathright did not serve in the Confederate army, claiming poor health and family and professional obligations. He, along with all other administrators, was dismissed from A&M in 1879. He died the next year. See *Handbook of Texas Online*, Molly Kate McCaughey and Nancy Beck Young, "Gathright, Thomas S.," accessed August 17, 2016, http://www.tshaonline.org/handbook/online/articles/fga45, uploaded on June 15, 2010, published by the Texas State Historical Association.

35. The *Weekly Democratic Statesman* (Austin), July 5, 1877, reported that "Cadet W. A. F. Trenckman [sic] . . . read an original essay on the subject of 'Science and Religion.' He acquitted himself creditably, and showed that he had studied his subject with care."

given the honor that is known today as valedictorian. With intense interest and to my great advantage I participated in the literary society, whose chief activity was debating. I also tried myself as a writer by making contributions to the college paper.[36]

In April 1879 a letter from my father brought the unexpected message that he was no longer financially able to send me to school, a message made all the more frightening by the addition that it was only through the sale of his cattle that he had been able to furnish the necessary funds for the purpose. I had always thought that he was well-to-do, for that was what others had led me to believe, probably because he denied himself every luxury. Things had gone with him as they had with most of the other Latin Farmers. Thus it was up to me to make my living in the future. I quickly decided to become a teacher.[37]

36. The valedictorian was the student with the highest academic rank in the class. Graduation at A&M in that era went by subject rather than a strict four-year term. Trenckmann had "graduated" in German already at the end of his second year and in all the subjects the school offered except for Latin, Greek, and mathematics by his third year. *Fourteenth Catalogue of the Agricultural and Mechanical College of Texas* (1889–90), 68–69, listing alumni. Apparently he could have continued a fourth year.

37. Trenckmann's father, who died in 1883, had greatly reduced his farming operation by 1880. He owned only one horse, his total livestock was valued at $145, and his only crop production was Irish and sweet potatoes, valued at $30. A year of study at A&M cost slightly over $200 including books, though this comes to about $4,400 in 2015 purchasing power. 1880 US Census, Cat Spring Precinct, Austin County, Texas, enumeration district 6, manuscript agricultural schedule, 16, accessed through ancestry.com.

More about A&M

In the issue of September 17 I did not accomplish what I had planned to do; hence I do not need to rush with the writing of my reminiscences and will even take a step backward in regard to the first period at A&M College. It is a well known fact that in spite of the obstacles it had to face, this institution is now attended by thousands of students each year and takes a high place among state schools that train young people for agriculture and related activities as well as for important technical careers.[1] The school has become a power through the zeal with which its students defend it. This loyalty always makes its appearance when there are propositions to cut down the legislative appropriations for the school.[2] For a long time that was not the case. To most farmers it seemed ridiculous that a

Originally published in *Das Wochenblatt*, October 1, 1931.

1. In the late 1920s, after the discovery of vast pools of oil in West Texas, Texas A&M and the University of Texas began sharing the Permanent University Fund. This allowed steady growth at A&M despite the onslaught of the Great Depression. By 1931 the School of Veterinary Medicine, the Agricultural Extension Service and Experiment Station, and the Texas Forest Service had broadened the mission of A&M beyond what it had been in Trenckmann's student days. More than twelve hundred former students had served as officers during World War I.

2. In the 1910s and early 1920s, before the Permanent University Fund was put on a sound footing and split between the two major state universities, funding often varied depending on the whims of the governor and members of the state legislature. Supporters of the University of Texas or A&M competed for a share of the budget and often fought with each other. Occasional talk of combining the two schools surfaced, but supporters of each side resisted.

school should presume to educate young people for farming, and during the first years only a small portion of the students came from the country.

The newspapers often ridiculed the institution, declaring that it served only to take the farmer's son away from the farm. My first newspaper article to appear in print was written in answer to this charge, but it furnished little forceful evidence because I could not deny that up to that time almost nothing had been done toward educating farmers and technicians.

How could it have been otherwise? The college was in no way equipped for the purposes for which it was founded: to prevent an appropriation from going to waste that had been made by Congress to the individual states for the purpose of establishing an agricultural and mechanical college in which military training would be offered. In the first two years the school did not even possess a plow, nor a hoe, and not until the third year were fruit trees planted there; but the students were not even allowed to watch the planting. The technical training was in the same deplorable state. The only tool that we could handle was an ax loaned us by the college carpenter to chop up planks for splinters to start fires. The equipment for the teaching of chemistry and physics was inadequate, less than small high schools now have at their disposal; but even if the equipment had been more adequate, not much would have been accomplished, for our faculty of six men had not been educated for the training of specialists.

At that time, only eleven years after the end of the Civil War and five years after the end of the Reconstruction Period and its mismanagement of the South, the chief consideration in the selection of the faculty had been that only Southerners free from every influence of the hated Yankees were to be permitted to teach in the school. Our professors had been educated in schools in which ancient and modern languages, literature, some mathematics and world history, and a very little natural science were taught. All but one of them were of advanced age and could hardly be expected to change their ways. The only exception, our commandant and teacher of applied mathematics, at least possessed a good surveying instrument and succeeded in giving his students good training as surveyors. All natural sciences were taught by a seventy-year-old Presbyterian minister, who was also our chaplain. He meant well, dear old Dr. Martin. But our course in agriculture was pure schoolbook instruction. In botany we made exactly two field trips, and on one of them we learned how, after much consulting of books, we could determine the name of a plant. To his chagrin, his rarely conducted chemical experiments often failed. But he was certainly not to blame for the fact that on one occasion all the students had to flee coughing from the Main Building because good-for-nothing students who had probably neglected to prepare their lesson had spread chlorine gas throughout the building. I must commend him, however, for the fact that he as a minister of one of the strictest Protestant churches, did not condemn the geologists as being unchristian for their estimation of the age of the earth, but reconciled their conflict with the Bible by saying that days in the Old Testament may have meant geological epochs.[3]

So in this educational institution, in which young men were to be trained for their future professions, I learned nothing that I could use in any profession except possibly a little bookkeeping; nevertheless this school was probably the right one to prepare me for my later life. I had acquired an interest in many things, particularly in world history, geology, chemistry, astronomy, botany, and English literature, to which I had been a complete stranger. The fact that I had two years of French and three years of Spanish, graduating in both, probably did not enable me to instruct Mexicans in chopping cordwood, nor would my French have been understood in Paris; but my reading knowledge of both these languages did preserve me from the assumption that only the English and German-speaking peoples are fitted to be the bearers of culture and that other peoples are inferior. But for my

3. C. P. B. (Carlisle) Martin, DD (presumably Doctor of Divinity), was listed as professor of chemistry and natural sciences and practical agriculture in the first *Catalogue of the Agricultural and Mechanical College of Texas* (1876–77). Born in Vermont in 1814, he had lived in Georgia since the 1830s and was president of an agricultural school there in 1860. If Trenckmann had known more about the varieties of American Protestantism he might not have been so surprised that a Presbyterian could accept the findings of modern science. In the late nineteenth and early twentieth centuries, leading Presbyterians often sought to balance faith and science, and they resisted the call from others in their denomination to cling to biblical literalism. See Bradley Longfield, *The Presbyterian Controversy: Fundamentalists, Modernists, and Moderates* (New York: Oxford University Press, 1991).

teaching career I was probably better prepared when I left Maetze's school at the age of thirteen. To prepare myself for that career now would hardly have been possible, even if my finances had not almost struck bottom, for there was no teacher training school in the entire South at that time. But already in 1880 A&M College was directed into the course for which it was intended by dismissal of the entire faculty. In their close living together on the small clearing between two forests, the professors, the majority of whom had been heads of higher teaching institutions, had gotten into such a state of constant dissension that this step became necessary.[4]

So I was to be a teacher and I, the son of a successful teacher, having grown up in a community in which the schoolmaster was the most highly respected man, was glad to be a teacher. But I was soon to discover that it wasn't easy to get a teaching job. At that time (1879) the school situation in the old German settlements in the Eastern part of the state had improved greatly, even though the schools weren't quite so good perhaps as those in the great closed settlements of the Adelsverein in West Texas, in which professional teachers who desired to remain true to their profession like Herman Seele had been early settlers.[5] Before the Civil War, during the war, and in the decade that followed it, it had been impossible for many of the German communities to hire any teachers at all. In others instruction was imparted by men whose lives had been wrecked: aristocratic and non-aristocratic former officers, bankrupt merchants, etc., who having failed utterly in their attempt to find mountains of gold in this country, finally sought jobs as schoolmasters in rural communi-

4. The faculty had deadlocked over whether to promote student John C. Crisp, who had made a disparaging remark about the mathematics professor. On Saturday, November 22, 1879, the board requested the resignation of the entire faculty; by Monday a new president and several faculty were in place. Dethloff, *Centennial History*, 1:58–65.

5. The Adelsverein (Society of Nobles) brought some seven thousand immigrants to Texas in the 1840s and founded the towns of New Braunfels and Fredericksburg, which along with their surrounding counties were about 85 percent German in 1870. Hermann Seele was the first teacher and later the mayor of New Braunfels. *Handbook of Texas Online*, Edward C. Breitenkamp, "Seele, Friedrich Hermann," accessed July 19, 2016, http://www.tshaonline.org/handbook/online/articles/fse06, uploaded on June 15, 2010, modified on May 6, 2016, published by the Texas State Historical Association.

ties because they felt no inclination to do strenuous physical work. Many of them drank to excess; of that brand there were many. At one time my father had four mule drivers, all noblemen, working in his gin. In the stronger schools of the three German counties quite a few trained in German teachers' seminars, as well as other men of higher education, were active—like Egmont Bretschneider on the Bernard—who had enough experience to excel in their calling.[6] These were supported by their own communities but at pitifully low salaries compared to today's. Millheim was probably the only country settlement in Austin County in which the year's earnings of the teacher substantially exceeded five hundred dollars.

So far as I can remember, no female teachers were employed in the German schools, but all the more of them taught in the small towns with two or more private schools. In these the daughters of former wealthy slaveowners taught the courses in which they had been trained. Arithmetic was practically never taught, for that was considered unsuitable for ladies; but on the other hand, there was often much training in declamation. In the neighboring Washington County instruction was for the most part given by ministers of the Lutheran or Evangelical denominations. There too it would have been impossible to find employment. At this time, by the way, more good German teachers came to Austin County; e.g., C. Klaerner, Theodor Buehring, and H. Wurzlow.

After I had knocked at doors in vain several times and was becoming discouraged, my old teacher brought me the news that the teacher's position at Hermann's Academy was vacant through the resignation of the principal. He himself, as a member of the board of supervisors, would support my application. In answer to my doubts that I was prepared to teach in an academy, he told me the history of the school with its high-sounding name. It was in a critical condition. Except for the few pupils who came from elsewhere, I would mainly have to teach elementary subjects, and under those circumstances I would have an excellent opportunity to show what I could

6. Austin, Fayette, and Colorado counties. Egmont Bretschneider, from the city of Altenburg, immigrated in 1851 at age seventeen, came to Cat Spring in 1867, and was a schoolteacher for twenty-five years. *Cat Spring Story*, 26. *Weimar Mercury*, January 25, 1908.

do. I applied and in the middle of August I was elected to be the principal and the only teacher of the academy.[7]

Before my election took place, I went through an embarrassing hour. With my fatherly friend and supporter I had taken a room in the upper story of Mrs. Henrichsen's Hotel in Frelsburg. Her food and beds were excellent, but her floors were exceedingly thin. Through them I could hear every word that was spoken under me in the room in which the directors of the academy were assembled. Some of what I heard was not all complimentary to the young man who bore himself so soldierly but who had never taught before nor attended any teacher training school. On the other hand, the conversation was full of praise for my rival applicant, Mr. Gertner, who had been educated for his profession in Germany. Finally I could stand it no longer. I rushed down the steps and excitedly explained that I was withdrawing my candidacy to keep from creating dissension. Five minutes later I was elected. For the school the choice of Gertner might have been a better one; but for him, since he later received a position as teacher of German in A&M College, it turned out to be a lucky break.[8] The worthy directors afterwards became my good friends and even regular readers of the *Wochenblatt*.

The next thing that was required of me was a certificate that I had a right to teach in a public school. The acquisition of such certificates was probably the only thing that was left from the Republican

7. Trenckmann's children in translating his autobiography called the school where their father first taught "Hermann's Seminar," but "academy" seems a more accurate translation. This school was created during the Republic of Texas era and intended to be a university, but it took until 1870 for it to be organized and its first building constructed. Lack of funding and lack of interest caused the state to sell the land and building to the Frelsburg public schools in 1871. City schools struggled in the 1870s, especially after Governor O. M. Roberts vetoed public school funding late in the decade, but city schools with local support, like Frelsburg's, proved reasonably stable. See Frederick Eby, *The Development of Education in Texas* (New York: MacMillan, 1925), 157–92; *Handbook of Texas Online*, "Hermann University," accessed August 23, 2016, http://www.tshaonline.org/handbook/online/articles/kch07, uploaded on June 15, 2010, published by the Texas State Historical Association.

8. Immigrant Marie Ewald Bernhard George Gartner was listed as professor of modern languages for the 1880–81 and 1881–82 terms of the college and as professor of ancient and modern languages in 1882–83. *Fourth, Fifth,* and *Sixth Annual Catalogues of the Agricultural and Mechanical College of Texas* (1879–82). However, the president reported that Gartner had died in February of 1883. *Ninth Annual Catalogue of the Agricultural and Mechanical College of Texas* (1884–85), 6.

regime, which had created the first public schools in Texas. There was no state superintendent of schools, and the examining board in Colorado County, to which I was to go, consisted of three lawyers. In Austin County too there was no teacher on the board. After boning up till my brain fairly smoked to pass the test, I rode off to Columbus. The elderly examiners sent me to their young colleague Mr. Sandmeier. The latter had attended Texas Military Institute. He inquired about cadets who had transferred to our school. We had a stimulating conversation, after which he wrote out a first class teacher's certificate for me without any examination. I had a similar experience when in the next spring I had applied for a teacher's certificate in Austin County. District Clerk Thomas, a good politician, gave me some compliments, conversed very interestingly, and I got my certificate without having to answer any questions. Not a few candidates for teaching positions would be delighted if certificates were so easily obtained today.[9]

My next problem was to get pupils on my list for the academy, for whom the state at that time paid $1.50 a month for four months.[10] During my search on horseback and afterwards on foot I gained a discouraging insight into conditions in Frelsburg. Probably two-thirds of the population were devout Catholics, whose children were taught for fifty cents a month by nuns and also free of charge if that seemed advisable. About one-fourth were Lutheran, and most of them sent their children to Pastor Gerstmann, who taught the parish school. The remaining one-twelfth, often designated as heathens, consisted of businessmen and a few artisans. These were on much better terms with the members of the two churches than the latter were with each other. To such a division into almost enemy camps I was utterly unaccustomed. It was terrifying to me. At A&M, where

---

9. Initially Germans strongly supported public schooling, which they had known from their homeland, but were apprehensive that it might "de-Germanize" their children. The superintendent of public instruction was a German immigrant, Jacob DeGrees. His position was abolished when Democrats regained control and the Texas Constitution of 1876 was passed. Until the early twentieth century, schools were largely under local control with very few statewide standards or requirements. See Eby, *Development of Education in Texas*, 157–239.

10. It may have paid slightly less, because Trenckmann later lists a sum of $4.50 for four months.

all denominations were represented, I had never dreamed that such a state of affairs could exist.[11]

For five months I taught with great zeal in Frelsburg, and many of the school patrons were kind enough to tell me later that I had been a good teacher. I myself have often thought back on my pedagogical sins of that time. I raced the beginners through the three Rs and found great satisfaction in the fact that little Theodor could multiply and divide seven or more digits so rapidly without understanding one thing about the real meaning. The most beautiful day of my Frelsburg time was undoubtedly the Saturday after the end of my first school month, the day when I could get my first self-earned money—something over forty dollars—in Columbus and buy myself a new suit. It had gotten too cool for light summer clothing in the meantime, and I did not like to stand before my pupils in a uniform with many shiny buttons. As an unnecessary luxury I bought a bed with springs such as I had become accustomed to in College.[12]

When the four months for which the state paid were over, only half of my students appeared for instruction, and I discovered that that was the custom in the community. Pleasant prospects! Since at Christmas I had given free rein to my long restrained love for giving and had even bought my first overcoat, I was in debt with the prospect of a monthly income of a little more than twenty dollars. I got a small supplement by teaching evening school, in which grown young Catholics learned elementary arithmetic and English and a few Lutherans from the country received further education. They were all ambitious, fine young fellows, and the fact that they later became faithful *Wochenblatt* readers lets me conclude that I must not have been too bad a teacher.

11. Despite their similarities in liturgy and views on matters such as alcohol and parochial schools independent of government interference, German Lutherans and Catholics remained highly antagonistic throughout the nineteenth century. In Prussia, mixed marriages accounted for less than 5 percent of the total in 1867. To this day confessional Lutheranism officially regards the Catholic papacy (though not necessarily the pope personally) as the Antichrist. Despite proposals within the last decade, the Catholic excommunication of Martin Luther has never been revoked, although even his "Battle Hymn of the Reformation," *A Mighty Fortress*, is in the Catholic hymnal. In practice, the laity has become much more tolerant.

12. By about 1880 in Texas, beds with a base of metal springs wired together were beginning to replace cotton rope, wooden slats, or rough cloth as the bottom support for mattresses stuffed with feathers or cotton.

However, since a clique of young Frelsburgers under the leadership of an Anglo-American perpetrated all sorts of mischief, barricaded the streets, moved small buildings to unsuitable places in the town, cut off the tails of carriage horses, and began to pester my evening students by untying their horses and chasing them away, my pupils became restless, and I had to look forward to the loss of this supplemental income too. I was sleeping poorly on account of financial worries.

A tragic event brought me to a decision that I often regretted later. I was returning on a Saturday morning from an unsuccessful possum hunt when a messenger on horseback was awaiting me with the news that my beloved oldest brother Emil Trenckmann, teacher in Shelby, had died suddenly of a lung hemorrhage (*Lungenschlag*). Just a week before, he had been singing gaily with the music-lovers in Frelsburg, and at their request had accepted the direction of a newly organized singing society. A few days after his burial I received a letter from my sister-in-law, who was both mother and sister to me, with the news that the Shelbyites—"Roedersmuehler" they usually called themselves back then—wanted me to take over their orphaned school.[13] She hoped I would accept. I was drawn as if by horses to Shelby, where during frequent visits I found what I had so long missed—a happy family life. I rode to Post Oak and faced the revered Dr. Becker in his little study to tell him the circumstances, and after some hesitation, he consented to release me from the Hermann's Academy. I am still ashamed when I think back on the day when I *deserted* my post, and I say to myself, "Your father would never have done that."

In this long chapter I have covered only half a year. From now on it must go faster, for otherwise I shall not finish this year. However, a description of school conditions of those days may be of interest to many people.

---

13. This singing society, the Harmania [*sic*] Verein, apparently sponsored Emil's gravestone. Shelby is in northwestern Austin County near the border with Fayette County. It was long known as Roeders Mill after Otto von Roeder, who built a grain mill at the site in 1841. See *Handbook of Texas Online*, Christopher Long, "Shelby, TX," accessed August 31, 2016, http://www.tshaonline.org/handbook/online/articles/hls41, uploaded on June 15, 2010, modified on February 4, 2014, published by the Texas State Historical Association.

More about the Academy;
Teacher in Shelby

First of all, another backward glance at the Hermann's Academy, which I left under such embarrassing circumstances.

Old Homer tells the story of the unhappy king's daughter Cassandra. When after a long siege the Greeks departed from Troy in their ships, leaving behind a gift in the form of a large wooden horse, Cassandra warned her countrymen with the words, *"Timeo Danaos dona ferentes!"* (Beware of Greeks bearing gifts.) No one listened to her, since prophets were not generally well received when they make unwelcome prophecies. The Wochenblattmann can attest to this when he prophesied that forty-cent cotton would bring evil consequences.

Such a Grecian gift was the land donation that the Congress of Texas made in the year of 1844 to the Germans in the state for the founding of a university. I was pleased when I read that it had been made as a reward for the bravery of the Germans in the war to free our state from Mexican rule. Even though the gift—a league of land—was really a rather small one, I am always pleased when German doings receive recognition. Recently when I read the acts in question, it almost seemed to me that the gift had been made in jest rather than in gratitude. It came as the result of a request from thirty-eight

Originally published in *Das Wochenblatt*, October 29, 1931.

citizens of the counties Austin, Fayette, and Colorado, headed by Friedrich Ernst, the first German settler in Texas; L. C. Ervendberg; and H. Amthor. The act provides that a league of government land shall be surveyed for the founding of a German university, that the university shall stand under the direction of a board of trustees chosen by the membership and that it shall be erected in the neighborhood of Mill Creek or Cummins Creek, that the members of the University Association shall each pay fifty dollars into the treasury or give fifty acres of land to the university, that it was to have four faculties—theology, jurisprudence, medicine, and philosophy—in fact to have more high faculties than our present state university. It exempts the gift from taxation, gives the university the jurisprudence to punish for the sale of spirits within a restricted area, requires that the president be a professor, that the professors must know the German and English languages and be Protestants, but that otherwise full religious freedom is to prevail.

This act was later amended to provide that the university might be built elsewhere in the state than near Cummins or Mill Creek and that the religious requirement in regard to the faculty be dispensed with. Mr. Ervendberg, a highly educated, ambitious man, attempted without success to have the university erected in West Texas, for San Antonio and New Braunfels, which first came under consideration, already had good German schools to meet all their needs. After the war a league of land had been surveyed in Gillespie County for the university, and since in the original act of donation the value of an acre of raw land was estimated to be one dollar, the value of the gift can easily be figured out. Later citizens of Austin and Colorado Counties joined for the founding of the university, which they gave the modest name of an academy. They decided to build it in Austin County if that county raised the greatest amount in membership contributions; otherwise in Frelsburg, which is only a few years younger than Industry.

Colorado County raised a little more money than Austin County.[1] With the available sum a well-built two-story modern structure

---

1. In fact, it was German lobbying rather than Anglo gratitude that led to the grant; otherwise, Trenckmann's account is quite accurate. A league of land came to 4,428 acres, so its value was less than five thousand dollars, given the location a

with two classrooms downstairs and four living-rooms upstairs was erected a half-mile from Frelsburg, and it was separated from the town by a road that was impassable in wet weather. Sometimes my pupils had to climb a fence to avoid this road in a wet season. I am told that two blue-blooded gentlemen were the first teachers and that after school hour, having freely imbibed intoxicating liquor, they sometimes beat each other up. The result was that fewer advanced pupils from a distance attended the school. My immediate predecessor, Professor Holmy, was an excellent mathematician who attracted a few students for higher training from neighboring counties. When he gave up his post, probably because the money realized from the sale of university land had all been spent, it was decided that for the time being the school would be supported by the money that it brought in. Later on it was kept going as an ordinary country school, and although the balance of the land donation after sale had been given to it and in spite of the zealous efforts of Dr. Fehrenkamp, it was unable to move any farther ahead under the prevailing circumstances. The school building burned down a few years ago, and with it the efforts of ambitious Germans to have a school for the higher education of young people of German descent were canceled.[2]

I was in Shelby in the spring of 1880 till August 1883 and can say that I taught with good success. The membership of pupils increased so rapidly that the old schoolhouse was hardly adequate. Another school in Shelby, taught by Pastor Moegle, a worthy Lutheran minister but poorly grounded in the English language because of his Swabian dialect, slowly disintegrated.[3] I had the

---

dozen miles west of Fredericksburg. All told, land grants of 172,319 acres were made by the Republic of Texas in support of various educational institutions. Shares in the university, which initially were to sell for fifty dollars, were reduced to fifteen dollars in 1870, but to little avail. The charter for Hermann University was revoked in November 1871, and its two-story stone building was sold to Frelsburg schools. Biesele, *History of the German Settlements*, 215–16; *Handbook of Texas Online*, "Hermann University."

2. German Texan Dr. Bernard J. Fehrenkamp (1855–1928) studied medicine in Philadelphia and was a physician in Frelsburg.

3. Rev. Johann Moegle, born 1830 in Wurttemberg, had been in Texas at least since 1860, when he married in New Braunfels.

pleasure of bringing about the abandonment of the spring "cotton chopping" vacations. When I taught until late in August in order to make up time lost through illness and death in families, almost all the children attended to the last day. With the exception of a few lazy and thoroughly spoiled youngsters, I could not have wished for more industrious and willing pupils.[4] I should like to note that a child's conduct in school is not always an indication of his future. This fact is proven by the youngest son of Dr. Bernhard Witte, who was given the full freedom of youth as demanded by his father and who, although he played hooky half of his school time, afterwards became an exceptionally skilled physician, greatly in demand for stomach disorders.[5]

Since I taught German and English in all my six grades, I had to work very hard and often keep late hours checking the written work of my pupils.[6] Still I found time to acquire new skills. I learned to play a little pool—this game and billiards were played in all saloons at that time—and a card game known as "Schafskopf," and Solo with the farmers, Skat with Heinrich Otto, John Stahlbaum, and the merchant Karl Korff, who were famous for their skill at cards. I had to pay plenty of apprentice money, as we sometimes played the whole night through. Sometimes I found time for a hunting or fishing trip. In these pastimes I learned how to understand mature men, some even of advanced years, from all parts of Germany. I learned to speak to them in their native dialect, even in that of Wittgenstein.[7] Shelby

---

4. In the 1880s the public school year in Texas varied from four and one-half to eight months, and schools were often let out so students could help with farm chores such as chopping the weeds and thinning the cotton plants in late spring. The school year typically did not begin until cotton was harvested in September. See *Special Report of the State Board of Education for the Scholastic Year Ending August 31, 1883, Ninth Report* (Austin: State Printing Office, 1883); *Biennial Report of the State Board of Education for the School Year Ending August 31, 1886, 11th Report* (Austin: State Printing Office, 1886).

5. Dr. Otto Witte (1854–1928), a nephew of Trenckmann's sister-in-law, studied medicine at the University of Louisville and practiced in Shelby, Texas.

6. For an account of the school based heavily on oral history, see Elvie Lou Luetge, "Shelby: A Rural School in a German Immigrant Setting," *East Texas Historical Review* 18, no. 1 (1980): 29–40.

7. German dialects were often the subject of inside jokes and needling, but there was nothing particularly difficult about the Wittgensteiner dialect, although it did contain elements of both Low and High German.

possessed a number of interesting original characters, for example, a Mr. Brandt, who was passionately fond of running around barefoot, made artificial fertilizer, and constantly quoted Liebig. Often highly cultured men of advanced years came to visit from the neighboring Latium—I learned much from them.

Although it had been settled very early, Shelby was undoubtedly the most German of all the places where I have lived for a longer period of time. Otto von Roeder, who came to this country with his parents in 1834, was an enterprising, energetic man. Already in the early 1840s he had built a mill there, probably chiefly for his own needs and those of nearby Industry (thus the old name "Roedersmuehl," which the old settlers would not give up). By 1845 this mill came into the possession of August Vogelsang. About the middle of the forties came Vanderwerth, Rothermel, and Ohlendorf; by 1846, Witte, Bernshausen, Wagner, Schmidt, Henniger, Hetzel, Albrecht, Rudloff, Frentrup, Roski, Krebs, Voelkel, Wunderlich, Brandt, Goebel, teacher Suerth, and Otto. Most of them had come to this country as colonists of the Mainzer Adelsverein, but on hearing reports of the fate of the New Braunfels settlement when they landed, they preferred to seek a new home near the old German settlements in Austin and Fayette Counties. The majority remained there, as did many of their descendants; however, most of the young people whom I taught turned to the south and west for homes, where good farmland was still to be had at a lower price, or they went to the cities.

Since 1854 Shelby had had a German school. It was under the direction of Suerth and perhaps held in the same solidly constructed building in which I and so many others taught. Already in 1852 a singing society was founded there, which held big *Saengerfest*s and which continued to exist until the death of my brother. An agricultural society, an offshoot of the Cat Spring society, was founded there too by F. Fisseler.[8] In contrast with Industry, Fredericksburg and many of

8. Mathias Suerth, born 1816 in Prussia, apparently arrived in Austin County in 1854. He was listed as an election judge in Shelby in 1862, 1864, and 1866, was elected justice of the peace in 1858, and served at least until 1863. The 1870 census lists him as a farmer, but he is shown as a schoolteacher in 1880, living next door to Trenckmann and his sister-in-law. Christian Friedrich Fisseler had immigrated from Waldeck in 1852 and was a substantial farmer in 1870 and 1880.

the other German settlements, Shelby was not one "long intestine," but the business houses, the workshops, the hotel, the gin, and the mill were all closely concentrated, and the cemetery touched the limits of the town.

The farmers in the vicinity, industrious, efficient men, had soon acquired a comfortable living. Already in the seventies the partly hilly black land had risen in price to thirty or more dollars an acre, while in Millheim the price of equally good land was only one-third as high, sandy prairie land cost from twenty-five cents to a dollar an acre, and state land was still to be had by new settlers as preemption. The broad, grass-covered prairie, which I had seen on my first visit from above Fordtran's place to Schoenau and then further to the west and north, had been fenced in; the stretch of road between Industry and Shelby had been increased by one-third because of the farms that crossed it. At the same time, because of the owners' desire to save on acreage, the road was so narrow that in rainy seasons the Shelbyites who were called to jury duty and the doctor could often make it only on horseback. In other matters these farmers were certainly not stingy. When it was a matter of getting a new gathering place for festive occasions for Shelby, which had only a small dance hall above Scharnberg's Hotel, John Stahlbaum and I on a single morning's ride were able to sell enough shares to farmers in a few hours to make it possible to begin with the building of the Harmoniehalle at once.[9]

It was the custom in Shelby to pay the school all the money at the close of the school year, and down to the last cent, I received all the money due me within a week after I had sent out the bills, with the exception of that of a young tenant farmer from whom I could hardly expect payment. I found a strange form of credit system there. Many had the merchant charge everything until they had sold their cotton. Then they paid and certainly before the new year because the merchant Korff, who had the main business, charged

9. Harmonie Hall in Shelby is still in existence and still hosting dances, although its sign claims a founding date of 1875, five years before Trenckmann's arrival. The town had hosted a major *Saengerfest* in 1867 celebrating the Prussian victory in its war with Austria.

ten percent interest from January the first on, but he hardly ever had a chance to collect the interest. He was my banker too and gave me credit or advanced me money until I drew out all my state money in the spring.

When I got my state money in the spring of 1881—$4.50 per capita for about sixty pupils—it amounted to a sum that made me feel rich. On the return trip by train, I spent the night in Brenham, waiting for a chance to ride home. As I was walking around a bit, I saw a real gambling game in a popular delicatessen store for the first time in my life. I watched for a while to see how the players were winning or losing as the ball rolled down. I had about ten dollars in silver in my trousers pocket. I put up some money, won a good deal and lost more often. Soon the gambling fever had me. My right hand was magnetically drawn to my coat pocket with the package of notes with which I could win back my lost money. When I held it in my hand, I realized that this was the fruit of all my labors of three long months. I shoved the money back into my coat. Realizing how difficult it was for me to resist, I made a resolution: *Never again!* This resolution I have kept under difficult circumstances, even when charming young ladies wanted to sell me chances for a charitable purpose, often for artistic products of their own hands. To be sure, the game of Skat, which I enjoyed playing for twenty-five years and have had to give up for lack of time, I do not consider a gambling game, but always felt that in Skat the winner is rewarded for his skill.[10]

Since I have mentioned young ladies, association with them— and there were many charming young ladies in Shelby, some just pretty and some real beauties—I did not find in Shelby either. Such contacts were to be found only in ballrooms. In Shelby only one ball a year was held—the Christmas ball. I could not dance, since from childhood I became dizzy after only two turns. When I climbed a

10. Skat is a three-person game played with a thirty-two-card deck. Each player is dealt ten cards, and the remaining two cards form the skat and are placed in the middle. Players bid for the skat according to their estimate of the value of the tricks they anticipate taking with each suit having a different value. The game was developed in Germany early in the nineteenth century and remains popular in German-speaking areas. See David Parlett, *The A–Z of Card Games* (New York: Oxford University Press, 2004).

pecan tree to reach the high limbs, I never dared look down for fear of tumbling. Besides, as I have related in the *Wochenblatt* before, the teasing of my brothers and sisters had made me girl-shy. My young female students were fond of me, and I was fond of them. I immortalized myself in their little albums with verses that I composed for them. Many of them have long since become grandmothers, but I believe they still consider me their friend. On the other hand, I got along fine with older women; for example, Grandmother Witte. Best of all, I got along with my kind, self-sacrificing sister-in-law, who found consolation in her widow's sorrow in caring for her children and for me. Then there was her eighty-year-old mother, Grandma Witte, whose husband I was told had left Germany with a whole sailboat loaded with goods to build a new estate in Texas. He had sold his beautiful German estate after many vain efforts to prevent the construction of a railroad through his property. Here he erected a storehouse in an area that probably no railroad would ever be built through.[11] Grandma Witte could tell entertainingly of olden days.

One story that interested me particularly was of the beginning of the Civil War. Near Shelby a company of cavalry, in which brother Otto and cousin Hermann served as volunteers, was drilled by Captain van der Heuvel, who fell later while leading them when his young German soldiers threw away their tin-tipped lances and depended on their revolvers to take a Yankee battery by storm and turned the tide of the Battle of Val Verde.[12] I learned later that he

11. The Wittes immigrated in various stages, but the biography of son Charles Otto, who settled in Charleston, confirmed much of the story and located the family estate in Kleefeld near Hannover, through which a rail line was undertaken in 1842. J. C. Hemphill, *Men of Mark in South Carolina: A Collection of Biographies of Leading Men of the State* (Washington, DC: Men of Mark Publishing Company, 1907–9).More detail on the Shelby Wittes is found in Frank W. Johnson, ed., *A History of Texas and Texans* (Chicago: American Historical Society, 1913), 3:1437–39.

12. Captain Marinus Heuvel commanded Company G of the 4th Regiment, Texas Cavalry, in which Otto and Hermann Trenckmann served. It was almost exclusively German, with many Austin County names. Captain v. d. Heuvel and one of the privates were killed and ten wounded, including Hermann Trenckmann. Their role in the battle is described thus: "Although McRae's battery poured a deadly fire of grapeshot into the charging Texans, the Rebels fell upon the Union artillery with a hand-to-hand

sought death because of a disappointed love for the beautiful sister of my sister-in-law. She chose a young Norwegian architect, who took her from Texas to his home in Christiania.[13] Grandma Witte remains in my memory as the original picture of a gay-hearted old German "Gutsfrau" who was accustomed to living on a grand scale.[14] I found happy companionship in my nephews and the younger nieces. In Shelby I became acquainted with a beautiful family life.

I realized that in forty years of teaching, standards had progressed and began to study the newer pedagogical works. I also tried with perseverance but without noticeable success to improve my scrawly handwriting by copying the entire dozen of Spencerian copybooks. I had my pupils copy the models that my deceased teacher-brother had made on cards. He had beautiful handwriting. At that time printed copy books could not be obtained for country schools.

The year 1883 brought a great sorrow to the family of my brother and me. Not long after Christmas Grandmother Witte died of pneumonia. Up to this time she had kept her strength and had read a whole stack of magazine novels, per week. At the beginning of her illness and apparently still full of life, she calmly announced, "In

---

savagery rarely seen in the annals of American military history. Within eight minutes the Texans had overrun the Union guns." *Handbook of Texas Online*, Jerry Thompson, "Valverde, Battle of," http://www.tshaonline.org/handbook/online/articles/qev01. A company muster roll was published by Leonie Rummel Weyand and Houston Wade in *An Early History of Fayette County* (LaGrange, Texas: *LaGrange Journal*, 1936), 307–9.

13. Emil Trenckmann's sister-in-law Wilhelmina Witte married Norwegian immigrant Paul Due on August 3, 1858, in Austin County. In 1860 they were living in Charleston, South Carolina, where Due was listed as an architect and where a Witte brother had settled. Several of their later children appear in Norwegian baptismal records. Heuvel was living in the household of Wilhelmina's brother and next door to another brother in 1850 and was unmarried at age forty-three when he enlisted.

14. Her husband, Ernst Witte, had leased a domain with fourteen hundred tenants before purchasing an estate near Hannover. Hemphill, *Men of Mark*, 437. The palatial Witte house in Shelby, completed in 1860, is pictured in Kenneth Hafertepe, *The Material Culture of German Texans* (College Station: Texas A&M University Press, 2016), 136–38. It is now a museum: Texas German Society, "Witte-Schmid Haus Museum, 'Das Haus,'" http://www.texasgermansociety.com/DasHaus2014.html.

nine days it will all be over." A week after her my sister-in-law died. She had over-strained herself at nursing.[15] Soon thereafter it was my beloved sister Anna. She left seven small children and had been a truly self-sacrificing heroine.[16] Although he could have had the best of care from his daughter-in-law in the home of my brother Otto in Millheim, my father insisted that he would never be a burden to anyone. Having loved Anna more than any of his other children, probably because her mother had died shortly after Anna's birth and he had had the care of her, he soon followed her into the grave.[17] Brother Otto found him dead before his bed in his old home when he came to pay him a morning visit. Of nine brothers and sisters, only Brother Otto and I now remained alive.[18]

That fact strengthened a conviction that had entered my head when I was a boy: I too would not live long and should not marry. A kind of heart cramp had been seizing me often in the past three years. It occurred the first time while I was on a ride from Millheim, where I had visited my aged father for Christmas. I had ridden the whole way in the rain but protected by my yellow slicker. My horse and I had been driven downstream a piece in the high water of Pastor Creek. I reached Shelby at midnight. In order not to awake anyone, I kept on my wet clothes, wrapped a woolen blanket around me, and lay down to sleep. Such are the follies of youth when one

15. According to an unofficial source, Christianna Elizabeth "Lisette" Witte died on November 1, 1882. According to her modern gravestone, Johanna Witte Trenckmann died on January 18, 1882, but in view of Trenckmann's account, 1883 seems more likely. Find a Grave, "Christianna Elizabeth 'Lisette' Linnemann Witte," http://www.findagrave.com/cgi-bin/fg.cgi?page=gr&GRid=31594888.

16. Anna Frederica Trenckmann married Fritz Engelking on December 4, 1872, and was living with him and their five children on the farm in 1880. She actually died on December 11, 1882, barely thirty-two years old.

17. Anna was only two weeks old when her mother died. It was more than seven months before her father remarried.

18. Trenckmann's father Andreas died on May 13, 1883, according to his letter to A. Regenbrecht, February 18, 1916 (Clara Trenckmann papers, privately held by Stuart Strong). The exact death dates of Trenckmann's mother, and brother Paul are uncertain; none of their three graves were recorded in the cemetery records of the Austin County Historical Commission. They were probably buried on their home farm, as Otto and his family were on theirs. Otto and his father both owned farms in the James Cumings League but were five entries apart in the 1880 agricultural census.

still thinks nothing can do one harm. It is an indescribable feeling when suddenly you cannot feel your heart beat, breathing stops, and your limbs tremble in wild cramps. They told me that I looked as if it would be all over with me in a few minutes. When I had one of those spells, the exceptionally capable physician of Shelby, Dr. Witte, arrived in a few minutes and gave me an ether injection. In a twinkling it was followed by warmth and a heavenly good feeling. I could understand why many a one becomes an ether addict in order to enjoy this wonderful sensation. Dr. Witte gave me many additional injections and finally, probably assuming that a neglected case of pleurisy might have left me with *Wasserausscheidung* (water on the lungs), gave me injections of bromine, which almost drove me wild without bringing permanent improvement. I also consulted old Dr. Herff, the leading authority in Texas.[19] He shook his head and said that my heart seemed to be perfectly normal. Later, two famous younger doctors in San Antonio explained that a change of climate and exercise in the open would be beneficial. Much later I reached the conclusion that my supposed heart ailment had a very prosaic cause—a digestive disturbance brought about by malaria, which I had contracted while camping in the woods.

At that time, I was seized with the wanderlust—a trait common to many Germans. I decided to emigrate at once and chose to go to Australia, which would have an entirely new plant and animal life to offer me and almost entirely new land, something that Texas no longer had to offer. I secured a passport, had Albert Jacoby make me a belt with a receptacle to hide my savings in gold pieces, and bade farewell to Shelby, which had received me in such a friendly spirit.[20] In Shelby I was leaving August Voelkel, a life-long friend. In the

19. Ferdinand Herff was a skilled surgeon trained at German universities. He was a political émigré who led the communistic Bettina colony, later settling in San Antonio. *Handbook of Texas Online*, Vernie A. Stembridge, "Herff, Ferdinand Ludwig," http://www.tshaonline.org/handbook/online/articles/fhe27, uploaded on June 15, 2010, modified on April 18, 2016, published by the Texas State Historical Association.

20. Trenckmann's passport application was dated July 26, 1883. Australia was a rather exotic destination for Americans, only 7,472 of whom were enumerated in the 1891 census there, a testimony to Trenckmann's sense of adventure. But his frame of reference may have been Germans, who had a considerably greater Australian presence of some 45,000 in 1891,

thirty years that he has been my agent, I have never been able to persuade him to keep his commission. It was farewell with the intention of starting the long journey as soon as an inheritance matter was settled. I paid last visits to my old A&M schoolmate, W. M. Sleeper, in Waco and then to Uncle Jockusch and his family in Galveston. There I received the message from the administrator, E. G. Maetze, that it was absolutely necessary for me to remain in the state a few months longer. These few months grew into forty-nine years. Neither he nor I had taken into account the slow pace of the Texas courts.[21]

21. The settlement of the estate was only dated January 22, 1885. Austin County Deed Records, Book 3, p. 253.

Schoolmaster Again

After three or four weeks of uncertainty in Galveston, a letter from Mr. Maetze brought me the news that it might be a year before I could leave the country if everything was to be properly settled. Uncle Jockusch advised me to stay in Galveston and gain mercantile experience, which might help me in a strange land. He introduced me to the heads of several big German firms, who were his friends, and gave me a brilliant recommendation. The gentlemen were polite but replied, "Perhaps in a few months when business picks up." From the account of my life they probably deduced the correct view that this farmer's son, who had been a country schoolmaster for four years and carried his head quite high, would hardly suit as a merchant's apprentice. That was a cooling agent for my self-esteem. I had learned to consider myself quite important in Shelby, where the children all seemed to like me, the mothers seemed to look on me favorably, and in spite of my youth the fathers counted me in on important undertakings.

Idleness became unbearable for me, although Galveston offered plenty of entertainment. Cousin Julius, who was nearly grown, took me out fishing in his little sailboat on the bay, and in the home of my uncle I had the opportunity to meet many nice young people at

Originally published in *Das Wochenblatt*, November 19, 1931.

a literary evening and at rehearsals for a German comedy. Among them was William Bohn, who had just emigrated to Texas and who later in Austin became a strong supporter of the *Wochenblatt*. I also heard much good music. Cousin Clara sang beautifully and was an excellent pianist. As always, Galveston seemed a bit of paradise to me.

Here again I am reaching back a long, long time to my first trip to that city. I was an eleven-year-old boy, and, if I am not mistaken, it was in the beginning of April when my little mother took me on a two weeks' visit to Galveston to celebrate the birthday of her brother. What an exciting trip that was! First in the horse-drawn wagon to Alleyton, the nearest railroad station of the present Southern Pacific Railroad, and if I remember correctly, its terminal point. On this ride the giant, broad-limbed live oaks thrilled me. At eleven o'clock we got into a chair car, which seemed a veritable palace to me. The journey lasted twelve hours, for the rails were shaky, and in the Brazos Bottom all the male passengers had to get out and help shove the cars back on the track. Outside the Brazos Bottom only wide, uninhabited prairie except for the small railroad station buildings and a few huts. Old Harrisburg—the railroad did not go through Houston at that time—was the biggest town. After Harrisburg it got dark and I gazed steadily through the window waiting for the big event, the ride over Galveston Bay. I have never again been so thrilled as I was when at last I could see the whitecaps in the moonlight and hear them splashing against the bridge pilings.[1]

When I awoke the next morning at daybreak, I had a big scare. When I looked out of the south window and far and wide I could see nothing but water—Uncle's house stood and still stands on

1. Railroad construction began in Texas in the 1850s as Texans sought to move beyond the limitations of shallow rivers and muddy roads. But it was not until after the mid-1860s that construction boomed. Local and state governments offered incentives for much early construction, and since railroads provided the more feasible form of transportation, cities rose or fell according to their ability to gain access to railroads. The earliest railroads stretched out from Galveston and Houston to the agricultural regions in the interior, and railroads reached Dallas, Austin, and San Antonio by the mid-1870s. See *Handbook of Texas Online*, George C. Werner, "Railroads," accessed August 18, 2016, http://www.tshaonline.org/handbook/online/articles/eqr01, uploaded on June 15, 2010, published by the Texas State Historical Association.

Avenue H near the courthouse, and from there to the Gulf were only isolated houses. A hard downpour after midnight had put everything under water, which soon ran off. The grand style of living that prevailed in my uncle's home, the many well-dressed people, the elegant dinners, which were served at 5:00 in the afternoon—all this abashed me. I did not know what to do with my hands and feet. In the evening, however, at the big birthday party when I had my first taste of champagne at the children's table, and the oldest daughter of the house, the gentle, calm, wise Mary, took charge of me, I began to find Galveston a very nice place. Mary is still living and to me she has not changed one bit. I found boy company from the families of Runge and Wagner.[2] We ran along the strand to the tip of the land tongue, which was much longer at that time, and to the market. Near it I found what I had been long hunting for—Holstein's Bookstore. Every morning I visited the beach, the market, and the bookstore, where I spent most of my savings and gift money on books.[3]

When I visited Galveston for the second time after Christmas 1883, it had become a different city, with its Tremont and Beach Hotels, a few paved streets, and proud mansions. In place of gas lights and mule-drawn streetcars had come streetcars motored by electricity and electric lights, and the Oleander City was the most beautiful one in Texas.[4] Cousin Lula took her country cousin under her special supervision and took great pains in trying to make him a man of the world. Later she continued her help in letters to me. My young cousin Julius took me out in his boat. When I cast out my line the first time, not far from the wharf, I pulled it in a few minutes later with three fish on three hooks: sea trout, pompano—small but

2. Jockusch lived across from the courthouse on the corner of 20th Street; the site is now a parking garage, but houses on the next block are still quite presentable. Mary Jockusch was six years Trenckmann's senior. Immigrant merchant Henry Runge had two sons Trenckmann's age. Commission merchant Theo Wagner's son was a couple of years younger. Germans made up about one-fifth of Galveston's population in 1870.

3. Isadore Holstein had a cover ad in the 1872 city directory promoting his German and English books and a German circulating library on 173 Tremont Street.

4. Trenckmann is confused here; the first electric streetcars were introduced in Galveston in 1891, but the city did install electric street lights in 1882, the first in Texas to do so.

considered the finest—and a very small shark. Never again have I fished with so much luck.[5]

Much had changed in the Jockusch family, too. The great financial crash, which began in Europe with the World's Fair in Vienna, had brought financial ruin to my uncle, who before with the firms of Kaufmann & Runge; Focke, Wilkins & Lange; Gus Heye & Co.; and Wagner had been predominant in the German business world of what was then the only important Texas port city.[6] As German consul he had been solicitous about the welfare of German immigrants. Although in the seventies he himself was still active at a small salary, Cousin Clara gave music lessons, and Cousin Lula was employed in the Customs office. But the representative old Galveston families, Anglo-American as well as German, had not distanced themselves from the Jockusch family, as often happens elsewhere, so there was a fine sociability in their home. .

Now go on! In the hope of getting permission to leave the country I went to Bellville, but again Mr. Maetze informed me that I could not go now. On the street I met Senator Chesley, the chairman of the school board, and was introduced to him. Mr. Chesley said I had come as if in answer to a call and that I must take over the principalship of the Bellville school, since the present principal, Professor Paulus, had suddenly resigned to accept a better paying position in Terrell.[7] I did not hesitate long, accepted for one year, and shortly

5. Galveston was the largest city in Texas in 1880 with a population of more than twenty-two thousand, putting it ahead of second-place San Antonio and third-place Houston. By 1883 Galveston had a diverse population with many cultural and economic connections to New York, New Orleans, Havana, and Western Europe. It served Texas as a commercial and banking center as well as its main seaport. See David G. McComb, *Galveston: A History* (Austin: University of Texas Press, 1986), 42–120.

6. The 1873 World Exhibition in Vienna simply happened to coincide with the Vienna Stock Exchange crash on May 9, 1873, which triggered an international financial crisis. Its American manifestation, known as the Panic of 1873, was set off on September 18, 1873, by the insolvency of Jay Cooke & Company. The ensuing depression, the most serious up to that point, persisted through 1877. In the 1870 census Jockusch reported fifty thousand dollars' worth of real estate and fourteen thousand dollars in personal property.

7. New Hampshire–born lawyer Alvah Chesley had come to Texas in 1863 and represented the 12th District in the Texas senate for the 1883–84 term. David Paulus, the son of a physician from Copenhagen, was a normal school student at High Hill in 1880 and a county judge in Hallettsville in 1900.

thereafter I was a teacher again with a monthly salary of $80.00 for ten months—at that time considered quite good—and three women assistants. For my classroom I had the auditorium of the former Unity Hall; one of the assistants had the stage, while two small wooden houses attached to the building housed the other two. All of these rooms were harder to heat than the schoolhouse in Shelby had been. The environment of the schoolhouse was unfortunate. Close by to the northeast was the jail with its noisy black and white prisoners and sometimes even a raving insane occupant. To the northwest was a saloon with customers, mostly young Anglo-Americans from the country, who tried to flirt with our older girls. I appealed to the saloon keeper, a good man but too easygoing. I told him this would have to stop, and it did.[8]

I promptly found good lodgings in "Bachelors' Hall," formerly Dr. Cocke's office next to H. Miller's store. Here, Charley Miller, the young lawyer whom I had had to take under my wing when he entered A&M College; his younger brother Herman; Fritz Roensch; and Bernhard Dornberger had their sleeping quarters.[9] The last three were employed in Miller's store. I was also fortunate in finding an excellent boarding house conducted by Mother Harigel. It was very reasonable, though not quite so ridiculously cheap as Shelby, where I had paid ten dollars a month for board and lodging. Among the regular guests I found two especially congenial ones: William von Rosenberg and Albert Saft, who shortly before had established a book and novelty store.[10] At court sessions the German jurors and witnesses from all parts of the country came to still their hunger at

8. Unity Hall, on the site of the current city hall, was built as an entertainment venue in 1873 and was sold to the Bellville School District for four hundred dollars in 1881; it served as the public school for about twenty years. In 1904 it was sold to the Bellville Turnverein, renovated, and returned to its original purpose under the name Turner Hall.

9. The Miller brothers later became Trenckmann's brothers-in-law. Roensch, exactly Trenckmann's age, had immigrated from Prussia in 1871 and later became a merchant in Bellville. Bookkeeper Bernhard Dornberger, who had immigrated in 1884, lived next door to Trenckmann's nephew Otto in 1900.

10. Charles J. von Rosenberg, born in 1857 into an elite family of Forty-eighter immigrants, was a clerk in Bellville in 1880 and later became a businessman in La-Grange. Albert Saft was a Jewish immigrant who arrived from Germany in 1877; in 1910 he ran a bookstore in Hallettsville, where he also led religious services in Hebrew and English. "Encyclopedia of Southern Jewish Communities—Tri-County

twenty-five cents for an ample meal. Here I made acquaintances from all parts of the county that were advantageous to me later.[11]

The teaching in the Bellville school, with its eight classes, was much more advanced than in Frelsburg and Shelby; and since in addition to the German classes I had charge of the upper grades, I had to cram higher mathematics for a few weeks. What had seemed obscure to me in algebra in the past cleared up rapidly in the course of teaching it to others. The task of being principal was much more difficult for me. Fortunately the teachers of the lower grades were happy choices, and they lightened my problems considerably. The girls in the upper classes were well advanced teenagers. Some of them came from elsewhere and some were Bellvillites who had been kept out of school for a while because their mothers considered my predecessor too youthful.[12] These grown ladies caused me considerable embarrassment, but little by little one adjusts himself to every situation, and I must say that I profited from teaching these nice young women.

Bellville, where I expected to stay the year, which extended itself to twenty-six years, was at the time in a state of business decline from the boom that had started about New Year of 1880, when with the arrival of the Santa Fe it had become a railroad town. Then a number of very pretentious brick houses had been built on the square to replace old wooden structures. Mr. H. Miller had built one two blocks to the east. The number had rapidly increased with the arrival of Jewish firms and a few professional men and artisans. All but two of the Jewish firms—Stern Brothers, well-educated men who had recently emigrated, and Wolf and Lewis—had soon moved elsewhere, but the German element of the town had received an

---

Texas: Columbus, Hallettsville, La Grange, Schulenburg," http://www.isjl.org/texas-tricounty-encyclopedia.html.

11. Male German Texan participation in the jury process suggested that they were accepted by Anglo Texans as roughly equal before the law and in politics. Well into the twentieth century women, African Americans, and Tejanos faced difficulties or were excluded from juries. See *Handbook of Texas Online*, Joseph W. McKnight, "Jury Trial," accessed August 19, 2016, http://www.tshaonline.org/handbook/online/articles/jzj02, uploaded on June 15, 2010, published by the Texas State Historical Association.

12. His predecessor, Paulus, was three years younger than Trenckmann, so barely twenty when he left.

increase of young blood.[13] The trade territory had decreased rather than increased with the railroad, for Sealy, only eighteen miles to the South, was growing rapidly and drawing trade from as far as Millheim and Cat Spring. The two stations of Peters and Kenney had also established businesses, and for the lowland farmers along the Brazos, who at that time harvested considerably bigger cotton crops than today, Hempstead in Waller County was much more accessible than Bellville. The businessmen of our city took great pains to draw the cotton trade. It was much more customary then than today for the farmer to buy heavily at the place where he sold his cotton and other products. For a time they were successful; but then the construction of the M.K.&T. Railroad from Sealy to New Ulm created two new railroad towns to the west, which hurt the cotton trade. The merchants of Bellville were restricted to a much smaller trade territory.[14]

A real stroke of luck was the creation of the Farmers Alliance, which had its headquarters in Bellville. This attracted much trade, which remained after the failure of the Alliance store. Merchants, fearing ruin because of the competition of the Alliance, had lowered prices and increased their efforts to please their customers. A rumor that Bellville would cease to be the county seat had been stopped by a popular election in which the proposal to move it to Nelsonville had been defeated.[15]

13. In 1880 four-fifths of the five hundred inhabitants of Bellville were white, among them fifty-four persons born in Germany and more than one hundred of German parentage. Aaron Wolf and Isaac Lewis were listed as Russian Jewish merchants in Bellville in 1900; the Stern brothers could not be identified but later sponsored half-page ads in the paper.

14. The Gulf, Colorado and Santa Fe Railroad reached Bellville in 1880 and within months increased the population from three hundred to over five hundred, but the Missouri, Kansas and Texas (M.K.&T., or Katy) line came through in 1892 ten miles to the south. Kenney and Peters were on the Santa Fe about halfway from Bellville to Brenham and Sealy, respectively. Still, more than eighty-six hundred bales of cotton were shipped from Bellville in 1898. When Trenckmann arrived in 1884, the town had two weekly newspapers, a dozen general stores, and three saloons. *Handbook of Texas Online*, Christopher Long, "Bellville, TX," http://www.tshaonline.org/handbook/online/articles/hgb05, uploaded on June 12, 2010, modified on May 2, 2016, published by the Texas State Historical Association.

15. The Southern Farmers' Alliance began in 1877 in Lampasas County, Texas, and it eventually had almost three million members across much of the country. German membership and participation as indicated by the Cat Spring Agricultural Society

Following this, the decision was made to erect a new courthouse in place of the old red brick box, and for those times it was to be quite a stately building. This event was celebrated with a big barbecue, which, next to a public execution, probably attracted more people to Bellville than any other event of the past or future. More than ten thousand people are said to have feasted in the park just acquired by the Turnverein Gut Heil. Farmers of the neighborhood donated fat calves, beef, and hogs for the fest, and the Bellvillites furnished coffee, bread, and other edibles. The citizens of Bellville showed the hospitality for which they have gained a lasting reputation; it was a veritable feast of joy.[16]

At that time Bellville was nearly half German.[17] All the larger business establishments with the exception of the two Jewish firms were in the hands of Germans. From the beginning there were capable, educated men among these Germans who would not allow themselves to be dominated. When through the efforts of Senator Chesley Bellville was incorporated as the first independent school district in the state, Unity Hall, which at that time had served as a temple of the Muses for the Germans, was given to the school on the condition that permanent instruction in German would be given there.[18]

---

minutes and mention by Trenckmann again suggested that German Texans were at least partially integrated into the world of Anglo Texans. There was a separate alliance for African American farmers. The Southern Farmers' Alliance tried several economic strategies to deal with fluctuating prices for cotton and other farm commodities. These included forging trade agreements with local merchants and setting up their own alliance cooperative stores. See *Handbook of Texas Online*, Donna A. Barnes, "Farmers' Alliance," accessed August 19, 2016, http://www.tshaonline.org/handbook/online/articles/aaf02, uploaded on June 12, 2010, modified on September 4, 2013, published by the Texas State Historical Association.

16. The new courthouse was constructed in 1888. The Bellville Turnverein, founded in 1885, later hired local contractor Joachim Hintz to build a twelve-sided pavilion, which was completed in 1897. It was purchased by the city in 1937 and gained recognition as a Texas Historic Landmark in 1996.

17. Like many ethnic boosters, Trenckmann exaggerated the size of the German community, which made up only one-third of the white population of Bellville.

18. After the passage of the Texas Constitution of 1876, the halting progress toward higher-quality free public education of the previous few years ended. By 1880 attempts to reinvigorate public schools usually centered on forming independent school districts in towns and cities. The Bellville district probably was formed about 1880. See Frederick Eby, *The Development of Education in Texas* (New York; MacMillan, 1925), 157–92.

The Germans lived in good friendship and harmony with their Anglo-American neighbors—court officials, doctors, etc.—but insisted on their rights. A pleasant sociability existed between most of the German-American and Anglo-American families. But at the time when there really were only private schools in Bellville conducted by Anglo-American ladies who were often lacking in certain branches, particularly in arithmetic, most of the Germans sent their children either to the outstanding Piney School, which was under the direction of an exceptionally capable teacher, Professor Emil Koch, or later to Professor Beyer's private school. With the exception of the small post oak clearing where lived a class of Anglo-American people similar to the hillbillies near Austin, most of the land around Bellville was owned by Germans who had come to Texas early. On the black land to the south, however, lived industrious German farmers who had come in the seventies and who conducted their own schools and maintained their own associations, such as the Piney Agricultural Society, the Concordia Singing Society, and the Coshatte Turnverein. All these had erected their own halls for many happy celebrations. Many of the children of Anglo-Americans who lived near these people learned to speak German well.

There was no lack of spirit of enterprise in Bellville. It evidenced itself in efforts to improve the roads, which needed improvement badly. The sand surrounding the town on three sides was a "horse killer" in dry times. People from other areas made fun of the town, insisting that a lady from Bellville could easily be recognized by the climbing walk that she acquired in her effort to pull her feet out of the sand. Present-day visitors to Bellville will find this hard to believe. For many years the Bellvillites have tried to improve their sandy roads by covering them with red clay. They made the road through the frequently flooded muddy grama grass prairie to Millheim passable in all weather by building a causeway. Efforts to improve the school have always been in evidence. Near the end of the first year of my principalship an effort was made to abolish the school tax. Some patrons thought I was aiming too high; others objected to paying the tax. But the people of Bellville voted the proposal down. The money that I needed for equipment to teach physics and chemistry and a small collection of minerals was obtained at a school entertainment. A money collection was used to buy a nice little library. Even

Petrus Wolnitzek, the most original among all the old-time originals in Bellville, gave me $2.50 for the school library. All the other solicitors had refused to tackle him because consistently he had refused to give; besides that, he cherished a deep dislike for school children. Perhaps he had learned that I was making every effort to keep my pupils from annoying him just to see him burst out of his door and to hear him scold them in Polish, English, and German.[19]

The parents insisted that I was capable teacher; at least they said so in my presence, and many of my pupils tell me that to this day. I reproach myself for not having maintained stricter discipline, since I preferred smiling children to those with long faces. I worked hard, often, as my wife told me later, much too hard and too long, in order to give special attention to this and that detail that seemed important to me, often somewhat awkwardly at setting up necessary equipment for the school.

There was plenty of entertainment in Bellville. When the president of the school board called my attention to the importance of setting a good example by avoiding the many saloons, I answered that I would visit them when I so desired but would never leave them tipsy. At Hermann Schlosser's I enjoyed many a game of pool, and in private homes and in the Turner Hall I gave lessons in playing Skat until instruction became unnecessary. My pupils excelled their teacher. Often I went quail hunting or rode to Millheim to try once more to shoot prairie chickens. I made frequent hunting trips to the Bernard with Charley Miller, who had a good hunting dog and was the better shot than I.

Best of all was the fact that I was gradually drawn into a jolly circle of young folks. We had organized a literary society. Since we couldn't agree on a better name, we called ourselves the Y.F.S (Young Folk's Society), which my merry father-in-law-to-be, H. Miller —interpreted to stand for young fools' society. The membership consisted of an equal number of young men and young ladies. From

19. Peter Paul Wolnitzek, born 1822, immigrated in 1856 from Silesia and ran a furniture store in Bellville. The state of Texas rewrote its school laws in 1883 and 1884 just as Trenckmann began teaching in Bellville. More tax money was provided for the support of public education, school districts were allowed, and the districts could tax in support of the schools. See Eby, *Development of Education*, 193–213.

them I learned at last how to take out a young lady and deliver her home properly. Music and amusing games furnished more of the entertainment than literature, but these evenings became so stimulating to me that I was even inspired to write poetry, and after one of them I found myself the blissful fiancé of Miss Tillie Miller. From the beginning of our acquaintance we had been engaged in a teasing battle of wits.[20]

At first we kept our engagement a dark secret, for her exceptionally practical mother had visited our bachelors' quarters and had sharply criticized the disorder in my room and the extravagant number of not-worn-out suits that I had. She thought her father too would object. As a merchant he had a good head for mathematics, but otherwise he was a genial, liberal soul and particularly adept at composing jingles. Out of love for their daughter both of them gave their consent without much hesitancy, and on April 20, 1886, we were married in the midst of a jolly circle of friends. Rhinewine, champagne, and "Bowle" (punch) loosened tongues and made our wedding unforgettably merry. I had gained a splendid comrade, who although of a very different temperament from mine, had the same goals in life that I had. She has clung to me faithfully through the good and the many bad days, and for forty-five years has made great sacrifices without a murmur of complaint. From her I learned to love life and many other things, even though I was an inept scholar in practical matters. There can be nothing better than our life together has been.

20. A German proverb states, "Was sich liebt, das neckt sich," or, as the editor was told as a child, "They tease you because they like you."

The Principal
Becomes an Editor

Naturally, as a married man I gave up all plans of going to Australia or anywhere else in the world. I had come to like Bellville so well that I was ready to spend the rest of my life there. Whoever knew the Bellville of that time will readily understand why. I felt I was a true Bellvillite and took an interest in all of its enterprises. I was particularly active in the *Turnverein*, which, with Albert Saft as director, really did gymnastics or at least attempted to and at the same time upheld the German language. Our newly erected, roomy, and practically arranged Turner Hall became the headquarters for all German entertainments. I also took a lively interest in county politics, and naturally in the teachers' association, the County Institute. As a member of the board of examiners I gained an insight into the school situation of the county. By this time a second generation of Germans were beginning to seek teaching positions—among them a number of Maetze's later pupils. Although they had no higher education, two of these—F. C. Kloss and Reinhold Regenbrecht—have been successful teachers all their lives.[1]

Originally published in *Das Wochenblatt*, December 10, 1931.

1. Regenbrecht reportedly had only six years of schooling and was picking cotton when informed of a teaching opportunity, but he passed the teacher's exam within a few weeks. Fred C. Kloss was born in Texas in 1873 and taught school at Millheim for several decades. *Cat Spring Story*, 55, 70–71.

The German country schools now began to employ women teachers. I observed with regret that a number of German communities began to count on the state school money, which had been increased, for the payment of teachers' salaries; i.e., on the state's maintaining the school without any contribution from the parents. I foresaw the result that the schooling of the children would be of a poorer quality than it was at a time when the teachers had received a higher education in the schools in Germany and that the parents might lose interest in schools that cost them nothing. In giving examinations to prospective Negro teachers I gained an insight into the thinking of the somewhat better educated Negro of that time. Often he attempted to cheat or by means of flattery or bribery to gain the eagerly sought certificate. In order to keep all teacher positions filled, we had to let many, including white aspirants with meager knowledge, slip through with third-class certificates.[2]

The discharge of my duties was not made difficult for me in Bellville, but the more I tried to improve myself through reading the more I became convinced that for the best success in teaching, thorough pedagogical training in a good teacher's college is necessary. Texas had only one, and it was still in its infancy.[3] I had my family—two boys had made their appearance by this time. I had no wish to leave them. I felt that my goals were gradually turning away from school. We had purchased something more than half an acre of land that had formerly belonged to the Harris family to the east of our home. There I could return to my old love—gardening and raising fruit. Upon the death of my revered father-in-law my wife had inherited a tract of about sixty acres next to the Turner Park. He had planted a sizable Herbemont vineyard on it. Grape culture had taken hold in Austin County at that time but was soon halted

2. African Americans were relegated to separate schools in the 1880s and had no schools in Bellville. Throughout that decade there were twenty to twenty-five African American schools in the county. See the *Biennial Reports of the State Superintendent of Schools*.

3. Sam Houston Normal School in Huntsville was founded in 1879. *Handbook of Texas Online*, Joe L. Clark and Nancy Beck Young, "Sam Houston State University," accessed July 21, 2016, http://www.tshaonline.org/handbook/online/articles/kcs02, published by the Texas State Historical Association.

by the black rot, which caused the grapes to dry up. Shortly before his death my father-in-law had bought Le Conte and Kiefer pear trees. I planted these, stomping them in with my boots because a long rainy period had made digging impossible. They all grew, and many of them are still bearing heavily today. Our grapes bore so well that in spite of the fact that many were stolen we had enough to eat and to give away to our heart's content and to make a big whiskey keg of wine.[4]

I noticed that I was drawn more and more to the garden and to the grape vines; and while I had formerly in my teacher's zeal often rung the closing bell too late, I now found myself watching the hand of the clock move to the hour of four. In my opinion the teacher's calling is such a noble one that it is only for those whose love for it does not diminish despite the petty annoyances connected with the profession. So there gradually ripened in me a resolve to make a change in my life. My wife encouraged me. My salary had soon been raised to $900 per year, which was considered good for the principal in a town with the population of Bellville. We wanted to get ahead and carefully kept our cashbook. But when the year came to an end, it showed only a very small balance. Our older son was beginning to be hard on his clothes, outgrowing them fast, and the younger one was becoming very active. I believe that the school board would have increased my salary if I had asked for it, but I did not want to do this as long as my assistants were getting only 40 to 50 dollars per month. The school tax was inadequate. Bellville was standing still. Finally the decision was made, but we had not solved the problem of what I would undertake.[5]

4. In the nineteenth century, German Texans tended to farm more intensively and to have higher levels of productivity per acre. They also emphasized market gardening, the sale of fruits and vegetables, and wine making more than their Anglo Texan or African American Texan counterparts did. See Terry G. Jordan, *German Seed in Texas Soil: Immigrant Farmers in Nineteenth-Century Texas* (Austin: University of Texas Press, 1966), 192–203.

5. The *Galveston Daily News* announced on June 23, 1891, from Bellville: "The graded school of this place closed with fourteen graduates, the largest class we have ever had. Professor Trenkmann [*sic*], who has been at the head of the school for the last eight years, retires from the profession, and Texas looses [*sic*] one of its best educators."

The mercantile business appealed to us. J. G. Wessendorf, who was retiring from his long held position as stationmaster, offered me a partnership in a general merchandise business. Though I was not qualified, I was about to accept. My practical mother-in-law settled that matter with the assertion that partnerships are no good. All at once—we do not remember who thought of it first—we decided that I should found a German newspaper. My old teacher Maetze told me that in Austin County I could not count on more than three hundred readers, and an increase in circulation from distant points for a paper published in Bellville could not be expected. The town already had two English newspapers, and Sealy had one. Other friends advised against it or shrugged their shoulders but could not dampen my enthusiasm. The necessary funds were available to me, and the orders were sent off for a very good printing shop for those times.

The conditions of the time had a lot to do with our decision to enter into a risky enterprise. It was a boom period for the German Americans. They had grown greatly in numbers through the big immigration in the two preceding decades, receiving increases in the number of farmers and well-trained craftsmen as well as in venturesome and enthusiastic young people. Carl Schurz, the greatest German American, had been dead for five years. This man who had introduced civil service reform and by his example had shown that a good citizen must turn against his own party when it gets on the wrong road, had been buried with honor, tendered only the greatest in the nation. His teaching that the immigrant should become a true American but should at the same time preserve the language and the intellectual treasures of the land of his birth had made a deep impression on the German Americans. Barthold and others were wielding a great influence in politics.[6]

6. Trenckmann misstates the year of Schurz's death, which was 1906, but otherwise the characterization is accurate. Richard Bartholdt (1855–1932) immigrated from Germany at age seventeen and worked in journalism until being elected to Congress as a Republican from Saint Louis (1893–1915). See Hans L. Trefousse, *Carl Schurz: A Biography* (Knoxville: University of Tennessee: Press, 1983); Richard Bartholdt, *From Steerage to Congress* (Philadelphia: Dorrance, 1930).

In the cultivation of music the Germans, who had introduced male choruses, were the leaders. They took the lead in school improvement. Many of the large cities in the North maintained German theaters. The German *Turnvereins* had become important in the country, and the Turner enterprises gave the impetus to a general introduction of gymnastic exercises. German daily newspapers were exercising great influence, and German weeklies shot up like toadstools in the warm rain. Politicians eagerly wooed the German vote through flattery and learned to drink and to appreciate *Koch-kaese*.[7] For some years the National German-American Alliance had been affecting conditions beneficially. This organization, which had spread rapidly, later turned more of its attention to fighting prohibition and any restriction of immigration than to the preservation of German cultural treasures. It came to an inglorious end in 1917, when it was falsely accused of disloyal activities and its leaders declared it dissolved. The celebration of German Day had rapidly taken hold in all the larger German settlements, and here in Texas the Order of the Sons of Hermann was working diligently for the preservation of the German language and customs in accordance with its most important purpose.[8]

This and the growing prosperity of the Germans had brought about a greater respect for them and a greater recognition of their worth, but it had also awakened jealousy. This jealousy was particularly evident in the Southern states, where so many plantation and slave owners had become impoverished. In many counties they saw their lands fall into the hands of German immigrants, while they themselves became more and more dependent on the good will of these newcomers in Texas, who had bought their lands; possibly as

7. *Kochkaese*, cooked cheese, was an especially smelly German delicacy, at least as the editors' grandmothers made it. What they "learned to drink" was of course beer.

8. The National German-American Alliance was an umbrella organization for the promotion and preservation of German culture. At its peak in 1916 it claimed well over two million members, but given its umbrella structure, these were nominal memberships through its affiliated local organizations, not necessarily committed to its larger purposes. Its German name, the Deutschamerikanischer National-Bund, should not be confused with the pro-Nazi Bund of the 1930s.

office seekers they were forced to give their so-called German friends assurances of their love and esteem. That considerable bitterness resulted among them is understandable. This fact was brought to my attention through some of their children, my pupils, who were less cautious in hiding their thoughts. I considered myself capable of helping to heal the breach, and I hoped to influence the Germans in taking a more active part in other phases of politics and to seek a more powerful assertion of their rights than the question of prohibition, which was gradually becoming a burning one. I particularly wanted to help the newer immigrants to an understanding of American institutions. I wanted to impress upon them Carl Schurz's teaching that in order to become good Americans they must remain good Germans; i.e., they must preserve in their homes the German language as the bearer of German culture.[9]

The die was cast. Moved by the slight fear that in our new life we would have to live sparingly, I had bought from Mr. Wessendorf, who had in the meantime become bank cashier, the bookstore formerly owned by Saft in order to have a small but sure income. We had selected the name *Wochenblatt*, not realizing that a paper by that name was being published in Fredericksburg; it was little known until Robert Penniger became its editor.[10]

The first issue was to appear at the beginning of September. Printing type was at hand and also a typesetter from Saint Louis named Schubert—a loyal soul. But the press we ordered from Connecticut had failed to arrive. From telegrams we discovered that it had gone

9. Trenckmann articulated his life's mission in this paragraph. Cultural differences, particularly surrounding Sunday laws and Prohibition, often sharply divided Germans and Anglos, and as the later pages of his autobiography make clear, World War I and the arrival of the Ku Klux Klan in the 1920s only made conditions worse. See Seth Shepard McKay, *Texas Politics, 1906–1944: With Special Reference to the German Counties* (Lubbock: Texas Tech Press, 1952).

10. German Texan Joe Wesendorf, exactly Trenckmann's age, was a railroad agent in 1880 and a bank cashier in 1900. Saft is probably Albert Saft mentioned above. The *Fredericksburg Wochenblatt* was founded in 1877. Penniger, a German immigrant, had worked on German papers in New Braunfels and San Antonio before he joined the Fredericksburg paper in 1888 and bought it in 1890. He edited it for two decades, taking the circulation from 850 to over 2,000. *Handbook of Texas Online*, Martin Donell Kohout, "Penniger, Robert G.," http://www.tshaonline.org/handbook/online/articles/fpe28, uploaded on June 15, 2010, modified on April 29, 2016, published by the Texas State Historical Association.

to Beeville instead of Bellville by mistake. Finally it came, and there also came to us Miss Anna Uhlig, the young daughter of a teacher. She proved to be a faithful and quick assistant.[11] We worked at high speed to get out the first issue, at first until late in the evening and then till midnight. On the last day Miss Uhlig kept setting type until 12:00 p.m.; Schubert and I did not stop until nearly breakfast time. I had often written for newspapers and had once represented Henry Mueller of the Brenham *Volksbote* for a short time as editor; but since I didn't have the slightest idea about the technical features of newspaper publishing, I soon had to call in another and still another helper. The bookstore was an obstacle. We were expected to supply the books for all the pupils when school opened. I soon realized that the two enterprises did not go together, but my wife, always willing to do her part, came to the rescue.

Issue Number 1 actually came to press on September 17 but was not completed until the next day and not until the gigantic Negro who served as motor for the press, rolling in sweat from turning the 1,500-pound roller, had perfumed the whole place but had not succeeded in driving away a huge crowd of spectators. At last 3,000 *Wochenblatt*s were printed, folded, addressed, and put into mailbags. They were addressed to the heads of all the German families in Austin County and to many more distant acquaintances. We went home dog-tired, but before supper we had to study the paper. To my disgrace and chagrin it had no editorial, due in part to the rush of the last days when so many unexpected advertisements came in that I had not got to this important feature of a family paper until Schubert announced that only half a column of space was left. In all haste I concocted a "Greeting to the readers," who I hoped would become *subscribers*. There were more errors than ads, but satisfaction triumphed over annoyance—a beginning had been made.

The chapter on my change of professions has become too long. I promise that it will be the last of this kind, and I shall try to complete the remaining forty years of my life very soon.

11. Beeville, Texas, lies between Corpus Christi and San Antonio, nearly two hundred miles from Bellville. Anna Uhlig Kirsten immigrated from Saxony in 1882 at age twelve, married in 1895, and settled in Houston. She had a seventh-grade education. Her daughter reported a German mother tongue in the 1940 census.

About the *Wochenblatt*
in Bellville

An examination of that first copy of the *Wochenblatt* shows clearly what changes can come about in forty years. Every Bellville business, naturally the bank, the doctors, the lawyers, and a number of craftsmen are represented in the advertisements, and Brenham too, by a big advertisement of A. A. Woehlers, whose place was known far and wide by the people who appreciated a good drink and tasty food. Since I had not had much time to solicit advertising, their number proved that a German paper was felt to be a necessity. Shortly before, LaGrange in the neighboring Fayette County had provided the veteran newspaperman Lehmann with the means to found the *La Grange Deutsche Zeitung;* a few weeks before that the *Seguiner Deutsche Zeitung* came into existence; the *Nord Texas Presse* of C. F. Altermann was started in November; and a few years later in Caldwell County, several thousand dollars were collected by the German citizens to found a German paper under the genial management but all too unstable W. Hofmeister. The *Friedrichsburger Wochenblatt*, which had been vegetating for a long time, awoke to new life under Mr. Penniger's energetic management and was soon

Originally published in *Das Wochenblatt*, December 30, 1931.

Wochenblatt offices, Bellville, Texas. Photo courtesy of Bellville Historical Society, Bellville, Texas.

well financed by a corporation.[1] My *Wochenblatt* retained the record of being published in the smallest town in which a German newspaper could exist.

Expressive of the spirit of the time is the first festival advertisement announcing the celebration of German Day in Bellville. It announced the participation of the German societies of the county, music furnished by three bands, gymnastic exhibitions and exercises, a parade, festival orators, and naturally a grand ball at the close. All this was carried out too and on an even grander scale than was expected.

This issue contained a first contribution from a coworker, the genial and original son of our Millheim neighbor, Sigismund Engelking, who under the title of "Mueller and Schulze" and in his own

1. The *La Grange Deutsche Zeitung* was founded in August 1890 with Hugo Lehmann its first editor. The *Seguiner Zeitung* was founded on August 20, 1891. In Dallas, the *Nord Texas Presse* was founded on October 14, 1891, with Hugo Moeller as editor; Charles F. Altermann took over as editor and publisher in 1893. In Caldwell County the *Lockhart Zeitung* lasted from 1906 to 1918. Arndt and Olson, *German-American Newspapers*, 619–34.

dry, witty style created characters similar to the two "Spiessbuerger" in *Kladderadatsch* but adapted to conditions in Texas. He kept up these contributions for some time. Some items in the issue call to mind the short duration of human life and fill one with sadness. Of all the advertisers none have been living for many years. But many of them like W. E. Luhn, Heinrich Louwien, C. F. Hellmuth, and the saddlemaker, Jean Baptist Bailleux, a Luxembourger with French sympathies but always my staunch friend, contributed for many years to the building of Bellville, left their stamp on the town, and are well remembered. The county and precinct officers whose terms were announced have all passed away too, as have all fifteen of my first *Wochenblatt* agents. Of all the names that appear in it the only man living is the honest, devout John Brooks, who was at that time one of the officers of the then powerful Farmer's Alliance.[2]

Many festivities have since taken place in Bellville, but none was celebrated so enthusiastically as German Day, on which I reported in the issue of October 8. Nearly all, and certainly all the German business houses, were attractively decorated. A cold autumn drizzle threatened to spoil everything, but long before the sun came out many visitors had gathered on the square, and after an hour's delay the parade started downhill to the new Turner Hall. The bands from Millheim and Cat Spring and the first Bellville band participated, also the Cat Spring and Piney Agricultural Societies, the Cat Spring Turnverein, proudly mounted on horseback, the Schiller Lodge No. 4, O.D.H.S., the Piney Concordia Singing Society, the Coshatte Turnverein, and the Turnverein Gut Heil of Bellville. Among the best planned and most attractive floats were those of the Piney Agricultural Society, which presented German immigrants; the Center Hill School Society, which presented a German Sunday in an arbor; the Schiller Lodge, whose theme was "Faith, Love, Hope"; the float of the Coshatte Turnverein, with the members in their gym suits; floats presenting Germania and Columbia;

2. John W. Brooks (1856–1939), a Texan with roots in Georgia, was farming with his father, a mortgage-free landowner, in 1900. By 1910 he was a mortgage-free farmer himself, married with a family. He later worked as a surveyor. Through the 1890s Germans in Austin County supported attempts by the Farmer's Alliance to ease the burden on farmers of fluctuations in the money supply and the price of farm commodities and supplies.

and another showing Arminius (Hermann) with his foot planted on the neck of the conquered Roman.[3] A very realistically constructed Elbe boat piloted by Wilhelm Scholz created much amusement. In the hall Dr. H. F. Tietz read a pleasing poem that he had written for the occasion, and Hermann Schlosser read an eloquent festival poem by F. Westermann. The Piney Concordia sang under the direction of its aged but capable leader Friedrich Raube. Then the unforgettable teacher C. F. Reinecke of Millheim delivered a typical, forceful German Day oration. Finally, the entire audience sang words adapted to the occasion to the tune of the *Wacht am Rhein*. A joyous, enthusiastic festival mood prevailed.[4]

In the second issue a loyal friend of the *Wochenblatt*, Theodor Buehring, who conducted a model school in Welcome until he became editor of the *Brenham Volksbote* and who taught children manners as well as books, sent in his first report on a well-attended *Saengerfest* in Welcome. Participants were the singing societies of Brenham, Nassau in Fayette County, Helvetia of Schoenau, and Welcome, including nearly a hundred singers. This issue also contained the announcement of another German Day celebration, that of the Harmonieverein in Shelby. The club kept up its German Day celebrations regularly, even during the First World War and thereafter.

The number of coworkers on my paper grew rapidly. Fritz Westermann furnished humorous verses under the name of "Fritz Schwart and Coarl Witt." His son Heinrich soon started his forty-year career of magnificent contributions: nature studies, travel experiences, local reports, and articles under the pen name of H. W. Schnueffelmaier. In one of these articles he recommended the cultivation of the "earth cherry." Wm. Hagemann of New Ulm, who cultivated grapes on a large scale, wrote helpful and stimulating articles of grape culture. W. Freckmann of Sealy furnished an amusing travelogue in which

3. The Germanic prince Arminius led a revolt and virtually annihilated three Roman legions at the Battle of Teutoburg Forest in AD 9. German nationalists celebrated this victory and in 1875 erected a statue of Hermann (the German form of his name) brandishing his sword against France—the tallest in the world until surpassed by the Statue of Liberty. Fergus M. Bordewich, "The Ambush that Changed History," *Smithsonian Magazine*, September 2006.

4. German American Day was first celebrated in Philadelphia on October 6, 1883, the two hundredth anniversary of when the thirteen German families who founded Germantown first landed in the city.

he ridiculed Governor James S. Hogg's zeal for enforcement of the Sunday Law. C. F. Hinkel of Weimar soon began sending in poetry and prose. Adolf Billig of Sealy wrote on historical and agricultural subjects. Frank Lotto and later Gustav Hoppe of New Ulm and many others helped to create and maintain interest in the *Wochenblatt*. I am convinced that probably never before in this country had a German paper had so many fine voluntary coworkers, who even furnished their own paper and stamps, as did the *Wochenblatt*. I interpret this fact to mean that they found something in it that they deemed worthy of support.

Soon after the first issue appeared I faced the most difficult task of a newspaperman—to report the death of a person who was dear to me. In the issue of October 8 I had to report the passing of a gifted pupil, the wife of my brother-in-law Herman Miller, the former Lieschen Machemehl, who died soon after the birth of her first child. In the following week it was my old teacher, E. G. Maetze, who had accomplished so much to the honor and credit of the Germans in Texas and who had always been my good counselor. The huge crowd that followed the remains of the Warrior for Freedom in Two Worlds and their sincere sorrow gave proof of the fact that his work in Austin County was appreciated.

Soon I had cause to write my first political article. Our then governor, James S. Hogg, had instructed the county attorney to enforce the Sunday Law with rigid strictness. The Germans and Bohemians of our part of the state had been keeping the Sunday just as it was kept in their homelands. All business houses and all saloons were wide open. Before and immediately after the close of church, Sunday was one of the principal trade days. Festivals where beer was sold were held preferably on Sunday. This command from Austin was held to be an abuse of power, and I voiced my sentiments in this regard, perhaps a little too sharply. As far as I can recall, no arrests were made. In any event there were no convictions, and the Sunday Law remained a dead letter for a long time among an otherwise law-abiding citizenship.[5]

5. Sunday laws governed what businesses could do on a Sunday, reflecting a melding of Protestant morality and state government. Typically such laws regulated the sale of alcohol, the hours businesses could operate on Sunday, and the sale of

Shared fears and sorrows cause two people to understand and appreciate each other even better than shared joys. In November of this same year our second son, 21 months old, who had previously been in the best of health, became ill. After considering the case from every angle, our family physician pronounced his illness to be a slow fever. He prescribed all sorts of remedies to no avail, and soon we had to admit to each other that the life of our child hung in the balance. Convinced that the doctor was unable to diagnose the case, I called four of the best doctors available to our home one evening. And after I had listened anxiously to their endless discussion, I finally turned the case over to the youngest of them—Dr. August Schenck of Kenney. He changed the whole treatment, and in two weeks, during which my wife hardly left his bedside to change clothes, our son was saved. In order to spare his colleague, Dr. Schenck had not pronounced the disease as typhoid but had treated it as such.[6]

During this time my foreman Schubert, who found the Texas winter disagreeable, had resigned. I had had to employ and train new help, had to be away from home till long after midnight and sometimes till daybreak. I could only very rarely relieve my wife at the sickbed. Even then, she could not rest. Those weeks of fear and anxiety we two shall never forget. I knew then that my wife was not only a beloved comrade but a woman whose capacity to sacrifice for her loved ones was unlimited.

We spent many happy Christmases, but none that was brighter than the next because of our joy over the fact that our child was spared for us. Then too I received a wonderful Christmas gift from my wife—one long, narrow box and other important looking small boxes. The narrow box contained a Mustang mailer—a simple machine with which we have printed the names and addresses of our subscribers on the paper ever since—1,400 names per hour when I was going strong. (This mailer and my big paper clipping shears are about all that is left to me now of the earliest *Wochenblatt*). In the

---

some other products. Such laws became more common toward the close of the nineteenth century, and some remained in effect into the twenty-first century.

6. Schenck was born in Bellville in 1867, the son of an immigrant merchant. Typhoid is a bacterial infection spread through poor sanitation and contaminated food and water. It is often accompanied by fever and extreme fatigue and weakness.

Wochenblatt printing press, Bellville, Texas, about 1900. Photo courtesy of Stuart Strong, Austin, Texas.

other boxes was type for the names. The tiresome job of writing the addresses of my readers, whose number had risen almost to a thousand, was over.

For a few years things went ahead smoothly. The *Wochenblatt* gradually found an entrance into neighboring counties, and departing Austin County readers took it with them to their new homes. I had sold the bookstore because the operation of it took too much time from my newspaper work, and with the money I had bought a small press for job printing so that I could add to my income with job work as my competitors were doing. It brought me little profit. I set my prices too low. When I sold it fifteen years later, I estimated that I had profited only a few thousand dollars, not counting my time and that of my printers. Since then and particularly since the World War prices for this type of work had been adjusted to overhead to make job printing a paying business.

In the fall of 1894 cotton prices were at the lowest that we had ever experienced, coming unexpectedly with a bumper crop after prices had been steady for a long time at between seven and ten

Trenckmann family at work setting the *Wochenblatt*, Bellville, Texas, about 1900. Photo courtesy of Stuart Strong, Austin, Texas.

cents for middling, and the farmers had been able to get ahead very well in a time of cheap merchandise and low taxes. Prices for cattle, poultry, and other farm products were much lower, too. Conditions were bad, lamentations were loud, and for two years I sent out no bills. In order to save expenses I often stood at the type case myself, ran the little job press, and through overexertion contracted a stomach ailment that plagued me for a dozen years. I had heavy expenses from my illness, and the editress was burdened with a husband who was on a strict diet and whose food required special preparation. Coffee, vegetables, fruit, and hot sauces were strictly forbidden. I missed the strong coffee most.

In 1898 the boll weevil made its entrance into Austin County, destroyed the crop in the wooded lowlands, where from great tall stalks that no stalk cutter could cut up, the farmers made hardly a bale from fifty acres. On the uplands they did not do so much damage. This infestation struck only the "Bottom" farmers, few of whom were Germans.[7]

---

7. Boll weevils spread from Mexico into South Texas in the early 1890s and migrated north and west from that point. Boll weevils emerge from hibernation in the spring, feed on the tender new growth of young cotton plants, and then lay eggs in

After a severely cold winter—zero in February—the year 1899 brought the worst flood that had ever hit the southeast quarter of the state. Near the end of June, when during a period of rosy crop prospects I had sent out the little booklet *Austin County* as a supplement, it poured for three days almost without interruption. More than twenty-five inches of rain fell. On the grama grass prairie and in the bottom fields Mill Creek rose high above the ears of the cornstalks. From the courthouse tower it looked to the south and east as if an arm of the sea were spreading out. The inhabitants of the river bottoms had to flee and lost their homes and part of their cattle. They could not get back to the devastated lands until late in autumn. Thousands of Negroes, who had lived there as tenants, had to be fed. The flood damage had been terrific from Waco on down to the south. Everything on the Brazos south of Navasota had been destroyed. Near the coast it was reported that the Brazos and the Colorado had joined.[8]

In other parts of the state good crops had been harvested, and there was great eagerness to help. Carloads of used articles of clothing, bacon, etc., arrived in Bellville. The Negroes led a jolly life in their camps, feasting without work. Their wives strutted about in the cast-off silks and satins of white city ladies. Later, smallpox broke out among them, adding greatly to the problems of the people of Bellville, who had to carry the main burden. In the late autumn the order was given that there would be no more food for them without work. They were ordered to clean up the flooded fields on which houses had been built for them. The owners of farms labored

---

the emerging buds and bolls. The bolls fall from the plants, and the eggs hatch in a few days. Colder temperatures reduce the survival rate of boll weevils in the winter, and that may explain why the bottomlands, more protected from sharp plunges in temperature, had more boll weevils. Early planting and more rapidly maturing cotton varieties also reduced damage from the insect. See *Handbook of Texas Online*, Frank Wagner, "Boll Weevil," accessed September 02, 2016, http://www.tshaonline.org/handbook/online/articles/teb01, uploaded on June 12, 2010, modified on December 4, 2015, published by the Texas State Historical Association.

8. The Brazos flood inundated some twelve thousand square miles, killing nearly three hundred people, leaving thousands homeless, and causing an estimated nine million dollars in damage. *Handbook of Texas Online*, Curtis Bishop, "Brazos Flood of 1899," http://www.tshaonline.org/handbook/online/articles/ydb01, uploaded on June 12, 2010, published by the Texas State Historical Association.

with great industry, and in the spring after the flood everything flourished even in fields that had been exhausted from fifty years of cultivation.

On the eighth of September, before the heavy crop was half harvested, came the worst Gulf storm that had ever struck Texas, bringing death to thousands in Galveston, destroying every wooden building to the north as far as Alvin, and even houses in Sealy, and completely ruining all unharvested crops. The Wochenblattmann spent the hours during which the storm attained its height in the Santa Fe depot in Sealy in the only old but well built room that remained standing. For the last hours before midnight I was the sole occupant. Toward midnight there came a brief pause, which enabled me to see the destruction the storm had wrought. The wind had changed but was still very strong, not strong enough, however to destroy houses. Since all lines of communication had been torn down, no one knew when a train would arrive. So the next afternoon, Mill Creek being impassable, I walked the last six miles home on the railroad track to find out what had happened to my family. Pushed along by the strong south wind, I covered those miles in seventy minutes. In Bellville the damage had been comparatively light and north of us quite insignificant.[9]

The boll weevil damage had decreased in South Texas after the severe cold of 1899, but in 1900 the little pests appeared in increasing

9. On Saturday, September 8, 1900, one of the deadliest hurricanes in the history of the United States struck Galveston, Texas. Galvestonians had known a storm was in the Gulf of Mexico since September 4, when news of a hurricane over Cuba reached the island. The storm strengthened, however, after moving west from Cuba, and because of the limited communication and tracking systems of that time period Galvestonians knew few details about the storm until the morning of September 8. Despite being warned by Isaac M. Cline, the local person in charge of the Weather Bureau, to leave the island, or at least to move away from the shore, few moved out of harm's way. As the tide rose and winds increased, wooden structures along the beach collapsed, and the debris acted as a battering ram that destroyed structures further inland. Eventually as many as eight thousand out of the city's almost forty thousand residents were killed, and perhaps as many as twelve thousand died on the island. As Trenckmann reports, the storm caused damage far inland. See *Handbook of Texas Online*, John Edward Weems, "Galveston Hurricane of 1900," accessed September 6, 2016, http://www.tshaonline.org/handbook/online/articles/ydg02, uploaded on June 15, 2010, modified on March 21, 2016, published by the Texas State Historical Association.

numbers on the upland farms and, in spite of the many advertised methods of eradication, spread over the whole county. Only the Cleveland prairie was spared, possibly because of its exposure to strong south winds. The cotton crop was reduced to less than half. When the autumn *Volksfest* was held in New Ulm in the fall with a distribution of all sorts of prizes, many farmers were entitled to the prize offered for the smallest cotton crop, since they had not harvested a single bale. The prizewinner harvested less than one picking sack. Those were bad days again, since farm products brought little money. The farmers living around Bellville who liked to try new things experimented with castor beans; but as they attempted to harvest their crop, beans hopped away from them, and what they managed to gather brought only a small price. They tried potatoes and made a good crop, but the merchants soon found their warehouses overstocked and were forced to refuse to buy. They, as well as the inhabitants of other settlements, have since experimented with many other crops, but most of them have gone back to King Cotton as the chief supplier of cash.[10]

Whoever gets the notion that there was nothing but gloomy talk during this difficult time is badly mistaken. The Austin County Saengerbund, formed early in the nineties, annually celebrated a fine joyous *Saengerfest*. Bellville held a successful state Skat tournament—the game had spread among the farmers. Numerous organizations held their annual summer festivals, Christmas celebrations, and dances, though not as many as occur nowadays.[11] It appeared that the sharp reduction of credit brought on by poor crops and low prices resulted in fewer people being deeply in debt, and hence there were fewer of the common complaints about being short of cash.

10. Cotton was one of the few crops that could produce at least a limited yield even in the worst of conditions, and it had a ready market. Local bankers and merchants were also far more willing to extend credit on the prospects of a cotton crop than on any other crop. It took the New Deal programs of the 1930s and the growth in economic opportunity brought by World War II to move the majority of Texas farmers away from cotton.

11. Skat is a notoriously complicated three-person card game beloved by Germans, involving bidding and tricks. The *Galveston Daily News*, August 22, 1896, p. 4, announced that the fifth state Skat Congress would be held on August 30 in Bellville, with Trenckmann as president of the committee.

State Politics

I have already mentioned the fact that since my boyhood I have always been greatly interested in politics and that I went into the newspaper business partly to stimulate interest in politics among the Germans, where interest, particularly among the younger men, had been deplorably small because after the election of Coke over Edmund J. Davis it came to be the rule that everyone nominated for state office or for Congress by the Democrats was sure of election. Although I always called myself a Democrat and a strict follower of the teachings of Thomas Jefferson, the execution of my original purpose occurred with the intention of always submitting the facts of exposing even the sin of the Democratic party and of frankly expressing that I sometimes jumped at conclusions and gave wrong counsel.[1]

Originally published in *Das Wochenblatt*, March 3, 1932.

1. The Civil War left much bitterness between German Texans and Anglos, and this bitterness sometimes played out in politics, with the Germans siding with African Americans in backing the Republican or Unionist factions in Texas politics. We have little evidence of the political affiliation of Trenckmann's father after the Civil War, but the Cat Spring Agricultural Society, of which he was a member, did suggest support for the Union League. See *Cat Spring Agricultural Society*, 31–34. Tellingly, Austin County had a murder rate only one-fourth that of nearby Anglo counties such as Brazos and Brazoria in the early years of Reconstruction. Nicholas K. Roland, *Violence in the Hill Country: The Texas Frontier in the Civil War Era* (Austin: University of Texas Press, forthcoming, 2020), chap. 6.

So it was, for instance, in the case of James S. Hogg. In the first political campaign after the founding of the *Wochenblatt* I did everything I could except resort to untruth to gain votes against him in the primaries, and after the primary campaign, which ended with a split and two Democratic tickets, I continued to work against him until the November election. I did not like the type of campaign that Hogg was conducting the first time. His manner of courting popularity by the use of coarse jokes and bad English, and preferring to drink in public from a gourd, smacked of the tricks of a demagogue. I despised demagogues as leaders of people. I felt that his insistence upon the strict enforcement of the Sunday Law by our county attorney was directed particularly against the customs of the Germans. His program in the campaign for reelection, the chief plank of which was the establishing of the Railroad Commission to determine freight rates, seemed to me to be directed against free competition and therefore to be undemocratic. Besides, I was young enough to be influenced by my environment, by good friends and by the *Galveston News*, which had been in our home as long as I can remember. In any event, I proceeded to attack Hogg editorially and was happy to see the Germans in Austin County, nearly all of whom were readers of the *Wochenblatt*, take part in the primary convention for the first time and to note that they voted in the November election for George Clarke of Waco, the "Little Giant."[2]

Later I came to realize that demagogic methods might be excusable, sometimes even necessary, to win over the ignorant and unthinking for something that is beneficial to the general public, and also that something had to be done to prevent the railroads from preferring certain shippers of raw materials and manufactured foods at the expense of small city and country merchants and farmers and thus building up larger cities and enriching certain industries and corporations, while at the same time ruining others. Further, I realized that a governor was obligated to see that the officers of the criminal courts

2. The 1892 Texas gubernatorial election was one of the most interesting and exciting elections in the state's history. Three candidates were on the ballot in the general election: James S. Hogg for the Democrats, George Clark for the conservative Democrats, and Thomas L. Nugent for the Populists. Hogg won a plurality of the votes and was reelected. See Barr, *Reconstruction to Reform*, 125–42.

carried out their official duties when he was requested to see to the stricter enforcement of the Sunday Law. The requests may have come from people in the county who wanted to irk the Germans and Bohemians by stopping festivities and the sale of beer on Sundays, and perhaps also from businessmen who could not or did not want to keep open on Sunday. Certainly Hogg did not concern himself as to whether our county attorney carried out this directive, and Attorney Glenn contented himself with publishing the order. The Austin Countians held this publication strongly against him. But they got great amusement out of a travel report by W. Freckmann in which he stated that after Hogg had demanded the closing of saloons that sold beer on Sunday, including Scholz Garten, the governor and a good friend from East Texas entered Scholz Garten after a long walk and asked the barkeeper for beer for two. He refused to serve them. Did this really happen? Freckmann loved his little jokes. You will have to ask old-timers in Austin to verify this story.[3]

At that time the views of the people in the smaller towns of our state were greatly influenced by Galveston, whence most businessmen obtained their wares. Galveston wholesalers were their friends, and glib-talking drummers who called on them influenced their views. Most of these salesmen were mature men who brought not only the newest jokes but much that was worth knowing to them but naturally reflected the views of the wholesalers. To these men Hogg, with his demands for uniform freight rates that might cut their profits, was an abomination. Clarke, who with the railroads had the business world of the state with him, was their man. Hogg got an unexpectedly big vote in Austin County; not only most Anglo-Americans but also the Negroes voted for him solidly, in spite of the fact that the Negroes of that time were rated as Republicans and the Republican State Convention had given its support to Clarke. Hogg had won the Negro vote with a few words in Bell-

---

3. William Freckmann had emigrated from Germany in 1885 and was a tax clerk in Houston in 1900. Scholz Garten, an indoor-outdoor beer garden just four blocks from the capitol, was and is a favorite watering hole for Texas politicians. *Handbook of Texas Online*, Nick Roland, "Scholz Garten," accessed August 16, 2016, http://www.tsha online.org/handbook/online/articles/xds12, uploaded on July 14, 2016, published by the Texas State Historical Association.

ville. When he was to speak in the Turner Hall in which every seat and standing place was taken, half a dozen Negroes were standing in the entrance door. Hogg called to them, "Come on to the front, boys. You shall hear what I have to say." The fact that these Negroes took places near the stage in front of white women lost him a few white votes but brought him the solid Negro vote. I am convinced that the colored vote getters, who were paid by the Clarke Club to win votes against Hogg and gave assurance that they were succeeding, all voted for Hogg. Later, when the demagogue Hogg left office in debt, I learned to value him as a real friend of the people.

I had a great aversion for the system that existed at the time of making nominations by means of primary meetings and county and higher conventions on account of the experience that Austin County had particularly in electing representatives to Congress. Walter Gresham of Galveston, who had served one term and had gotten credit for securing appropriations for Galveston harbor, offered himself for renomination. He was opposed by Jonathan Lane of Fayette County, and if I am not mistaken, by Burgess of Gonzales County and Duff of Brazoria County. I did not particularly like Gresham. He was too smooth for me, too free with his compliments, but my whole environment was supporting him, and because Lane's too obvious flattery of the Germans was objectionable to me, and Duff seemed too young and too oratorical, I decided for Gresham, silently hoping that for want of a two-thirds majority a more prominent man who might be an honor to the district would later be chosen. Too late I learned that Duff, a true idealist, was the best man.

In Austin County Gresham won after a hot election. As had been expected, the district convention was locked, since Gresham could not get the two-thirds majority, even though Brazoria County gave him its few votes. The friends of the other candidates had declared from the beginning that they would prevent Gresham's nomination, and finally that they would propose Miles Crowley of Galveston if those instructed for Gresham refused to change their vote. After a full week's convention in Hallettsville, during which my wife's uncle, Karl Langhammer, and I had excellent quarters with the William von Rosenberg family and I played Skat with likeable Hallettsvillers when there was a pause in the voting, I was called back to the *Wochenblatt*.

It must have been another week before the convention closed with the nomination of Miles Crowley, an uneducated but clever leader of the dock workers in Galveston, who caused the district to become an object of ridicule. When he sought reelection, the delegation from Fayette County, which was to blame for his original nomination, maneuvered the nomination of J. H. Shelburne of Bellville. If I am not mistaken, this was at the instigation of C. J. von Rosenberg of LaGrange. The latter, although popular among the Bohemians and Germans, was not a superior orator, hence he was defeated by R. B. Hawley, another wealthy Galvestonian and the nominee of the Republicans. Two years later Hawley, who was supported by the business world and spent much money, defeated Robson of LaGrange. His successor was George Burgess, a good orator and a capable man but occasionally a heavy drinker. The fact that he was on one of the rare but long-lasting drunken sprees during the tragedy of the storm broke his political neck.[4]

Through the census of 1900 Austin County was put into a new district with Harris, Fort Bend, Waller, Grimes, and other more eastwardly lying backwoods counties. In the first congressional election Tom Ball of Huntsville, undoubtedly a very gifted, personable man, who never mentioned the subject of prohibition in Austin County, was elected without opposition. The next election brought a life-and-death struggle between two Houston men: Holt and Ewing— as unwelcome a situation as the Hallettsville convention had been. After weeks of wrangling, John Pinckney of Hempstead, about the most objectionable man to the citizens of Austin County, was nominated as a "dark horse." The fact that he lived in Hempstead spoke

4. Texas had thirteen US congressional districts in the 1890s, and Austin County was in the 10th District. Then as now, the Texas legislature set the districts. See Texas Legislative Council, Historical Maps, congressional maps, http://www.tlc.state.tx .us/redist/history/maps_congress.html. Trenckmann is mistaken about who was serving in Congress from Galveston during the 1900 storm. Robert B. Hawley, a Republican, served from 1897 to 1901. Trenckmann also failed to mention German Texan and African American support for Hawley in both of his successful runs for Congress. See *Handbook of Texas Online*, Anne W. Hooker, "Hawley, Robert Bradley," accessed November 13, 2017, http://www.tshaonline.org/handbook/online/articles/fhabd, uploaded on June 15, 2010, published by the Texas State Historical Association. Also see *Galveston Daily News*, October 17, 22, 1896; "TX District 10," Our Campaigns, https://www.ourcampaigns.com/RaceDetail.html?RaceID=376368.

against him with us. This nearby town, in bad repute throughout the state for its frequent murders, was commonly known as Six-Shooter Junction. I knew a few very fine families who lived there, and I sympathized with them because of their disturbing environment. Then too, Pinckney was an ardent prohibitionist—a fact that really went against the grain with us. We forgot that circumstances in Hempstead furnished abundant justification for his objections to the sale of whiskey. Pinckney himself was killed in a courthouse shooting. Later I learned from dependable people facts about him that proved him to be a completely just and noble gentleman. His successor in Congress, John Moore, also nominated by the two-thirds majority rule in a locked convention, was a landowning millionaire from Fort Bend County and a thoroughly respectable man who voluntarily refrained from seeking reelection. Finally, Joe Eagle, who had been a Populist in his youth, a very capable right-thinking man and a real Democrat, was elected to Congress, and for the first time in a long while Austin Countians could be proud of their representative in Washington.[5]

In the years that we were in one district with Houston in Harris County and the timber counties east of the Brazos, the Austin delegation had usually been excluded from the organization of the district conventions. All our county resolutions were blocked, the opposition having elected the chairman and filled committees beforehand, thus depriving us of all influence in the convention—an old political trick. So it is understandable that long before its passage I became a zealous supporter of the Terrell Election Law and worked hard for a completely new system of nominations.

It is true that the primary system did not bring about a favorable change either for state officers or for Congress. Our representation in Congress has become weaker on an average under it; we have elected governors and other high state officials who have done everything for the state except reflect credit to it. But I doubt that retain-

5. Joe Eagle (1870–1963) ran unsuccessfully for Congress as a Populist in 1896. He served six terms as a Democrat, 1913–21 and 1933–37, where he was a strong advocate for farm credit and New Deal programs such as Social Security. *Handbook of Texas Online*, Alwyn Barr, "Eagle, Joe Henry," accessed August 07, 2016, http://www.tshaonline.org/handbook/online/articles/fea01, uploaded on June 12, 2010, published by the Texas State Historical Association.

ing the old system would have achieved better results. The cause for the deterioration is in my opinion not the primary system that prevented nominations by deception and other disgraceful maneuvers as well as bitter animosities, but it is the apathy created by the primary system, which left the whole state to be run by one party whose principles had become extremely vague. In former times the two-thirds majority rule prevented the nomination of candidates for office and sometimes brought about the choosing of an extremely able man who would never have thought of being an office seeker. It is doubtful that that would still be possible today when personal and capitalistic interests manipulate politics. In retrospect of the battles of that time, I cannot understand why otherwise sensible representatives of country legislative districts even recently have strained themselves to prevent Harris, Dallas, and Bexar Counties, which have the required population, from forming their own congressional districts. The counties with a small population that are put together with great cities into one district remain powerless. Only a few purchasable vote getters benefit, and the big city controls.[6]

In the nineties, especially in the latter half, there were hot political battles in the whole country. Then as now the fall in prices of farm products and the closing of many industries created discontent. The result was a populistic movement whose good inner kernel was really socialistic but in which very soon selfish demagogues, competing for high office, took over the leadership, and the party became quite powerful in Texas. With the able and irreproachable Nugent as candidate for governor, it can be blamed for the fact that Culberson, an extremely popular man, was reelected with only a plurality instead of a majority because the Republicans, whose party was taking the crawfish route, had its own candidate.

Bryan, the silver-tongued, brought about the end of the Populist, or People's party. With his alluring Free Silver program he enticed its members to come under the Democratic flag. In Texas and in many other states the Populists remained permanently with the Democratic party because that party adopted many of the Populis-

6. Voter turnout plunged in Texas after the introduction of the poll tax and the primary system in the first decade of the twentieth century. Blacks were barred from voting in the Democratic primary, and that became the key election in determining who held office. This caused a loss of interest in voting.

tic reforms on its platform but never brought them into law. With a flourishing economic situation the rapid rise of the Populist Party was soon forgotten. Those who remain true to its principles to the extent that they did not become Socialists always support the party that makes the most enticing promises. Bryan was almost elected. The fact was recognized, however, that his election and the carrying out of his program would have done great harm to the country. For years he deprived the Democrats, who had made him their leader, of any hopes of winning an election. It was not until 1912, when Wilson was elected, that they succeeded, and there only because the Republican vote was split between Roosevelt, who had a lot of Populist votes, and President Taft.[7]

Since my Hallettsville experience I had refrained from becoming a candidate to the congressional convention but for a long time participated regularly in the state conventions. As a member of the organization committee in Dallas, where Campbell finally won out over Colquitt, whom I preferred, and of the Resolutions Committee in San Antonio, where the Prohibitionist Campbell was again nominated for lack of an anti-Prohibitionist opponent, I had an excellent opportunity to study the procedures of large conventions, and I found little in them to rejoice over.[8]

7. William Jennings Bryan was the Democratic candidate in 1896, 1900, and 1908, losing with a smaller share of the popular vote each time. The 1896 election brought a realignment, strengthening the Republican hold on the Midwest, where many Germans and urbanites were repelled by Bryan's crusading Fundamentalist style and his prohibitionist leanings. In the South, the Populist threat of an interracial coalition of sharecroppers provided the impetus for black disenfranchisement. Wilson won in 1912 with only 42 percent of the popular vote.

8. Thomas M. Campbell served two terms as governor from 1907 to 1911, and like his mentor, James S. Hogg, he helped pass significant laws regulating big business. He was the governor while Trenckmann served in the legislature. See *Handbook of Texas Online*, Janet Schmelzer, "Campbell, Thomas Mitchell," accessed September 14, 2016, http://www.tshaonline.org/handbook/online/articles/fca37, uploaded on June 12, 2010, modified on February 24, 2016, published by the Texas State Historical Association. Oscar B. Colquitt followed Campbell as governor, serving from 1911 to 1915. Unlike Campbell, he opposed prohibition and was supported by most German voters. See *Handbook of Texas Online*, George P. Huckaby, "Colquitt, Oscar Branch," accessed September 14, 2016, http://www.tshaonline.org/handbook/online/articles/fc032, uploaded on June 12, 2010, modified on February 24, 2016, published by the Texas State Historical Association.

Another regrettable and unfortunately never entirely missing factor in politics, the willingness to offer bribes, I was to encounter twice as the publisher of a newspaper. Before the primary convention the incumbent of a state office who was an office seeker visited me. I had previously felt some leanings toward him because I had read good things about him and usually preferred an older man to one much younger. But when he began to tear down his opponent, reporting that the latter, who when a sheriff had collected mileage money from the county while he had free passage on the train, doubts arose in my mind. And when he pulled a big roll of bills out of his purse and said, "I need the Austin County vote," I showed him the door and became an enthusiastic supporter of his young opponent. The latter was elected and held the office to the general satisfaction for a long time. Since that time no office seeker has made me a similar proposition.

Another experience was very embarrassing for me. In the congressional campaign I was an active supporter of Ewing. On the day of the primary convention in Austin County, a Houston man who had arrived on an early train stepped hurriedly into my office and informed me that he had to rush to Nelsonville in order to assure the delegation's instructing for Ewing by means of money bribes. I told him it was highly probable that he would be thrown out if he came to Nelsonville with such propositions and that I myself would fight the votes of Nelsonville if he attempted anything of the sort. Nelsonville instructed for Ewing without his visit, but from that day on my enthusiasm for Ewing was dampened. The Houston man later held a high judicial position and was lauded in his eulogy as one of the finest in the state. It is possible there was a change to respectability in him. I am still amused when I think of the astonished faces of a few Galvestonians who, as managers of a booster delegation of several hundred, arrived in Bellville in the forenoon of the day of the county convention to work for Gresham. I told them the best thing for them to do was to let me lock them all up in my printing shop. I knew how much damage a delegation of city men in stiff shirts and shined shoes could do among a group of sturdy farmers.

War and Politics

The last decade of the nineteenth century brought a change in the policy of the country toward the outside world the results of which we can judge better now than we could in the beginning stages. From the time that the Thirteen Colonies had freed themselves from British rule there had been an effort to increase the union of states directly to the west within the southern three-fifths of the part of North America that lies in the temperate zone. Under the leadership of fur hunters and space-seeking pioneer farmers the Mississippi was soon reached and crossed. After Jefferson's great land purchase from Napoleon to help the latter overwhelm the British, who were constantly opposing him in North America, the Stars and Stripes were carried to the Pacific Ocean in the Northwest and then, upon the annexation of Texas and the speedy victories over Mexico to the Southwest, into the golden land of California. The gold booty acquired in California and the railroads built over the mountains to the west coast brought rapid settlements. With these, however, a limit seemed to beset further advancement. The attempts to acquire Canada during the Revolution and in the second war against England had failed. And while American troops had put those of Mexico to flight and taken possession of the Mexican capital, it became clear that the Spanish-speaking population of Mexico, like the French

Originally published in *Das Wochenblatt*, April 28, 1932.

speaking population of Quebec, and the British of Toronto, did not wish to become Americans. The conquest to the north and south to subjugate unfriendly and nonassimilable people in large numbers, which we could have gained by going against our own principles of the Rights of Man, we could not attempt.

The American spirit of enterprise had up to this time been fully occupied with the settlement and profitable development of the West and the reconstruction of the South, ruined and impoverished by the Civil War. For both projects much foreign money was put to use and a tremendous immigration from North Europe had furnished a large part of the necessary physical labor. Their industry conjured up income-bearing property of the forests, the wide plains, and the rich mines under the ground. By means of factories in the New England states, and through profits in the sale of farm and grazing lands, which had been bought at dirt cheap prices or acquired at no cost at all by means of land grants, many Americans had become extremely wealthy after the Civil War. Now no longer able to increase their wealth so rapidly, they sought new opportunities for gain—the neighboring foreign lands, especially in the West Indies and particularly in Cuba. The revolutionary attempts of the Cubans, who in spite of much bloodshed could never be completely subdued, gave the American daily press, which beyond a doubt was acting partly on the orders of the young American sugar trust and the American owners of sugar plantations in Cuba, an opportunity to stir up our people against the Spaniards. Through exaggerated and invented accounts of brutality they managed to incite a war against Spain to free the Cuban patriots. This propaganda was handled just as zealously and as successfully as was the propaganda to induce the United States to go to war against Germany and Austria from 1914 to 1917.[1]

The sinking of the American battleship *Maine* in the harbor of Havana was presented by the press as a ruthless plot of the Spaniards, in spite of the fact that not the least proof of the sinking by the Spaniards existed and none has ever been found. It became clear

---

1. In the wake of the Spanish American War (1898), Carl Schurz, the most prominent German American at the time, was vice-president of the Anti-Imperialist League, which many fellow ethnics supported.

that our government, knowing that an investigation would clear the Spaniards, did not want to permit it. War was declared, and President McKinley, who knew the truth and did not want war, dared not take a stand against it. In a short time the weak Spaniards were conquered almost without resistance. Spain had to give up her island possessions, and thereby we acquired a dozen million unwilling subjects and exercised a sort of dominion over Cuba, Haiti, and San Domingo.

The American dollar, behind which stands the American flag, is active in the entire West Indies and in Central and South America; and in the effort to protect it or the money lenders, a great deal has happened that is unbecoming to the role of an unselfish stronger brother who is supposed to protect the weaker members of his family. As president, by means of a corrupt revolution that forcibly separated the Panama area from Colombia, Theodore Roosevelt brought to our country a small but commercially and strategically important addition in the narrow strip of land required for the building of the Panama Canal, which brought the East and the Pacific West so near to each other for the use of our naval fleet and commerce. Roosevelt himself, who as a publicity seeker stands alone in world history for attaining nonpecuniary goals by means of skillful publicizing by reporters, became the leader and hero of the Rough Riders, vice president, and then president. He has shown other ambitious young people the way to the highest office in the land, an office that lends more power than any other on earth except perhaps that of Joseph Stalin. His success strengthened jingoism more than ever. Following his paths, our country became a war power and a world power and a victory bringer in the World War, from the peace terms of which not only Europe but all other parts of the earth are suffering, and even many capitalists who became rich from it.[2]

---

2. Trenckmann was correct in pointing out that in 1903 US warships intervened to ensure the success of the Panamanian Revolution against Colombia. Panama became a protectorate of the United States, and construction of the canal followed. The various treaties that ended World War I split apart the German, Austrian, and Ottoman Empires. The Russian Empire had already fractured as a result of the stress of war. Assigning war guilt to Germany, and the outrage this provoked among Germans, was widely seen as one reason for the rise of Adolph Hitler, and this may have influenced Trenckmann's early 1930s appraisal of the war's end. He also resented the harsh treatment of German nationals after the war.

Does all of this belong under the title An Account of the Life History of the Wochenblattmann? Many a one will ask that question. It does insofar as the phases of American history have influenced me and kept me from taking the wrong path. While I insist that I am completely peaceable by nature—my wife has often expressed the opposite view—there must have been a portion of fighting spirit in me from childhood. When our teacher had thrilled us with exciting accounts of the most important events in Texas history and we had read Barnes's "History of the United States," I was a fiery Texan and an American patriot. In the numerous free hours of my youth when it was too hot for other activities and I had nothing to read or study, my favorite sport was war games. In the soft sand and shade of the trees I would set up companies, then regiments, and destroy them or take them prisoner. In these games the weaker side was always victorious. My soldiers consisted of rusty nails. These were Texan or American patriots engaged in battle against superior forces, who were represented by discarded matches. Under my supreme command the matches were mowed down in rows. These war games I continued for many year without nails and matches in fantastic stories of revolutions and wars, which I spun out for months on horseback, behind the plow, or on the hunt. And always I was in command, remained victorious, conquered countries, whole continents, and completely unexplored territories in them. Then for three years I wore the gray uniform of A&M College, for two years the epaulets of a lieutenant; and although as quartermaster I was excused from drill in the last years, I did imbibe a good portion of esprit de corps, which is related to the military spirit.[3]

So it came about that I admired the great conquerors of olden times, even Frederick the Great, in spite of his invasion of Saxony without a declaration of war, and Napoleon, in spite of the devastation he wrought in Europe and especially in German lands and his oppression of freedom after a fight for freedom had gained him his top position. I sought to condone many events in the history of the Republic of Texas and of our country that could not be justified from a moral standpoint and acted like a good "hurrah" shouter at "spread eagle" speeches.

3. Glorification of war was a common late-nineteenth-century trait, especially among those too young to have experienced the horrors of the Civil War.

When the war against Spain was declared, not a few good comrades from A&M College volunteered for service, and the Galvestonians, at least judging by the *Galveston News*, trembled in fear of a bombardment by the Spanish fleet. I felt a momentary impulse to follow their example. This war had not lasted long, however, when I began to have doubts as to whether the declaration of war against Spain, whose government had done the utmost to deprive us of any grounds for war, was justified. I began to wonder whether the Spanish governor, General Weyler, was really the bloodhound that he was represented to us to be, and whether our nation would do itself honor in conquering an enemy that in desperation could with great difficulty send only a few battleships under the brave Admiral Cervera to the harbor of Cuba.[4]

When the war was over and the peace treaty concluded, I experienced a complete change of heart, which for the first time in years I sought to express in verse and in a rather long poem at that. In this poem a courageous, noble young American goes to war in the belief that he is fighting for the freedom of a cruelly oppressed people. He contracts an incurable disease. After it becomes clear to him that only the financial interests of individuals have brought us into the war and that after the victory our government has decided on a policy of conquest, our young hero on his deathbed utters the hope that before he draws his last breath he will hear that Cuba and the Philippines have gained their freedom. I sent the poem to the *Dallas-Galveston News*, which had been fairly independent in politics and had theretofore accepted every contribution from my pen. For weeks I received no word. Finally I received a letter praising my work but stating that the publication would not be in the spirit of the times.[5]

Later my good friend Faiszt sent me articles from Arkansas that exposed the manner in which the big railroad systems of his state

4. For his harsh occupation policies, General Valeriano Weyler was dubbed "Butcher Weyler" by the American yellow journalists agitating for war. At the battle of Santiago de Cuba on July 3, 1898, the Spanish fleet under Admiral Pascual Cervera was destroyed, and more than three hundred crewmen were killed, while the Americans suffered only one man killed and another wounded.

5. Apparently the poem was never published; since it was in English, it was inappropriate for the *Bellville Wochenblatt* as well.

were making unlawful profits with the aid of their tapline roads and told how organized operators were taking vast timber supplies and compelling the independent operators to sell their valuable holdings for nearly nothing or ruining them by refusing them transportation and even resorting to force when necessary. Furthermore, he stated that the lower and higher courts were helping them and that the federal courts refused to proceed against such acts of violence. These things seemed unbelievable but were so clearly proven and so sensational that one might assume that every newspaper would be eager to publish them as a precious scoop. Faiszt had sent his proofs to a number of the biggest daily papers, including two socialistic dailies, for publication. Almost without exception the editors manifested great interest and seemed eager to publish them, but they had never been published. When he sent them to me a few years later they appeared in the *Wochenblatt* as edited by my younger son.[6] Their publication should have given the readers an insight into the illegal acts of our powerful corporations, the subservience of our courts toward them, and the control exercised by the great corporations over the daily press. Since then I have received hardly any advertisements from railroads, and I have never sought them from other corporations. It became clear to me how very difficult it is for the editor of a smaller paper to bring the truth to his readers in regard to public questions, since he must glean the truth from the usually already muddied sources of the press agencies of the daily papers.

Such acts of violence as the railroads committed against the Arkansas lumbermen are no longer practiced by corporations. North Carolina and Kentucky have shown that within the framework of state and county governments that they helped to elect, everything that is necessary can be accomplished. The people receive protection of their interests from the daily press in a lawful manner. But no big

6. The name, if spelled correctly, is quite rare. Trenckmann may be referring to Elmer Faiszt, born in Illinois with German roots, a high school–educated railroad machinist and plumber who made his way via Sikeston, Missouri, to Buhler, Louisiana, where he served as postmaster from 1914 until shortly before he joined the US Army in World War I. He later lived in De Quincy, Calcasieu Parish, Louisiana, a railroad town dominated by the timber industry.

newspaper can make real profits without advertisements. Even the weeklies, which were independent thirty years ago and thundered out against monopolistic and capitalistic trespasses, have become very tame because of their need for welcome advertisements. The years that followed the Spanish War brought me the conviction that every suppression of justice toward other nations has brought shame to our republic and injured its standing in the long run and that every war of conquest is to be condemned in the same manner as robbery with a deadly weapon, for which our laws prescribe the death penalty or life imprisonment.[7]

The first half of the first decade of the new century was on the whole a good one for us. The economic situation improved slowly. The price of cotton had advanced gradually, and although the weevils prevented big crops, the farmers got ahead better, but not one of them owned an automobile as yet. The merchants extended credit more readily. The year 1904 brought a good cotton crop, free of weevils, because a period of continual rain, which lasted until June, had slowed up the planting. The freight division of the Santa Fe had been of some help to Bellville business. Our boys and girls were slowly growing up. The eldest began his studies at A&M in 1904 and finished his course in engineering after four years. Later, when he recognized the fact that Trenckmanns are not suited for real estate dealers, he became an enthusiastic farmer. Love for the soil must be in his blood, as it was in the blood of his Magdeburger ancestors and his grandfather and father. Even though they chose other callings for a time, they always thirsted to sow and cultivate.

In 1904 my finances were so much improved that for the first time since my bachelor days I undertook a more distant excursion—a trip to the World's Fair in Saint Louis. From the start I had bad luck. On account of washouts in northeast Texas I lost a whole day's time before I had gone 100 miles from Bellville. With a wife who feared bedbugs more than snakes, I certainly did not want to spend the

---

7. Restrictions of corporations' power in order to prevent them from taking advantage of their size and political influence were a common theme in American politics on the state and national levels from the 1890s to the 1930s. His comments may also reflect his concern that corporate power and interests led the US government to intervene in the affairs of distant nations.

night in Milano, so after hearing of the delay, I went to Rockdale, where I knew some kindred souls, and through the good offices and friendship of Mr. Meyer I was able to pay an afternoon's visit to the Busch Valley and make the acquaintance of some of its fine German population, of which F. Westermann had often told me.

The exhibitions at the fair were intensely interesting, but I had to hurry to get through in eight days. After I had spent too much time on art, ancient relics, and zoological and botanical exhibits, I had to skim through the remaining ones too hastily. To an editor an exhibition is only half enjoyable because he always has to think of the report he has to make on what he is seeing and scribble down notes. I attended to these reports with illustrated supplements that cost me more than the trip. Fortunately a newspaper man did not have to count the railroad fare because he got a booklet with as many free thousand miles as he requested in return for advertising.[8]

I had plenty to do at that time and had to limit my farming operations to raising a garden, watermelons, sweet potatoes, and sometimes corn for my horse. Once I raised potatoes on newly plowed acres, but that was chiefly to spread the Bermuda grass, which I laid in the furrows. Like the sandyland farmers of this region who are always ready for new projects, I had little financial gain from all this. County festivities took up a large part of my time. I was generally expected to speak at these affairs, which sometimes took place at a considerable distance, so that in that autoless time I often had to devote two days to such trips. But they had to be made in order for me to get better acquainted with the people and their conditions. They gave me pleasure and stimulation, but the speeches I made on such occasions were often difficult for me. I shall never forget the first one. It was at Post Oak Point, where I had many friends and good acquaintances from my Frelsburg-Shelby days. Following the example of Senator Maetze, I had my speech carefully written out and memorized, but on the stage I suddenly lost the thread. My knees

8. The 1904 World's Fair (officially the Louisiana Purchase Exposition) attracted an estimated twenty million visitors in its seven-month run. The fairgrounds extended over twelve hundred acres, with fifteen large exhibit palaces among its nine hundred buildings. The landscaping and buildings undertaken for the fair formed the basis for Forest Park and both the Saint Louis Art Museum and the Saint Louis Zoo.

began to shake, and I felt that I was losing my drive. That would never do. Suddenly in front of me I spotted a precious motherly little woman in whose wise features I read the fact that she understood my predicament and was on my side. With her help I got through with it, and from then on I have made it a rule to keep my eyes on the public. I stopped memorizing and overcame the obstacle but admit that I never felt absolutely sure of myself on such occasions.

In the year of 1906 I had an unusually large amount of speech making practice, for it was then that I got involved in something that I had never expected to do. I got into politics as a candidate, although I knew too well the problems they had with treating, which was in vogue then.

The decision to enter politics came about in the following manner. In a special session the legislature had adopted the well-known and in many respects ill-reputed Terrell Election Law relating to primaries for the larger political parties. After the observations I had made in the congressional elections in regard to the maneuvers by means of which the will of the majority of the participants was so often ignored, I had acquired a veritable loathing for the old system, and although it had been garbled by countless amendments, I saw in the new law a possibility for accomplishing reform. Besides, nomination on the primary ballot seemed desirable for my own home county. Although it constituted only one-fourth of the population, the colored element had been making the decisions in filling the county offices, for they voted solidly for the candidates selected by their leaders. I also knew that bribery of these leaders played a big part in the election for higher offices. Had I not seen out of my office door how vote getters, e.g., in the Hawley congressional campaign, were counting with happy grins their rolls of banknotes after their secret meeting? I had seen them marching into Bellville in endless droves to cast specially marked ballots, which had been distributed to them in owl meetings. Every candidate could have these printed to suit himself.[9]

9. In this passage Trenckmann reflected his close affiliation with the Democratic Party, the leaders of the elimination of black voters from meaningful elections in the early twentieth century. See the discussion of the poll tax and white primary in the Introduction.

I have always been in favor of equal justice for the colored people and for giving them equal voting rights. But I was convinced that their participation in elections as they were conducted in Austin County, and still worse other areas of the South, where laws were passed to hinder them from voting on account of illiteracy and where they were also kept from voting booths by intimidation, was harmful to them. It was harmful to them because it aroused bad feeling amounting to hatred in the white people, on whose good will they are largely dependent. Although there were not many Negroes in old Millheim, there were enough of them for me to know them from childhood and to realize that in their hearts, particularly in those of the most intelligent, hatred for the whites was fermenting. The fact that they had been slaves, that some of them had received cruel treatment, and that even by humane masters they had been treated as slaves is the explanation.[10]

I shall never forget how frightened I was as a small child by a husky twelve-year-old Negro boy whom my father had hired from his parents. We were digging for fishing worms, which I had to pick up, as I was too small to wield the spade. Suddenly he said to me, "When the Yankees come, you will work for me." I can't forget either how his sister turned her back to the white boy when she met him, lifted her skirt and called out in English Goetz von Berlichingen's famous invitation.[11] The father of these Negro children, who looked more intelligent than most Negroes, wore a silver plate on his head. It was said that some of his brains became exposed when he was angry. A white man was said to have caused the injury with a blow from a gun barrel when the Negro threatened to kill him. He was

10. German Texans or German Americans generally were certainly not immune to racism and exhibited a wide range of attitudes and behavior towards blacks, with whom their political alliance weakened over time. But as late as 1922, Republican congressman Harry Wurzbach of Seguin cast the sole vote in the Deep South in favor of an antilynching bill that passed the House, whereas Anglo-Texan Hatton Summers led the opposition. Cf. Walter D. Kamphoefner, "New Americans or New Southerners? Unionist German Texans," in J. F. de la Teja, ed., *Lone Star Unionism, Dissent, and Resistance: The Other Civil-War Texas* (Norman: University of Oklahoma Press, 2016), 101–22; here 113–18.

11. This "invitation" was made famous in a 1783 play, *Goetz von Berlichingen*, by Johann Wolfgang Goethe, where in Act III Goetz replies to the demand that he surrender his besieged castle with the Latin equivalent of "kiss my ass!"

one of the leaders of that faction of Negroes who at that time interpreted social equality to mean that they had a right to insult whites, including women on the streets, the type of thing that gave cause for the organization of the first Ku Klux Klan. On the other hand the great majority of the Negroes were harmless, had maintained much of their old respect for the whites, and looked to them when they needed help. Our old Sally, who had gone to her relatives on the other side of Bellville when emancipation was announced, came on foot several times a year with a sack to collect the discarded clothing of her former "Missus," bacon, and other items.[12]

Generally I got along well with the Negroes, my wife still better, because we understood them.[13] We closed an eye when trifles disappeared after their day's work. We treated them kindly and generously but never familiarly and overlooked careless work done when they were not supervised. The smartest ones, mostly preachers and teachers, were constantly trying to ingratiate themselves with the whites. They were skillful flatterers, and while they claimed they were teaching race politeness and humility, they were secretly inciting them against the whites. I am convinced that this situation has not really changed but only gotten worse by reason of the fact that many young Negroes wore the American uniform in France. The politics of this smarter but dangerous faction cannot have much weight except here and there in city elections, and that we owe to the Terrell Election Law. This law brought it about that the leadership of the Republican Party, after most of the white Republicans took part in the Democratic primaries on account of the prohibition question, became "lily white" and shut the door on the colored politicians who could no longer serve their purposes.[14]

12. The Trenckmanns reported no slaves in the 1860 census, but his "Christmas in Troubled Times" from 1863 mentions "Sally, the old black woman whom my father had bought less for the work she could perform than out of pity." However, since he was never assessed for a slave in the annual tax rolls from 1860–64, it is possible that they rented or "borrowed" Sally from her owner.

13. Father-in-law Miller owned a black domestic and her three young children in 1860. The Millers named a son Charles Stonewall in August 1862, a strong indication of admiration for Confederate general Thomas Jonathan "Stonewall" Jackson.

14. After 1900 Republicans, in an effort known as the Lily White movement, had begun to exclude African Americans from leadership roles in their party. Wurzbach

Others felt as I did about this question, and we undertook to bring about the nomination of county and precinct officers in primary elections. Of the incumbents of county officers only Surveyor H. J. Machemehl was willing to have his name placed as a candidate on the Democratic ticket. The others were afraid of the experiment, which was contrary to the old custom that an election did not end until the evening of Election Day, and declined our invitation. The able young attorney C. G. Krueger announced as candidate for county judge. Three additional candidates for county offices followed. It was generally accepted that the experiment would end in failure. In the hope of contributing to its success by my personal entrance into the campaign, I announced as candidate for the post of representative, without expecting to be elected against the quite popular incumbent, who was serving his second term and who had announced as Democratic candidate. Thereupon, the latter had his name transferred to the Independent ticket. Thus, a campaign was brought into being that lasted until November, to be sure, but with fewer candidates. Krueger and I undertook to acquaint the citizenry with the advantages of the new law in evening meetings—no easy task, because much of its content was confusing and contradictory. The participation in the primary election in July was much larger than had been anticipated.

Then the real battle started, since the incumbents, including those who were without opposition, largely stood against us. I accepted the invitation of my opponent to debate the campaign issues with him before the people of Austin County, and debate we did, sometimes as part of public festivities and sometimes in specially called meetings. As is usually the case in exciting elections, the debate did not concern itself solely with the condemnation or defense of the election law but came to personal abuse and defense of character. At midnight on Election Day I could go to bed with the assurance that although I was still a few hundred votes behind my opponent, I had enough votes coming in six outstanding precincts in the upper part of the county to give me a majority and that all candidates on the Democratic ticket had been elected. Since then Austin County

---

and the San Antonio area were exceptions to this trend, and Wurzbach often feuded with the leaders of the Texas Republican Party.

has held regular Democratic primary elections, and with only one exception the candidates nominated have always been elected.[15]

The campaign cost me a great deal of time. Never before or after did I get to bed so often long after midnight. Although my stomach doctor had forbidden me to drink beer, and for a long time I had been imbibing only postum—never coffee—and had been forgoing many of my favorite dishes, on the campaign tour I often had to make a meal out of warm bottled beer and canned sardines and crackers in some country store. When the election was over, I had gained fifteen pounds, and my stomach trouble had disappeared for quite a while. Much talking, just like singing, is undoubtedly good for one's health, even if it sometimes gets one into trouble. What was most beneficial to me was getting away from the typewriter and mixing with people. I never forgot this lesson, but unfortunately I could not follow it very well.

My experiences and adventures in the 30th and 31st Legislatures, the extra session of the 30th and the first extra session of the 31st, I have reported in detail to my old readers, who—thank God—so far as they are still living are still reading my paper. I will not repeat. In all four sessions I did not introduce a single bill and oftener than any other member voted against bills that had practically no other opponents. There were hot fights in the first in regard to the reelection of Joe Bailey as senator, the law concerning the tax question, the Bascom McGregor Bill relating to the regulation of saloons, and a change in the election law that brought us the foolish pledge; in the second they concerned Governor Campbell's repeated attempts to submit the Prohibition Amendment, banking laws, and the selection of school books.[16]

15. Trenckmann defeated C. C. Glenn 1,267 to 975 in the 1906 general election. See *Bellville Wochenblatt*, November 15, 1906.

16. Under Campbell's leadership Democrats passed numerous laws aiming at regulating business and stabilizing and promoting economic growth. Perhaps most prominent of these was the Texas Guaranty Fund Law, passed in 1909, which required all state-chartered banks to pay into a fund used to repay depositors who lost their funds when a state bank failed. This precursor to the Federal Deposit Insurance Corporation was meant to prevent runs on state bank such as had occurred during the financial panic of 1907. Texas was the fourth state in the nation to pass such a law. See Walter L. Buenger and Joseph A. Pratt, *But Also Good Business; Texas Commerce Banks and the Financing of Houston and Texas, 1886–1986* (College Station: Texas A&M University Press, 1986), 44–46.

These battles brought me many interesting acquaintances and more insight than did the conventions into the heights and depths of politics. They showed me that among the prohibitionists, whom I theretofore opposed, there were very decent men—sensible and well-meaning on all other questions, and that among the leading anti-prohibitionists there were a few who were not guided by principles but on the contrary worked for money. These quickly turned pro with the tide and thanked their German friends with kicks. I also realized that the majority of the members of these two legislatures were honest, decent citizens whose ambition was to serve their constituents. They made most of their mistakes in their eagerness to win popularity with their constituents, who were less qualified to judge than they themselves. Often the prohibitionists erred because of their fear of antagonizing the heads of the Anti-Saloon League and the prohibitionist ministers. Many went wrong because they were too lazy to study the bills. I also learned that when it leads the orator to speak too long and too often, great oratorical skill is one of the surest ways of gaining unpopularity among one's colleagues and robbing one of influence, and that members who never make speeches or attempt to persuade their fellow members privately can nevertheless exert influence.

Mr. Werner from Guadalupe County, who represented his district for a long time, is an example. This man, who never asked to be recognized but studied all proposals for law thoroughly, has helped many a good bill through the lower house. The members sitting around him were nearly all prohibitionists. When it came to voting for a bill they had not studied, they let Werner be their guide, because they knew he was a man of integrity.[17] On prohibition questions they consistently voted against him. The legislative time was a great strain on me because I always had to help with the *Wochenblatt*, but it was an even greater strain on the editress. Although I seldom went to the theater, never played Skat, and occupied fairly cheap quarters, it made quite a hole in my pocketbook, too.

17. Fridolin Werner (1846–1929), who had immigrated as a young child and worked as a blacksmith and farmer in Cibolo, served two terms together with Trenckmann and the next term in the lower house of the legislature as a Republican. "Fridolin (Friedolin) Werner," Legislative Reference Library, Texas Legislators: Past & Present, http://www.lrl.state.tx.us/mobile/memberDisplay.cfm?memberID=3056.

The Move to Austin

The year 1909 brought us of the *Wochenblatt* a great change, to the editor and business manager, to his wife, and to his children, since all of them had almost from babyhood worked for the *Wochenblatt*—the move of the paper and family from Bellville, where all our children had been born and where I myself had been active for twenty-six years. The decision to make the change came rather suddenly. Our eldest son had graduated from A&M and gone to work for the Fairbanks Morse Works in Beloit, Wisconsin. He worked there until the short but serious panic of 1908,[1] during which for a long time nobody could draw more than five or ten dollars per day from the bank and everywhere factories were closing and workers were cut down in numbers or dismissed because Wall Street had drawn in all the money in the country and had lost much of it in wild speculation. In the next spring love had attracted him to Seattle, Washington, where the Axel Meersheidts, the parents of his bride, had moved

Originally published in *Das Wochenblatt*, May 19, 1932.

1. This panic actually occurred in 1907 and nearly destroyed the American banking system and dried up credit. The Panic of 1907 not only led to the creation of a state guaranty fund to maintain confidence in safety of deposits, but it also led to the eventual creation of the Federal Reserve System that linked all banks together and provided a safety net that limited bank failures.

after their return from Germany. We had to adjust ourselves to the fact that Washington would be the permanent home of our son.[2]

Our other three children wanted a college education; our son Willy was already in his sophomore year at the University of Texas. If we stayed in Bellville, we could expect to see him and the two girls at vacation time only, and after completion of their studies they too would find a sphere of activity elsewhere. There are parents who are willing to do with short vacation visits and letters in order that their children may have better opportunities and to give them up even to go to foreign lands. The majority are not so constituted; they would like to have their children, grandchildren, and if possible their great-grandchildren close by.[3] I know old German farmers who struggled and scratched to fulfill the goal of their lives—a farm in their neighborhood for each child. Some went too far in this effort in a time of rising prices, paid too much for neighboring lands, and plunged into debt. This desire is perhaps the quality that most markedly distinguishes men from higher animals, among whom mother love lasts only a few years at best. For parents the wish to transplant much of their own ways of thinking and feeling into their descendants is the rule, even among uncivilized peoples. We had that wish and told each other timidly and doubtfully, "To fulfill that wish we must move to Austin." We certainly had no desire to leave Texas.

We rejected the idea at first, for we had a good setup in Bellville, with relatives and friends there and in the surrounding country who were very dear to us. Bellville had become home for me too. The fact that as publisher of a German newspaper who was in the habit of speaking his mind I had enemies too who would welcome my disappearance from the horizon with pleasure was a reason for staying.

2. Axel Meerscheidt, a German Texan whose mother was a von Rosenburg, was a real estate agent in San Antonio in 1900 and in Seattle in 1910. He was well traveled, having visited Germany as a merchant in 1876, 1877, and 1885 and also having renewed his US passports in 1892. He and his family left Hamburg bound for New York on September 29, 1900. Robert Trenckmann married his daughter Beulah Anna on April 15, 1910, in Seattle and later became a farmer in Mason Co., Washington.

3. Some ninety letters have survived that Trenckmann wrote to his daughter Clara when she was living in New York and Europe from 1918 on.

Since the death of my father-in-law a sixty-acre tract of land near town, my wife's inheritance, had come under my supervision. I had selected a pretty grove on it as the site of our future home, had spent most of my leisure hours clearing moss, underbrush, and mistletoe from the beautiful young trees, had scattered pine seeds, and looked forward to growing Christmas trees for my grandchildren. Included in my plans were a garden and even a fish pond. How differently one plans at forty than when one is seventy! At that time I hoped to be able to retire at sixty; at seventy my great fear is that of being unable to carry on my accustomed work.

The thought that the move to Austin was the only solution kept popping up and finally ripened to a decision. The editress had a preference for Austin, since the time she had attended Mrs. Kirby's school there and had made acquaintances in fine families.[4] I myself had seen little of the city in the four sessions of the legislature that I attended, for when duty did not call me to the capitol, there was much letter writing to the editress and to my readers to be done. But a few occasions, such as the anniversary of the Cherusker Lodge on a Sunday afternoon in Pressler's Garden, a gathering place for congenial Austin Germans, and a *Saengerrunde* anniversary, had given me the opportunity to make promising acquaintances, and for a long time I had had a good friend in Ernst von Rosenberg.[5] Late afternoon walks in the idyllic surroundings attracted me to Austin. What drew me particularly was the hope of hearing instructive and interesting lectures at the university and possibly of widening my knowledge by

4. Alabama-born widow Mrs. H. C. Kirby established her Austin school, the Alta Vista Institute, in 1874. The school and its new building were touted in the *Weekly Democratic Statesman*, August 7, 1879. In the 1880 census she appears as "Keeper, Young Lady's Seminary," with her sister, a music teacher, and two assistant teachers in her household. Before the Civil War they lived in Washington County. She later had a long career as the first Dean of Women at the University of Texas. *Handbook of Texas Online*, Judith N. McArthur, "Kirby, Helen Marr Swearingen," accessed September 14, 2016, http://www.tshaonline.org/handbook/online/articles/fki32, uploaded on June 15, 2010, published by the Texas State Historical Association.

5. Pressler's Beer Garden was located near the river on the west edge of town. Rachel Feit, "Gardens of Eden: How Austin Used to Celebrate," *Austin Chronicle*, January 26, 2001.The Cherusker Lodge was named for the Germanic tribe from which the heroic warrior Arminius or Hermann came.

taking a few courses. This expectation was never fulfilled. Only rarely did I have a chance to hear lectures, never to register for a course. I had to study and work too hard to keep my little newspaper bark above water.

As soon as I had caught up with what I had lost during the sessions of the legislature and had laid the financial basis to what I had planned, namely to try to buy the *Texas Vorwaerts*, I went to Austin. I was convinced that this paper, which under the direction of Julius Schutz had won first rank in respect to circulation and influence among the German papers of Texas, was destined to take the crawfish route after the death of that able man. The great number of subscribers and influence had been built up through the personality and talents of the genial editor, who knew the art of impressing people and of vanquishing his opponents with tongue and pen. Wherever there were Germans in the state he had friends and admirers. He had the support of the Order of the Sons of Hermann, which owed its rapid rise chiefly to him. I knew that his successors lacked these qualities and felt certain that the second editor, Mr. Rumpel, who was sacrificing himself, could not hold the subscribers. I was informed that the *Vorwaerts* was not for sale.[6] So I went home realizing that a second German paper in Austin would have a hard struggle for existence. We decided to risk it.

In order to devote myself entirely to the paper, I decided to have it set up and printed in Austin. It was advisable because to rent the space necessary for my printing shop would cost just about as much as the printing. While I was seeking living quarters for my family and attending to these matters, the editress had sold what

6. Julius Schuetze, who had taught at the bilingual German Free School and tutored the governor's children during the Civil War, founded the *Texas Vorwaerts* in 1883 and edited it until his death in 1904, when his son Eduard took over. Charles F. Rumpel, who had immigrated in 1869, edited it from 1910 until its demise in 1914. Its circulation had fallen from sixty-one hundred in 1900 to forty-six hundred in 1910. There were slightly over eight hundred German natives in Austin in 1910 and a good sixteen hundred in the second generation. *Handbook of Texas Online*, C. A. Schutze Jr., "Schuetze, Julius," accessed September 14, 2016, http://www.tshaonline.org/handbook/online/articles/fsc18, uploaded on June 15, 2010, modified on April 15, 2016, published by the Texas State Historical Association. Arndt and Olson, *German-American Newspapers*, 615–16.

was salable from our belongings: our small herd of cattle, our big faithful horse, the phaeton, my beloved buckboard, which we had used to deliver mail at the railroad station and manure to the garden, in which my boys with me and other friends had gone hunting and fishing. We sold superfluous household goods and garden tools and gave away many implements in order to have room for what we were taking in one freight car. When I returned for pressing business, I had time to bid farewell to only a few friends. The others did not seem to take offense, however, for soon afterwards I received a message that I had to be in Bellville for an important meeting on the following Sunday. Deep in newspaper work and tired from overstrain, I made myself go.

The important matter turned out to be a farewell celebration in my honor on the Sons of Hermann Picnic Grounds near the Mill Creek Bridge. At that time the creek had not been made shallow by a canal. In this spot we had enjoyed many jolly lodge celebrations. The watch that was presented to me then still runs perfectly; the gold-knobbed cane which was to designate me to the people of Austin as a distinguished citizen I have really never used, since the rheumatism in my left knee disappeared with the change of climate, but it has played a shining part in many amateur theatrical productions. Naturally, these gifts and many other proofs of friendship pleased me, but it was pleasure mingled with sadness. On the long railroad journey back to Austin, the grinding wheels seemed to say, "You've left so much there in the friendships of your youth for which you will hardly find a substitute." Old trees do not easily take root, not even in fertile soil. Years later it happened to me that I started a letter with "Bellville, Texas," and once it even happened much later that when I was traveling from Brenham to Bellville and the conductor, an old acquaintance, asked for my destination, I answered, "Home."

On August 5, 1909, the *Wochenblatt* appeared in a completely changed format: printed on book paper, four columns and sixteen pages stapled together. I thought that this format would be handier for my readers than the big sheet. Book paper would furnish clearer print and would show off the illustrations to better advantage. I soon learned, however, that the change impressed many of my old readers unfavorably. They said, "It is not the old *Wochenblatt*."[7] In this first newspaper week, just as in the first issue week of September 17, 1891, I was able to appear in our newly rented home for breakfast only. Here my wife and children were arranging furniture and household equipment to make our home somewhat livable in a simmering summer heat such as we have not experienced since. For three weeks I sent out three thousand sample copies to previously gathered addresses. The success in Austin was satisfactory, also in the neighboring counties of Caldwell, Williamson, and Hays, where quite a few Austin County friends were living. The low price may have contributed; and of course something new is always attractive. My expectation that advertising would help cover the main expense proved to be a disappointment. With only half as many inhabitants, Austin at that time had just as many newspapers as it has now, and few businessmen were ready to try out a newcomer among them. Soliciting advertisements has always been one of my weak points, and in spite of his efforts, my good friend Henry Steussy did not have much success either. I saw my bank account dwindling. Our son Willy insisted on staying out of the university for a year to help his father.

We did not stay in the rented house long. It was situated in the valley near Shoal Creek, and our closest neighbors were colored—incidentally, orderly, industrious folks, at least the women. Often when I returned from the office at midnight, I saw them through the window still at work ironing clothes to earn something and pay for their little homes or to build new in the colored part of town. Heretofore we had always owned our home, and we didn't belong in a rent house. Besides, the editress, to whom I had dutifully confessed the status of our finances, decided to increase our income. She thought the easiest way to accomplish this was by furnishing board and lodging to university students. Having sold our home and pasture and garden in Bellville, we bought a two-story house on a narrow lot north of the university where a big Baptist Church now

7. *Das Wochenblatt* later went back to the standard eight larger pages found in most weekly newspapers at the time.

stands. My wife soon had all the rooms she could spare rented out to students. She had always managed her own household, but usually with some help. Now she was carrying a heavy load, since her only help was that which her daughters could give her in their free time. Often when I returned home late, I found her still at work.

The proximity to the university and particularly the Germania Verein, in which our son was active as one of the founders, brought us some relaxation. The editress and her friend, Miss Helene Bastian, enjoyed directing students in German plays. But the nearness to the university brought disagreeable features too—our sleep was interrupted at all hours of the night. Guadalupe Street, which was not paved at that time, was unbearably dusty, and the dust crept in through the thin walls, into which one could not even drive a strong nail to hang up pictures—a great annoyance and burden to the housewife. The small profit was not worth the effort. Most students possess a healthy appetite, and many a woman who likes to cook well and who has hoped to make a profit on boarding students to get her own children through the university has only gotten poor thereby.[8]

We bought a place on a branch near Waller Creek. An honest German carpenter, Max Schneider, put the house, which had been partially displaced from its pillars during the storm of 1909, on a substantial foundation and added two rooms and a sleeping porch for me. Now we felt at home again. Now I could climb around again and trim our fine live oaks to free them of parasites. I could put the place in order and plant trees and shrubs. Everything seemed to grow well. Our son built a treehouse for our youngest daughter in the biggest oak—a refuge for reading and afternoon naps. This neighborhood, once a wilderness known as Horst Pasture, was very different from our previous one in the university area, where everyone seemed to be concerned with making money. Here we found

8. Austin was a city of just under thirty thousand when the Trenckmanns arrived in 1910, but it had surpassed fifty thousand by 1930. German immigrants numbered slightly over eight hundred; including the second generation the city had a German community of some twenty-four hundred. Enrollment at the University of Texas was just over twenty-five hundred in 1909 but had shot up above sixty-two hundred by 1922 and was over seven thousand by the time of Trenckmann's death in 1935.

real *neighbors*, who shared each other's joys and sorrows and who worked together for improvements, such as, the building of a board-walk to the Duval streetcar on a street that was all but impassible for the ladies during rainy seasons.[9] At times things looked dark for us. Each of our daughters spent a year teaching in a country school, and the elder in the Austin City schools to earn money for further study.[10]

I was often away from home on a speech-making tour, sometimes during political campaigns, sometimes for the Department of Agriculture, then for a longer period as chairman of the Board of Directors of A&M College. In the political campaigns I made new acquaintances and gained interesting material, which usually brought new subscribers. My position on the Board of Directors of A&M College, which as a former cadet gave me great pleasure, I was forced to give up after a year and a half because performing conscientiously the special duties of chairman took more time than I had to give.[11]

At this time the battle for prohibition was going on uninterruptedly in Texas. In two terms Tom Campbell had been unable to get the submission of the Prohibition Amendment through the legislature because the necessary two-thirds majority in the Senate was always lacking. With the majority of the women, who controlled votes even though they did not yet possess the ballot, on their side, with three big Protestant church organizations and the Anti-Saloon League

9. In the 1910 census the Trenckmanns were listed as renting at 2103 Guadalupe Street, and in 1920, as owners at 2305 Trinity Street. In 1930 they owned a house worth seven thousand dollars at nearby 804 East 23rd Street; in 1940 (and 1935), widow Trenckmann was listed as the owner at 704 East 23rd Street, worth thirty-five hundred dollars—the same house with different numbering systems. This area was absorbed by the University of Texas in 1966 when the LBJ Library was constructed.

10. Rural county-operated schools that were not part of an independent school district were able to hire teachers without college degrees well into the twentieth century, and many young women, especially, financed their higher education by teaching in these country schools.

11. Living one hundred miles away in Austin, Trenckmann still gave German addresses at the Cat Spring Agricultural Society in 1910, 1911, 1912, 1913, 1915, and 1916. He was appointed to the A&M Board of Directors in January 1911 and served as its chairman until he resigned on September 1 of that year. Cat Spring *Minutes*, 253–78. *Thirty-fifth* and *Thirty-sixth Catalogue of the Agricultural and Mechanical College of Texas* (1910–12).

working for them, and supported by generous money donations from prominent prohibitionists, the Pros were working constantly. The Antis, however, depended on donations from the brewers, who, profiting from the sale of beer, had to contribute the money to fight prohibition. But small contributions from enthusiastic adherents are usually much more effective than big sums contributed by a few with personal interests in an election.[12]

In the year 1910 I made the biggest political mistake of my career. Four candidates opposed each other in the governor's race: Attorney-General Davidson from Galveston, Railroad Commissioner O. B. Colquitt, and two strict prohibitionists. Davidson's platform made important concessions to the prohibitionists; Colquitt's sounded straight anti-prohibitionist. Early in the spring, Tom Love, the confidant and chief adviser of Governor Campbell, had come to me and asked me whether I would accept the position of secretary of state, which would apparently be vacant soon. The salary of $2,000 would have been very helpful to me at that time. With the help of my son the *Wochenblatt* could have gone on, and I could probably have accomplished more than many secretaries of state who left the bulk of their work to the first assistant. I thought I guessed the purpose of proposition and answered, "Yes, if there are no political strings tied to it." I was convinced that Campbell wanted Davidson, who would put nothing in the way of a prohibition referendum if elected. Campbell knew that none of the prohibitionists could gain the victory. As I expected, I never saw Love again after that, and the incumbent secretary of state remained at his post.[13]

Although Davidson appealed to me more personally, I put forth every effort to elect Colquitt. There was something in the latter's face that aroused my doubts. Colquitt won by a big majority. He owed his victory chiefly to the German vote. Long before the primaries it became clear that nearly all the Germans would vote for him.

12. In 1911 Texans narrowly defeated a constitutional amendment that would have established statewide prohibition. For a fuller discussion, see the Introduction.

13. Love served three terms in the Texas legislature, 1902–1907, and thereafter served as a leader of the prohibitionists and the anti-Ferguson forces. *Handbook of Texas Online*, James A. Tinsley, "Love, Thomas Bell," accessed September 21, 2016, http://www.tshaonline.org/handbook/online/articles/f1030, uploaded on June 15, 2010, published by the Texas State Historical Association.

As a result other antiprohibitionists who had been wavering in their choice now turned to Colquitt. Every German Democratic paper, with the *Wochenblatt* as the first, declared for him, and the argumentation for him in my paper evidently contributed much. After he had held the office for a good while, I had to conclude that although he was intelligent and energetic, he was not dependable. In his later career he finally turned Prohibitionist. As a reward for his help in electing Hoover he received a fat federal office. I regretted the fact that I had helped elect him. Davidson's election would probably have brought us a second prohibition election sooner but at a good time for a great new victory. Much that Colquitt did influenced people who were not prohibitionists to vote with the Pros. Since then I have made it a rule to depend upon my eyes in judging people with whom I have important business. There is much to be read in faces, beautiful or not beautiful.[14]

In many respects Austin fulfilled our greatest expectations. From nearly all the Germans we received a hearty welcome. The whole family made fine connections and lasting friendships. The Sunday evenings in the Saengerrunde Garden, which was at that time still carrying the old name Scholz Garten, were as jolly and stimulating as one could wish. The state *Saengerfest*, and the Grand Lodge meeting, which were held there in our first Austin years, were something that Austin could point to with pride.[15] The German Day Association,

14. Oscar Branch Colquitt depended heavily on German Texan voters in his two successful campaigns for governor in 1910 and 1912. He also drew on their votes in his unsuccessful campaign for the US Senate in 1916. Trenckmann's opinion of Colquitt probably was colored by his abandoning the Democratic Party in 1928 and leading the "Hoover Democrats." Opposition to Al Smith, the Democratic nominee in 1928, was largely based in Texas on Smith's Catholicism and his opposition to prohibition. Most German Texans agreed with Trenckmann that Colquitt had abandoned them. See McKay, *Texas Politics*, 9–86; *Handbook of Texas Online*, George P. Huckaby, "Colquitt, Oscar Branch," accessed September 26, 2016, http://www.tshaonline.org/handbook/online/articles/fc032, uploaded on June 12, 2010, modified on February 24, 2016, published by the Texas State Historical Association.

15. The state *Saengerfest* was held in Austin on May 22–23, 1911. Governor Colquitt and Austin Mayor Wooldridge welcomed the singers at the opening ceremony, and Honorary Vice President Trenckmann also addressed the group. The group sang to capacity crowds both evenings, the program including selections by Bach, Haydn, Schubert, and Puccini. *San Antonio Express*, May 23, 24, 1911. Richland, Pfluegerville, and Dessau are all in close proximity in northeastern Travis County.

created solely for the purpose of celebrating German Day, arranged festivities that were not only gay but that also showed an eagerness to preserve all the German cultural heritage. The Sons of Hermann Lodges near Austin also arranged enjoyable founding and other anniversary celebrations. In Richland, which was entirely German, good spirits prevailed, and also in Pfluegerville and Dessau, where the population was mixed, a wholesome German manner of living dominated, and every child of German origin spoke the language. On the other side of the Colorado, where the Germans were pretty well scattered among Anglo-Americans and Swedes, exceptionally jolly festivities were held by the German organizations, and most of the children of the staunch old settlers still spoke and read German.

After Colquitt had served out his second term, the Antis won again with the election of James E. Ferguson. I very reluctantly supported his candidacy, believing that the Renter Plank, which brought him more than a hundred thousand votes, was doubtless unconstitutional and a real demagogue's trick. In a meeting called in San Antonio I got into an argument with my good friend Hugo Moeller, editor of the *Freie Presse*, who was determined to see Ferguson endorsed. But I was afraid that the endorsement of a man in whom none of my German friends who knew him better seemed to place their confidence would hurt the standing of the Germans. I can still hear Moeller pleading with the group, "We Germans don't want to crawl into a mouse hole." The leaders in San Antonio, with the exception of C. A. Goeth, expressed themselves similarly.[16] Goeth's calm, factual presentation and the fact that a prominent German, who had come as Ferguson's representative, advised against the endorsement because Ferguson (fearing that it would cost him votes) did not wish it, were effective, and no endorsement was made. Two years later the battle was renewed at the same place, and the endorsement of Ferguson for reelection was again defeated. It was entirely unnecessary anyway, because

16. Hugo Moeller (1863–1921), a native of Rostock, immigrated in 1884 and edited the *Freie Presse fuer Texas* from 1906 to 1920. Conrad Alexander Goeth (1859–1953) was a German Texan lawyer in San Antonio. His parents had originally settled in Austin County; his mother's translated memoirs were published as Otillie Fuchs Goeth, *Memoirs of a Texas Pioneer Grandmother* (Austin: Eakin Press, 1982).

with the exception of a small number of German prohibitionists, the German vote would go solidly against the Prohibition candidate for governor.[17]

A little later and shortly before the primary election the vice-president of the German National Alliance came to Texas. He and a few Texans had an election ticket printed in all the German newspapers of the state as a guide for the Germans. The result was that the branch of the German National Alliance, which had been formed a few weeks before in Austin because of the brilliant oratory of its president, Hexamer, immediately dissolved. The members considered it an insult that a gentleman from Indianapolis and a few Texans should dictate to them how to vote. On all these occasions it was shown that the immigrants who came to this country at an advanced age believed that the Germans should be instructed how to vote, while those who were born here felt themselves capable of making their own choices.[18]

The above account brings me to a catastrophe for humanity, which has had heart-stirring and disastrous consequences for the Germans of our country.

---

17. James E. Ferguson was one of the most controversial and colorful politicians in the history of Texas. He was elected governor in 1914 and 1916 but was impeached in 1917. He ran for several offices after that but lost those elections. In 1924 and in 1932 he helped his wife, Miriam A. Ferguson, win the governorship. See *Handbook of Texas Online*, Ralph W. Steen, "Ferguson, James Edward," accessed September 26, 2016, http://www.tshaonline.org/handbook/online/articles/ffe05, uploaded on June 12, 2010, modified on February 24, 2016, published by the Texas State Historical Association.

18. Although Trenckmann omits the "American," this is the same National German-American Alliance as above. Charles Hexamer was its first and only president. Trenckmann was described as "the one directing spirit" and was elected second vice-president of the Travis County Chapter of the Alliance in 1914. Originally German letters of Robert L. Soergel to Joseph Keller, June 28 and July 3, 1914, translated and published in US Congress, "Brewing and Liquor Interests and German Propaganda," serial set, Issue 7597, 1285–86.

World War

More than a year has gone by since I began telling about my life in the Forty Year Jubilee issue of the *Wochenblatt*, of the fate of the paper and at the same time of all sorts of things that I believe belong to the story of the Germans in some of the oldest settlements in Texas. To this account certainly belongs the report of what the World War brought the inhabitants of German descent in our state. It is not a happy chapter. It offers much that is depressing and some things that are humiliating, but on the other hand, much of which those of German blood can be proud. So even if one's family physician says that heart, lungs, and all other organs are still sound and will function for quite a while, one should not put off for too long a report that should be made.

A short time ago we presented the files of the first forty years of the *Wochenblatt* to the university for safekeeping. Here they are kept in a fireproof building, safe from sudden destruction. They are to be bound and made available to all. Since more interest has been shown recently in all that the Germans have accomplished in the nation and in Texas, students who are working on theses can consult them to learn what German organizations and German individuals accomplished in forty years.[1] There can be found a good part of the

Originally published in *Das Wochenblatt*, October 6, 1932.

1. Rudolph L Biesele earned his PhD at the University of Texas in 1928 and returned to the history department permanently in 1931, when he also published his

political history of our state. There can be found contributions from talented coworkers that are of permanent value.

I had not planned to found a local paper, although the *Wochenblatt* was published in Bellville with fewer than 2,000 inhabitants, and the majority of my readers were living or had lived in Austin County. I always tried to extend my fields to the happenings that were important to the Germans of the entire state. I have as far as possible in an eight-page paper reported all outstanding achievements of Germans in our country as well as matters of importance in regard to national and state laws, politics, and the most important world news, so that even those who have access to no other newspaper might be fairly well informed on current events. I believe that I accomplished these goals.

At the beginning of the second decade of this century things were going well with the Germans of Texas. The politicians had become aware of the fact that there were easily 50,000 German voters in the state election; competing for these votes, they sought to inform themselves about these voters in order to be able to win them with well-based flattery. Businessmen knew that in spite of the fact that prices for farm products were still very low, the Germans had gotten ahead and usually had cash money, hence they sought their trade through advertisements in the German newspapers, whose number at one time had risen to thirty. Some, to be sure, had gone under in the meantime. The fact that the *Victoria Deutsche Zeitung*, one of the oldest and most highly respected, was one of these indicated that the climax had been passed, for in the old German settlements already a great number of the young people no longer read nor wanted to read German.[2]

The German National Alliance, which had been founded more than a decade before, had failed to fulfill the expectations placed in it. It had centered its activities too exclusively on fighting prohibi-

---

History of the German Settlements in Texas. Among the more than one hundred master's theses he supervised were many on various Texas German communities. *Handbook of Texas Online*, Megan Biesele, "Biesele, Rudolph Leopold," accessed August 24, 2016, http://www.tshaonline.org/handbook/online/articles/fbi04, uploaded on June 12, 2010, modified on April 8, 2016, published by the Texas State Historical Association.

2. In fact, the Victoria *Deutsche Zeitung für Texas*, established in 1881, survived until 1918, according to Arndt and Olson, *German-American Newspapers*, 635.

tion and any attempts to restrict immigration—probably because its strongest financial support came from the brewers and the big trans-Atlantic steamship lines, thereby lessening its activities in the field of German culture that were emphasized in its constitution. The great German population of Wisconsin had soon broken away from its political leadership, and in Texas too its interference in elections had proven to be very inept. But through the introduction of German Day celebrations it had rendered a great service. In Texas, for example, in all cities having a considerable German population and in many small settlements the sixth of October became a German-American festival day. Shelby-Roedersmuehl, so dear to me, even held to this custom in 1917 after the Declaration of War and celebrated it again in 1932. Travis County had a Deutscher Tag Verein, founded for the sole purpose of holding worthwhile celebrations. One mistake was that in almost every larger German settlement a separate celebration was held instead of selecting a gathering place for all the Germans of the state. A greater number of participants would have made a more impressive occasion, as San Antonio has demonstrated this year. Among these celebrations were a few unpraiseworthy exceptions, their principal aim being the consumption of beer.[3]

In nearly all these celebrations orators explained the services of the Germans to our country as well as the accomplishments of the old Germany and what it has to offer us. As is proper on such occasions, the German song was rarely missing. In English speeches too the significance of the day was explained. Thus they not only helped to inspire German youth to hold on to German ways but also impressed those of other blood. Fine, really splendid *Bundes-Saengerfests* were held at that time, which made friends

---

3. Trenckmann again omits the "American" in the Alliance's name; in 1902 it did take over the sponsorship of the *German American Annals*, edited by the respected University of Pennsylvania professor Marion Dexter Learned. German Day celebrations were initiated in Philadelphia on October 6, 1883, commemorating the two hundredth anniversary of the arrival of the founders of Germantown, Pennsylvania. The first German Day celebration in Texas was in Houston in 1889, according to the *Galveston Daily News*, October 7, 1889, p. 3. Brenham first celebrated it in 1890. Newspaper mentions drop off precipitously after 1916, and most mentions in the 1920s were in "25 years ago" columns. The German Day festival in 1932 in San Antonio was attended by various travel groups from around Texas.

for the Germans among cultured Anglo-Americans, but the great expense of these led to the splitting off of the Gebirgsaengerbund.[4]

Here in Austin we were especially fortunate in that the state university under the leadership of Dr. Prokosch had a German faculty that was excelled only by that of Harvard and the University of Wisconsin. Our German Department attracted a large number of students. They had their Germania Club, which was in every respect a model organization and thoroughly German. The students controlled the group, inviting the people of Austin to their meetings. On their theatrical tours the students made good contacts in other cities.[5]

Shortly before the unholy World War broke loose over our earth a Deutscher Kulterverein was organized in a meeting in Dr. Keasby's home. Because of the enthusiasm expressed there for German culture and manners, this meeting remains unforgettable to me. Leading faculty members and also the president of the Presbyterian Seminary, Dr. Sampson, who had studied in Germany, participated, sang the old student songs, clinked glasses (*"rieben den Salamander"*), and lauded German education.[6] All seemed to be one heart and soul. As secretary, I wrote out the constitution of the society. I have never

---

4. The distance to the 1881 *Saengerfest* in Galveston led the societies in the New Braunfels–Fredericksburg area to split off and found their own society, whose name translates to West Texas Hill Country Singers' League. *Handbook of Texas Online*, Theodore Albrecht, "Texas State Sangerbund," accessed September 03, 2016, http://www.tshaonline.org/handbook/online/articles/xat01, uploaded on June 15, 2010, modified on May 11, 2016, published by the Texas State Historical Association.

5. A native of Bohemia, Eduard Prokosch (1876–1939) studied in Vienna and immigrated in 1898. He was a distinguished historical linguist who came to Texas from the University of Wisconsin in 1913 and was chair of the German Department when he was accused of disloyalty and fired by the University of Texas Board of Regents in 1917. From 1930 on he held an endowed chair at Yale. The Trenckmann daughters were members of the Germania Club and acted in their theatrical productions.

6. Lindley M. Keasbey (1867–1946) had studied in Berlin and Strassbourg and was professor of institutional history at the University of Texas. He had aroused controversy and lost his chairmanship of the political science department already in 1906 over allegations that he was a socialist, and he was permanently removed from the faculty in 1917 because of his pacifist activities. Thornton Rogers Sampson (1852–1915), an accomplished linguist, had studied in Leipzig, was elected to be the founding president of Austin Presbyterian Theological Seminary, and promoted the school's association with the University of Texas. *Handbook of Texas Online*, Walter F. Pilcher, "Keasbey, Lindley Miller," accessed September 26, 2016, http://www.tshaonline.org/handbook/online/articles/fke46, uploaded on June 15, 2010; "Sampson,

seen it again. It was never read. Before a second meeting could be held, the war had broken out, and everywhere the Germans were portrayed as barbarians.

We had all been happy over the German progress in science, trade, industry, and shipping. Proudly my wife had reported that on five different days she had attended lectures in separate fields at the university, which were nearly all delivered by prominent foreigners, none of them Germans, and that each of the lecturers had represented Germany as a model for the world. When I told her I feared that too many paeans of praise would only awaken envy and hatred, she accused me of being too pessimistic. It soon developed that for once I had been right. American scientists, who shortly before had joined in lauding Germany, were now among the most zealous in tearing her down. The envy of the learned is said to be particularly intense. I found other grounds for fear: the news about foreign policy in Europe showed clearly that arrangements between France, Great Britain, and Russia were directed against Germany. At that time I had received two letters from Germany. One writer indicated and the other clearly stated that he was expecting those three nations to arm for an attack on Germany. Both wanted to save themselves and their possessions by coming to the United States.

Only too quickly my fears were realized. After a short pause following the murder of the successor to the Austrian throne and his wife, an exceedingly sharp ultimatum was sent to the Serbian government. Then came mobilization in Russia and the declaration of war of the German government, which could not leave a fairly dependable ally in the lurch, against Russia and France, and on the first Sunday in August it was decided that Great Britain too would enter the war against Germany, ostensibly on account of the violation of neutrality of Belgium, which she had recommended shortly before when her interests crossed those of France.[7]

Thornton Rogers," accessed September 26, 2016, http://www.tshaonline.org/handbook/online/articles/fsa13, uploaded on June 15, 2010, published by the Texas State Historical Association.

7. While Germany was certainly not an innocent victim of World War I, there is a broad scholarly consensus that the "war guilt clause" in the peace settlement was unjustified, as was cogently argued most recently by Christopher Clarke, *The Sleepwalkers: How Europe Went to War in 1914* (New York: Harper Collins, 2013).

At midnight on the same day I had to make a long trip under the auspices of the Student Association of the University to visit a number of universities and agricultural and mechanical colleges in the central and western states for the purpose of reporting on them and pointing out in what respects our university was lagging behind similar institutions. I had never lost my interest in education in the twenty-five years that I had been in the newspaper business. During the time that I was a member of the Board of Directors of A&M College this interest had been reawakened, so I was pleased with my assignment. I could get away, since my son William could fully replace me. But on that critical day I would have liked to withdraw from my mission. Realizing that Germany would have an exceedingly difficult stand against the superior might of the enemy, I wrote an article appealing for collections for the German Red Cross as my trunk was being packed.

The appeal was published four days later and was among the first to appear in this country. An organization to support the German Red Cross was soon formed here. It was active until our government declared war on Germany, and it sent thousands of dollars over there, which were obtained from donations of one or more dollars and later in regular monthly contributions or by means of successful entertainments, despite the fact that most Germans were firmly convinced that Germany would win. Some clung to this belief until the great offensive of 1918 had failed. I was less optimistic, though I too concluded that even though Austria would accomplish very little because the majority of her people were not German and even antagonistic, Germany's army would prove itself invincible against the immense superiority of her enemy forces.[8]

Two weeks after I had left Austin, a book came into my hands in the Iowa State Library in Des Moines. This book brought a comprehensive report on attempts to avoid duplication in the three highest educational institutions of that state: its well-known agricultural school, its university, and its state normal school. In this book I found an article by President Wilson, of whose nomination I had heartily approved because as an ex-schoolman I expected great

8. Most German Texans supported Woodrow Wilson's claim to have kept us out of war in 1916 and supported neutrality. They also supported Colquitt in his 1916 race because of his opposition to entry into World War I. See McKay, *Texas Politics*, 64–73.

things from a scholar at the head of the government. This article showed clearly that he was an Anglophile and a self-righteous and stubborn man. I also learned that when leaving Princeton University, he had expressed the wish to find his last resting place in beautiful Old England. All these things made me fear that he would do his utmost to get our country into the war on England's side. In the spring of the following year, just at the time when Dr. Kuehnemann of the University of Breslau was making speeches here in favor of Germany, I received dispatches from New York that pointed out that our secretary of state, McAdoo, had been sent to South America to induce the South American governments to deny supplies of coal to German ships in their harbors and to prepare them for participation in a great alliance against Germany. From then on I knew that Germany was bound to lose.[9]

Nevertheless, I naturally did what little I could do in a German paper against the campaign of hatred that had already begun in the great dailies under the influences of the manufacturers of war materials, of others who were hoping for profit out of the war, and of the British millions. The Hearst papers and a few others, and most magazines that took an opposite stand, increased their circulation but all with the same lack of success that my colleagues were having.[10]

The outbreak of the war had several times seemed near but had been avoided by the concessions of the German government. And so in spite of the murders in Sarajevo, it was generally expected that there would be a peaceful solution. All the greater therefore was the general consternation when suddenly it was there. Armies of millions were on the march and were soon engaged in bloody battles. The stock exchange in New York was closed, trade had largely ceased, and in the next issue of the *Wochenblatt* there was no market

9. William Gibbs McAdoo was actually secretary of treasury from 1913 to 1918. He also suspended the New York Stock Exchange for four months in 1914, preventing the Allies from cashing in their assets.

10. Americans generally supported neutrality through the end of 1916, but in the Northeast those with close ties to Britain supported entry on the side of the Allies. Irish Americans, German Americans, and those in the South and West generally were strongest in favor of neutrality. For background on the German language press, see Frederick C. Luebke, *Bonds of Loyalty: German-Americans and World War I* (Dekalb: Northern Illinois University Press, 1974).

report because cotton and all other commodities largely destined for foreign lands had become unsalable—a foolish state of affairs, for surely German warships could not prevent these commodities, for which there was so much greater demand, from going into other countries. When I returned seven week later, conditions had not changed, and all good patriots were urged to buy cotton at eight cents a pound to prevent distress among the farmers who were harvesting their biggest cotton crop.[11]

The daily papers were doing a big business; everyone was thirsting for war reports. Around the bulletin board of the Polish daily paper in Milwaukee I had found a huge group of Poles assembled to read the latest war reports. What all was reported in the papers of that time and believed seems incredible today. So I read in a Chicago paper a comprehensive report of the arming of the Germans in Buffalo for invasion with several regiments of nearby Canada. Many similar scare reports were published at the time, found believers, growing in part out of systematic propaganda and in part out of the greed to sell extras at every hour. On my trip, which brought me in contact with nonvacationing schoolmen and hotel people, I found a fairly general aversion to the spreading of mass murder and a fear of the consequences for our own country. Those who could see farther feared too that we might be drawn in. Among those of German blood I found warm sympathy for Germany—even among many who had apparently shed their German ways and had not spoken a German word in some time but had found their German blood again when the hard-pressed land of their fathers was winning victories against a superior might. I found sympathetic people of Swedish origin in Wisconsin. The warmest sympathy I found among the young students from India at that university, where I had quarters for a longer period and where these young people were working their way through college by waiting on tables. Their sympathy grew out of hatred of British rule.

11. Cotton prices plunged at the start of World War I in 1914, and Texas farmers experienced hard time. Prices later recovered, and the war years were among some of the most prosperous in the history of Texas agriculture. As a result, the entire Texas economy flourished from about 1915 to 1918. After that the economy fluctuated wildly for a decade.

When I returned from my long trip, I fully realized how immense our country is.[12] After two days of hot weather in Minnesota, I found myself freezing in a cold, wet spell, and I praised the wisdom of the editress, who against my wishes had packed an overcoat and heavy underwear into my suitcase. When I crossed the Northeast corner of Iowa, it had already been freezing there, and from the train I saw wild ducks on the ponds. In Omaha roast wild duck was on the menu. When we got to Kansas after a ride along the swollen Missouri River, I shed my overcoat, and when I awoke in the Pullman the next night somewhere in Oklahoma, I was bathed in sweat. On Texas soil the next night it was summerish, and I found it hotter than I had ever experienced it. From the same train on which I had left Texas the state seemed changed, more beautiful. In August the prospects for a cotton crop had been miserable after several weeks of drought, but now the little crippled stalks had grown tall, spread out, and were full of bolls and blooms—the result of two days of rain four weeks earlier and the fact that drought and heat had killed nearly all the insects. Sixteen million bales, more than ever before, were harvested that year. Even after the fear of a foreign trade block had vanished, the cotton price remained miserably low.

The Germans of Austin, including staunch Socialists, were almost without exception of the opinion that Germany would win the war. The Sunday evening concerts of the Saengerrunde with invited guests at Scholz Garden were more strongly attended than before, and the subject of the latest German victory was so eagerly discussed at most tables that the audience forgot to listen to Besserer's Band. The morning paper was doing a good business with war news extras, often greatly exaggerated and strongly colored in favor of the Allies. It soon became evident how foolish the German government had been in declining to buy stock in the Associated Press, explaining that such a move might be interpreted as an attempt to influence the news service. The bulletin board of the *Austin American* was always surrounded by people waiting for the last dispatches. One loyal old Englishman seemed to be camping there. Due to the flood of extras the supply of wood pulp suitable for making paper became exhausted. Replacement had to come from Canada, and the

12. This section published in *Das Wochenblatt*, October 20, 1932.

price went up fivefold and caused the ruin of many newspapers. The Englishmen living in the United States stood as one man for their country and against the Central Powers, and since there were many wealthy and well-educated people among them, they exercised great influence, although many of them, including university professors, had never become American citizens. Many old friendships were severed; before that time Englishmen and Germans had gotten along well.

Many took it unkindly that the Wochenblattmann, who was exerting himself to the utmost for the cause of Germany and Austria, did not foresee the rapid victory of their armies, as did so many of his colleagues, and certainly not as did the newspapers and magazines published in Germany, which were avidly read here at that time. What pleased him most was a sign of real humanity that came after Christmas after months of so much bloodshed—the news that on Christmas Eve and Christmas Day the cannons had been silenced. The French did not fire a single shot when they heard the Germans, who were encamped opposite them, singing their Christmas songs. It let the momentary hope arise that the nations themselves, tired of murder, would press for peace. But as is nearly always the case, when a war gets under way, the voice of reason is drowned out by the cannon's roar and the occasional news of victory.[13]

Even when Italy, under pressure of being locked off from the sea and in its determination to be avenged on Austria and Romania, entered the war on the side of the Allies and forced Austria to exhaust its strength in defense against new enemies, the Germans in America clung to the hope of a victory of the Central Powers. They were encouraged in their hope when after the victory of the young Turks, Bulgaria and Turkey entered the war on Germany's side. They did not consider the fact that by reason of this Germany would be forced to extend her armies to Asia Minor and thus to dissipate the strength of her forces on two fronts—East and West. The progress of the war seemed to justify the optimists for a while,

---

13. Although there was more fraternization between Germans and British, including choral serenades and soccer games in no-man's-land, some also occurred on the German-French front. Stanley Weintraub, *Silent Night: The Story of the World War I Christmas Truce* (New York: Free Press, 2001), 25–26, 66–68, 94–95, 138–39, 150, 161.

especially after Russia with its huge army had been knocked out of the war.[14]

Others were not so optimistic. Carefully watching the policies of our government, they saw how, from the start, our country was permitted to become the goat and the great armory for the Allies. They noted how although that true friend of freedom, Secretary of State W. J. Bryan, often protested against Great Britain's violations of international law, she was never made to reap the consequences. They saw that thousands of Americans, mostly immigrants from Entente countries, were permitted to join the allied armies, while thousands of Germans who wanted to fight for the land of their ancestors could not get across. They saw that the export of war materials to the Central Powers was forbidden. In the light of all these facts more careful observers were finally convinced that the United States would enter the war on the side of the Allies and that with its great supply of men and money the defeat of the Central Powers was certain.[15]

In 1916 when the presidential campaign began, the Democrats gave as their chief argument for the reelection of Woodrow Wilson the fact that he had kept us out of the war, and that slogan gained him the majority of the German vote in the country, as the Republican candidate Hughes was clearly a British sympathizer.[16] Soon

14. World War I lasted from July 28, 1914, to November 11, 1918. Some nine million soldiers and as many as seven million civilians died during the war. The Russian Revolution of November 1917 knocked that country out of the war, and within months the new Soviet Union signed a peace treaty with Germany and the other Central Powers. In the west after years of stalemate and deadly trench warfare, a German offensive in the spring of 1918 made some progress, but with American help the Allies drove back that offensive and forced the surrender of all the Central Powers. See Hew Strachan, ed., *The Oxford Illustrated History of the First World War*, new edition (New York: Oxford University Press, 2014).

15. William Jennings Bryan supported a more neutral position in the war, opposed US loans to the Allies because "money is the worst contraband," pushed for a law prohibiting passenger ships from carrying munitions, and favored notifying Americans to avoid travel on belligerents' ships. But he was undercut by Wilson confidant Colonel Edward House and resigned his cabinet post on June 9, 1915.

16. In fact, Hughes was less sympathetic to the British than was Wilson, but both parties had the dilemma of trying to appeal to German Americans without repelling other voters. The German American vote was split, but Wilson actually lost some ground with them in 1916, and Hughes carried six Texas German counties, including Washington, Lee, Comal, and Gillespie. Luebke, *Bonds of Loyalty*, 190–94.

after, when Wilson in his notes called on the participating powers to start negotiations for peace, many believed that he seriously favored a peace without victory, but they were soon forced to see that the peace notes were sent only as a justification for our entry into the World War through the contention that only our huge strength could bring it to an end. In spite of all the propaganda, the great majority of the American people were still against our participation in the war, as was the majority in Congress. But the declaration of unrestricted submarine warfare (which only to keep from irritating our government had not been made at a time when the blocking of our export of war materials, provisions, and money could have brought about a German victory) now gave the president the pretext to force a Declaration of War by exercising his powers of appointment to higher offices and with the help of the hate propaganda of the entire daily press, which threatened everyone in opposition with political destruction. The war was there. The names of the few men of strong character in both houses of Congress who stood against all the threats shall never be forgotten by us.[17]

Over in Germany the German Americans were frequently accused of not exerting their influence strongly enough to avert this calamity, which had been foreseen for years. This charge is unjust. Their protest against the course of our government was doomed to failure, as it could reach only a small percentage of our people, while the English daily press reached all levels of the population and was controlled by big capital, which had already made huge profits out of the war—profits that would be lost in case of a victory of the Central Powers—and which could expect an even richer harvest from our entrance into the war, including the secured payment by the American government for supplies that had already been delivered.

Easter Sunday, the day on which the news of the war declaration came, was a day of mourning for the Germans in America, and into

---

17. There were six votes against the war declaration in the Senate, and fifty, barely one-fifth of the total cast, in the House, two-thirds of them by Republicans. Midwestern Progressives from Robert LaFollette (R-WI) and George Norris (R-NE) on down were the strongest opponents. Except for Nevada's single seat, the strongest antiwar delegation was from the most German state of the Union, Wisconsin, with 9 of 11 congressmen opposing. Two of the three from South Dakota opposed, and the Nebraska and Colorado delegations split evenly. The lone Texas opponent was Congressman-at-large Jeff McLemore, leading the legislature to eliminate his district.

the sadness at seeing their country at war with the land of their forefathers there entered a fear of threatening calamity, which material-
ized only too rapidly. With the calamity came much that was humiliating. Already in the first years of the war it was apparent that many
a German who before applauded the growth and power of Germany
under Kaiser Wilhelm was cautiously segregating himself from the
fellow members of his race for fear of being banned by the friends
of the Allies. After the war declaration the number of such persons
increased rapidly, and not a few men of German descent, as well
as recent German immigrants, attempted to display their American
patriotism by means of furious anti-German propaganda. With the
Declaration of War the American Constitution was suspended without any enactment of Congress. In contradiction of the Constitution
the general liability for army service was introduced, even in a war
that was taking place outside of our country. From Washington a
widespread spy system was organized and directed into the most
remote corners of our land. This forced everyone of German name
or German sympathies to refrain from saying or writing a word that
could bring him under suspicion. Committees were set up in all
counties to collect contributions for war loans and for the American
Red Cross, and whoever refused saw himself exposed to possible
violence.[18]

Here in Austin a worthy German who refused to buy war bonds
because he did not want to help kill his blood relatives remained
unpunished only after he had contributed all the more to the Red
Cross. In Ohio during the first days of the war—or perhaps it was
in Illinois—a harmless German was killed by a mob. The murder-
ers remained unpunished.[19] From all parts of the country came
reports of acts of violence on Germans and even of murders and no

18. The Confederacy and then the Union both resorted to conscription during the
Civil War. But First Amendment rights were seriously curtailed during World War I,
and very little was done to resist vigilantism.

19. This may be a reference to the lynching of immigrant Robert Prager in Col-
linsville, Illinois, not at the beginning of the war but on April 5, 1918: the only recorded wartime lynching of a German American. Walter D. Kamphoefner, "The
German-American Experience in World War I: A Centennial Assessment," *Yearbook of
German-American Studies* 49 (2014): 3–30, here 3–4.

reports of punishments for these acts. In Travis County, where there were repeated instances of the mistreatment of Germans, the courts acquitted the guilty, and they even received praise for their acts. Great excitement prevailed when the papers brought reports of the arrest of two Germans who were charged with having attempted to blow up a troop transport train between Austin and New Braunfels. They were two of the most completely harmless citizens of Austin, who had gone out at night with spade and pick to dig for treasures. The worst of the outrages by individuals and sometimes by mobs were directly traceable to the hate propaganda, which had originated long before the Declaration of War, that described German plots, first against Canada and later against munitions factories in our own country. Many a German who had experimented with the radio, which had just been introduced, was arrested and interned if he wasn't a citizen. It was immediately decided to take property of German aliens into custody, although a long-standing agreement with the Prussian government expressly prohibited this, even in case of war.[20]

The worst and the hardest blow for the German-Americans was the campaign against the use of the German language. It was decreed that in foreign language papers everything that was reported about war occurrences and about foreign countries in general should be followed by an English translation. This decree spelled the end of many German publications. After the first committee meeting before which I could gain a hearing, the Texas Legislature had postponed the decision to prohibit the teaching of German except in higher institutions. But soon after upon the recommendation of Governor Hobby, it was accepted. Hobby had originally been elected with the German vote, and this same governor later vetoed the miserable appropriation of $2,000 for the teaching of German in the University; so for a long time

---

20. During the war the state government suppressed the use of the German language and superpatriots used various state and local defense councils to suppress dissent and force German Texans to purchase Liberty Bonds. There were also reported cases of whippings and beating of Germans. See Matthew D. Tippens, *Turning Germans into Texans: World War I and the Assimilation and Survival of German Culture in Texas* (Austin: Kleingarten Press, 2010), chaps. 5–6; Gould *Progressives and Prohibitionists*, 225–27.

German, a prerequisite for acceptance into the medical schools, had to be taught as a Romance language. Our splendid German faculty was dispersed to the winds. Here in Travis County the sheriff, who had been considered a good friend of the Germans, traveled around with a man who had previously been a leader among Texas Germans for the purpose of impressing upon the people the fact that German should no longer be spoken on the streets or preached in the churches. Many of the German ministers refused to discontinue their German services and preached in English on alternate Sundays only. Some of them were shamefully mistreated in Texas and in other states for this reason. In the public schools many teachers felt obligated to spread the lies about the alleged atrocities of the German soldiers; e.g., cutting off the hands of Belgian children, plundering, and murdering. They presented the Germans as well-trained barbarians and thus stirred up their pupils against their own parents.[21]

The command of duty as well as the command of common sense in that time was for the German-American to respect and obey all justified demands of the government in wartime. Their sons went into the war and fought bravely under the American flag, while mothers and fathers trembled for them. They were known to have the smallest percentage of slackers.[22] In order to avoid acts of violence, one had to be careful, but caution was overdone in some cases. For example, in the New Braunfels post office the use of the German language was forbidden. I considered the voluntary disbanding at this time of the German National Alliance, which had a charter from Congress, as foolish, particularly as ridiculous charges were being made against it. It was also unnecessary that the annual meeting

21. By mid-1918 about half of all states had outlawed or curtailed German instruction in schools, and some states even forbade use of German on the telephone, in assemblies, or even in public generally. See Luebke, *Bonds of Loyalty*, 252–55. Some of these laws were overturned by the Supreme Court in *Meyer v. Nebraska* (1923).

22. Nationwide, German Americans' military participation rates were only slightly lower than the national average, consistently over 90 percent. The loyalty of German Texans was vouched for by an odd source, a Houston Klan newspaper: "The Records show that our soldiers of German descent fought as valiantly overseas as those of families of longer resident [*sic*] in America." But it still demanded that all preaching be conducted in English. Kamphoefner, "German-American Experience," 9–12, 24.

of the Sons of Hermann in Texas voted to take the most important paragraph in regard to keeping up the German language and customs out of the statutes, and at the same time to adopt an English constitution. The insurance commissioner expressed his astonishment to me that an organization in such good standing would take such a step.[23] Many German lodges were disbanded, banks Anglicized their German names, and even villages and streets with German names were rechristened.[24]

In this tragic time that made all true German hearts heavy, the Wochenblattman fared well enough on the whole. Postmaster-General Albert Burleson, a fellow student at A&M College, sent him the very first permit issued by the government to publish war news and war discussions without English translations.[25] Once he received a request from the Department of Justice to send them certain issues of his paper. He did so and offered to send copies of all issues since the beginning of the war. He never received a reply. A local organization that had units over the whole country on one occasion voted in a weakly attended meeting that the *Wochenblatt* should cease publication. When the editor learned of this through the newspaper, he kept himself in readiness to show the bringer of such a message the way to the door. Once a person representing himself to be a German

23. Under congressional investigation since early 1918, the Alliance voted on April 11 to disband and turn its assets over to the American Red Cross, even before Congress revoked its charter on July 2. Despite their concessions to wartime realities, the Sons of Hermann were still advertising seven weeks of free German instruction in the summer in the May 19, 1932, issue of *Das Wochenblatt*, with Trenckmann's daughter Else as one of the teachers.

24. Brandenburg, Texas, was renamed Old Glory; Germantown, a few miles west of Victoria, received the equally German name of Schroeder because it was renamed for the first local doughboy who gave his life, ironically the son of a German immigrant.

25. Burleson attended one year together with Trenckmann in the second year of the college's existence; his older brother Ford attended the previous year with him as well. One indication of Trenckmann's access to the seat of power was a 1918 letter he wrote to his daughter in Washington, advising her that if she was stricken with influenza and needed help, she should get in touch with Burleson or the local congressman James Buchanan, "for I can expect of both that they would do something for my daughter." Trenckmann to "Liebe Tochter" [Clara], September 29, 1918, Clara Trenckmann papers, privately held by Stuart Strong.

sympathizer and a victim of the hate campaign burst into his office and begged for help. The man's fright seemed exaggerated. I suspected him of being a spy, and the good advice I gave him made it clear that I was not inviting him to return. One lone person, a lady who seemed to be slightly off in the upper story, once asked the editor if he was loyal, but otherwise he was not molested.

There was a heavy loss in advertisements, but it was made up in part by the fact that the readers paid more promptly than before, and there were many new readers; some subscribed for a regrettable reason: after it had become an English paper, the *Texas Volksbote* had gone under. The same fate was dealt out to the *Cuero Rundschau* and the *Nord Texas Presse*. My colleague, August Haxthausen of Houston, too was forced to suspend publication of his paper, which had existed for a long time. In other parts of the country there was a mass dying of German newspapers, partly due to persecution and loss of advertisements and partly to a shortage of paper, just as there was a shortage of sugar and flour—these articles had come under government control. The suspension of each German newspaper meant

Wochenblatt ad on page 101 of the 1922 *Polk's Morrison & Fourmy Austin City Directory*. Used with permission of the Austin History Center, Austin Public Library.

a loss for Germandom, because readers who were attracted by local interest ceased to have a German paper in their homes.[26]

The pride in American citizenship, which so completely harmonizes with deep love and respect for the land of one's forefathers, was to some extent lost to the Wochenblattmann when he saw that this citizenship does not protect one when the United States is engaged in a war against the land of one's forefathers. I noted with pleasure that the best among the Anglo-Americans respected those Germans who did not stoop to slander Germany and interfered to prevent any injustice done them. Judge James R. Hamilton was one of these, and because he has not forgotten and because Hamilton is one of the best judges in the state, the Wochenblattmann intends to write his name on the ballot for governor, having no desire to vote for either Ma Ferguson or Orville Bullington.[27]

26. The Brenham *Texas Volksbote* folded June 28, 1918, shortly after eighty-three prominent Germans published a petition distancing themselves from the antiwar American Party. The Cuero paper succumbed on November 7, 1918; the *Nord Texas Presse* in Dallas went under on July 28, 1918. August (von) Haxthausen immigrated as a child when his parents took over the *Texas Deutsche Zeitung* in 1884, and carried on their work until 1917; in 1914 he was also president of the Sons of Hermann in Texas. See Arndt and Olson, *German American Newspapers*, 617–26. Nationwide, World War I reduced the number of German papers by half and cut their combined circulation by three-quarters. See Park, *Immigrant Press*, 310–20.

27. James Robert Hamilton, 1860–1933, was a district attorney and criminal court judge in Austin who charged a grand jury with investigating Klan violence in 1921–22. Because of a change of venue, he also presided over the Sealy Klan murder cases. Trenckmann is referring to the upcoming 1932 election, when Bullington was the Republican candidate and was defeated by Ferguson. *Handbook of Texas Online*, John D. Huddleston, "Ferguson, Miriam Amanda Wallace [Ma]," accessed August 31, 2016, http://www.tshaonline.org/handbook/online/articles/ffe06, uploaded on June 12, 2010, modified on June 8, 2016, published by the Texas State Historical Association.

Aftermath of the War
and Conclusion

When after the closing of the first forty years of the life of the *Wochenblatt* I undertook to report about the founding, the difficulties, the struggles, and the joys that the paper brought me, about the environment in which I grew up and worked during the course of my already long life and the things that came under my observation in the course of it, I intended to cover it all in the Jubilee number. That goal I failed to achieve. Many other valuable contributions that absolutely belonged in it were put at my disposal for the issue. After I had written enough for two and one-half newspaper pages and had covered only Millheim and the student period, I concluded that I would have to add *a couple* of continuations. My wife often warned me not to make my speeches too long, and she and surely many of my readers often had cause to criticize my long sentences. The admonitions and the criticisms were well meant and well deserved, so I must be afflicted with long-windedness. I will not even count the number of chapters in my story. In the preceding one—now over three months ago—I had announced the conclusion, but when one has many interruptions in a task, it gradually becomes distasteful. Besides, such a piece of work takes more time and thought than does

Originally published in *Das Wochenblatt*, February 16, 1933.

writing about recent happenings and experiences. But although it becomes difficult, I must keep my word—difficult because even though I can report much to the credit of the Germans of Texas, I cannot offer them a happy horoscope.

After the Armistice on November 11, 1918, the so-called Treaty of Peace had finally been concluded in Versailles—in reality the treaty was nothing but dictated decrees of annihilation for a brave but conquered enemy who had been completely vanquished by starvation. Here there were many thousands of German parents in mourning for their sons who had fallen in the war against the land of their ancestors, had succumbed to wounds or illness, had been crippled, or had returned home with permanently weakened constitutions. All were distressed over the terrible want in Germany and Austria and shocked that our government would not permit them to help. The fact that our government, together with the other Allies, prevented the resumption of free trade with the conquered after the end of the war will always remain a stain on the heads of these nations. One might have forgiven a Clemenceau for saying there were twenty million too many Germans, even though Bismarck after the Peace of 1871 had put all German railroads to work at carrying food for the suffering population of France. Paris was supplied immediately after the capitulation.[1] Clemenceau knew that with equal weapons and leadership Germany would always remain victor over France. His patriotism guided him to let his old enemy become impotent through mass dying.

Our President Wilson, however, had no such excuse for the unheard of cruelty to a whole people, to its aged; its mothers, now weakened by insufficient nourishment, had to see their nursing babies waste away because they had no substitutes for breast milk. As an American, one would like to believe that Wilson returned from Versailles the victim of a mental illness from which he never recovered. The fact that, so far as I can recall, no member of Congress of either of the two major parties appropriately denounced a

---

1. Trenckmann neglects to mention that Germany imposed an indemnity of five billion francs (about one billion dollars) on France in 1871, and German troops occupied the country until it was paid. Thus, there was some precedent for the reparations imposed on Germany at Versailles.

brutality the like of which had never been practiced before after a war remains a blot on our people.[2]

Appeals of German organizations to be permitted to send clothing and food across were briskly refused. Even in the late autumn of 1919, nearly a year after the end of the war, the news came that what the German women of Saint Louis had gathered to send to Europe as soon as permission came was forcibly taken away from them by returning American soldiers and used for other purposes. At last—it may have been about the beginning of November—came a short news dispatch that brought the good news that our secretary of state had announced that the sending of money, food, and clothing to our former enemy nations was now permitted. The joy was great, and here and in San Antonio we decided to organize at once to help women and children. In San Antonio federal officers declared that such a thing would not be permitted, and that city's organization was abandoned for a time. Although some timid souls were against it, about sixty men and women of German blood met here in Austin in Saengerrunde Hall. Dr. J. M. Kuehne was there too. The fact that a university professor would participate in such an organization was regarded by many as taking an unheard of risk. It did him no harm; on the contrary, it gained him greater respect. He was elected chairman and filled the post with tact, zeal, and sacrifice until the organization was disbanded.[3]

But soon visitors of a different sort appeared. Our sheriff and two United States officers from San Antonio seated themselves a little apart from the others without greeting anyone or saying one word. I explained to them at once that we intended to help our blood relations in Europe in their need and that we held the assurance that our government had given its permission, and that I would give

2. Germany was still not technically at peace even after the Armistice, and mutual mistrust exacerbated the situation, but the Allies did use the blockade to pressure Germany to accept the peace terms. Some food shipments began arriving in March 1919, but full resumption of trade was not established until the Versailles Peace Treaty was signed on July 12, 1919.

3. The Saengerrunde Hall, next door to Scholz Beer Garten, is still in use by the singing society. Johannes Matthias Kuehne (1872–1950), a German Texan farm boy from Hallettsville, was by 1923 a full professor in the University of Texas Physics Department, where he taught for fifty years and was instrumental in the founding

them full information as to anything that was said and done at the meeting. They asked for no explanations, but after the close of the meeting Dr. Kuehne and several other prominent participants were called before them and told that no collection and no gift shipment would be permitted until the news dispatch was confirmed by a dispatch from the foreign office in Washington. It was several days before an answering telegram came. The permission was granted, and soon the organization was at work.

In the second meeting great enthusiasm reigned, and more than a thousand dollars must have been subscribed. The relief work gave impetus to successful entertainments of various kinds, which brought in goodly sums and at which those present seemed to be heart and soul for the project. The willingness to sacrifice was great, not only among the wealthy but also among those of modest means: one workman gave a full month's pay; a stout laborer's wife, who did housework every day, came dragging along on foot for two miles one hot July day with a heavy bundle of good articles of clothing. She had begged them from Anglo-American families for whom she worked, for the German women and children. The zeal of many women and young girls was remarkable. What they collected in clothing, what they sewed, what good used clothing they repaired, and what they sent over in big boxes must have been enough to supply a fair-sized village in Germany. Big shipments of food—bacon, sausage, coffee, etc.—to which the German farmers contributed most liberally were sent over from here. Austinites and farmers contributed liberally to the shipment of milk cows; most zealous among them was Alvin Olle. My efforts to create a state organization that should start the ball rolling in hitherto inactive settlements was unsuccessful. San Antonio, New Braunfels, and Fredericksburg contributed magnificently, as did Uhland and Rogers Ranch. Astonishingly large contributions were made in Austin County and in Fort Bend County as soon as a really active man assumed leadership, for instance Hermann Shulze in Industry. A good state organization could have

---

of the MacDonald Observatory. The History of the University of Texas at Austin Department of Physics, https://web2.ph.utexas.edu/utphysicshistory/UTexas_Physics_History/John_Matthias_Kuehne.html.

accomplished much more. But on the whole the Texas Germans did a creditable job.[4]

When the worst need was over, our organization disbanded. It was soon apparent, however, that the big boom brought about by extensive loans to Germany was only temporary. A report in my paper concerning conditions in an orphan's home inspired my good friend Gustav Wiesner to send me a contribution of five dollars to send over. I announced that I was always willing to remit such contributions. In the course of perhaps two years I collected about $16,000 from organizations and individuals. The Vogelsang family in Milam County sent in over $2,000 alone.[5] I was authorized to send these contributions to any organization that I considered worthy in Germany and here. Some I sent to the Allen Campaign for Germany, and the rest directly to worthy organizations over there. The Ruhr invasion caused many contributions to come in. I had much paperwork with this last part of the relief work in Texas, but at the same time it brought me great satisfaction over the self-sacrifice of the givers and the confidence they showed in me.[6]

The period brought the German American a new trial; but this time it was directed against all immigrants, against the Catholics,

4. Alvin Olle (1876–1931), a native of Fayette County, rented a farm on the east side of Austin in 1920. Hermann L. Schulze, a merchant and banker, emigrated from Germany in 1879 at age ten but had visited Germany again in 1907. Uhland and Rogers Ranch were neighboring, quite small communities northwest of Lockhart. The success of these efforts was all the more remarkable given the continued criticism of all things German by Anglos in Texas and the birth of the Texas branch of the Ku Klux Klan at about this same time.

5. Gustav W. Wiesner (1852–1924) immigrated in 1868 at age sixteen and was a farmer in the Phillipsburg community between Bellville and Brenham. Ernest Vogelsang had immigrated with his family in 1850 at age twelve and initially settled in Austin County; he, two adult sons, and a nephew were all farming in Milam County in 1920; another nephew was an X-ray technician there.

6. General Henry T. Allen was a member of the American Expeditionary Force and then commander of all American troops on occupation duty in Germany. Retiring in 1923, he served as chairman of the American Committee for the Relief of German Children. "Henry Tureman Allen," Arlington National Cemetery Website, http://www.arlingtoncemetery.net/htallen.htm. When Germany failed to meet its reparation payments, French and Belgian troops occupied the industrial Ruhr region from 1923 to 1925, precipitating massive German inflation.

the Jews, and the Negroes, and against all persons with socialistic or communistic inclinations. All at once an announcement came that the Ku Klux Klan had been newly organized in Georgia. It wasn't long before it had spread over the entire country. But it was a different Klan from the one that began its dark work shortly after the Civil War in order to instill fear of the masked night riders in the worst element among the Negroes and to prevent them from committing acts of violence in the belief that the Union troops stationed in the South would protect them and the newly created courts would show them mercy. This Klan originated in the head of a money-greedy speculator, who brought it into existence by appealing to the prejudice against Catholics and Jews among several Protestant sects, to the anger over the increasing impudence of the Negroes, after many thousands of them had worn the American uniform, to love of sensationalism, and perhaps to the more praiseworthy desire to punish depravity. He managed to get a huge income for himself and to make himself supreme ruler over subjects bound by oath, whose number is said to have run into millions for a short time.[7]

Through the support of a great part of the membership of a number of Protestant churches, the Klan became so powerful that in Texas, Alabama, and Indiana it was able to elect its candidates for the US Senate; and it was only because prohibitionist Democratic leaders like Crane, Cone Johnson, Moody, and others supported the candidacy of the wife of former governor James E. Ferguson, whom they disliked, that a Klan member was defeated for the governorship of our state. In many sections a veritable rule of terror prevailed. It was worst in Washington County, due to the desire to

---

7. William Joseph Simmons founded the second Ku Klux Klan at Stone Mountain, Georgia, in November 1915. The Klan came to Texas in the fall of 1920, first starting in Houston during a reunion of Confederate veterans. It spread quickly and became politically active. In 1922 the Klan elected one of its own, Earle B. Mayfield, as a US Senator from Texas, but it receded in power and influence after Felix D. Robertson, the Klan candidate, was defeated by Miriam Ferguson in the 1924 Democratic run-off primary for governor. Martin M. Crane had been the lead prosecutor in the impeachment proceedings of Governor Jim Ferguson in 1917, and his support of Miriam Ferguson in 1924 was especially significant. See Brown, *Hood, Bonnet, and Little Brown Jug*, 49–252.

prevent the German voters, who were in the majority, from voicing their disapproval of Woodrow Wilson by voting against the Democratic Party.[8]

In the Trinity Bottom near Dallas, flogging and tarring and feathering were almost nightly occurrences for a long time. It is true that some of the victims were men and women of immoral character who may have deserved punishment. If married white men who lived openly with Negro women were put to flight by Klan warnings or Klan visits, it may have accomplished some good.[9] But when some of these same persons became strong supporters of the Klan in another city, when the Klan here and in other places operated gambling halls in the interest of their organization, when doctors and lawyers were mistreated to the advantage of their Klan colleagues, when Klan threats forced businessmen to sell out with losses, it was evident that depraved men were leading the movement. All those who were threatened and to whom life in a country under such conditions would have been unbearable should be everlastingly grateful to the courageous Anglo-Americans who stood against this grossest contempt of all law and order. That goes especially for District Judge J. R. Hamilton, who rendered the decision according to which the Klan oath would never protect anyone who testified falsely for the benefit of the Klan from being sent to the penitentiary. With that decision he dealt the Klan its hardest blow.[10]

8. Republicans carried Washington County in 1916, and it elected an American Party member allied with Ferguson to the legislature in 1920, but he was denied his seat on trumped-up charges of disloyalty. In neighboring Fayette County, Ferguson outpolled Harding nearly two to one, and the Democrats came in third in the 1920 presidential race. Walter D. Kamphoefner, "The Handwriting on the Wall: The Klan, Language Issues, and Prohibition in the German Settlements of Eastern Texas," *Southwestern Historical Quarterly* 112 (2008): 53–66.

9. The Klan did not always stop at flogging. A married Texas German in the vicinity of Somerville who was carrying on an affair with a black woman was fatally shot by a Klansman on his front porch before the eyes of his family while resisting a kidnapping attempt; his young daughter's finger was shot off in the process. Nathan D. Giesenschlag, "Sunk in Lake Somerville: Morality Plays and Murder in Burleson County, 1917–1923," paper presented at the meeting of the Texas State Historical Association, Houston, March 1, 2012.

10. Judge James R. Hamilton presided over the Criminal District Court of Travis County, and starting in 1921 he strongly opposed the Klan's attempt to impose their

With few exceptions the Germans did their part in getting rid of this shameful business. With them were the Swedes, Bohemians, Italians, Poles, and others. Only here and there a few of the second and third generations and politicians with selfish motives joined the Klan, but they soon regretted it. The Wochenblattmann is happy to this day that in his old home county, in Sealy, men of the above-named races gathered in great numbers to drive away a nightly Klan visitation from another county with gunshots, if necessary, and that in the little town of Orange Grove at some distance away the Germans did the same thing.[11] But the bitter memory remains with him that his fine friend Fritz Schaffner and one of Schaffner's sons lost their lives through Klan persecution.[12]

Defeat in the election and the penitentiary for some of the members soon brought about this dissolution, and peace returned.[13] Those whose nativist impulses brought them into it are for the most part still living and have not undergone a change of heart, but they will hardly attempt anything like it again. Since that time the German Americans have shared the fate of all Americans. The World War and the sympathy with and working together to help members of their race have had the result with many that the feeling of belonging to their race has become stronger. Good *Saengerfests* have been held by the state Saengerbund and the Gebirgssaengerbund,

---

own version of law and order in Central Texas. See Brown, *Hood, Bonnet, and Little Brown Jug,* 59–66.

11. Orange Grove, which had a *Wochenblatt* agent, lies west of Corpus Christi in a county, Jim Wells, that had only one hundred German immigrants and some three hundred of the second generation in 1920.

12. A dispute about the use of the German language at a political barbecue in Cat Spring between Schaffner's son Robert and a young Klansman escalated several weeks later into a shootout in Sealy that left four people dead (two on each side), another Schaffner son hospitalized for weeks with stab wounds, and a Klansman imprisoned for murder. Sheriff A. J. Remmert refused to allow masked parading. Kamphoefner, "The Klan, Language Issues, and Prohibition," 62–64.

13. The 1924 gubernatorial election revolved around support or opposition to the Ku Klux Klan. After an initial Democratic primary with numerous candidates, the runoff primary pitted Miriam A. Ferguson, the wife of former governor James E. Ferguson, against Felix D. Robertson, the Klan candidate. Texans elected a woman governor, and the leaders of the Democratic Party moved to eliminate all Klan influence in Texas. See Brown, *Hood, Bonnet. and Little Brown Jug,* 211–52.

and the one that is planned in Dallas will not be inferior.[14] German theater presentations have become more numerous in the colleges and high schools. Participation in the study of German has grown.

All of this is good to know, but unfortunately it cannot be denied that among maturing young people, only a small minority of whom have had instruction in German, the language of their forefathers is gradually being forgotten and that most of the second generation who can still speak the language seldom make use of it. It looks as if in a few decades the knowledge of German will be limited to the highly educated. If it is to be preserved by those of German blood as a key to its rich cultural treasures, every effort will have to be made to change this trend.[15]

14. A *Saengerfest* was held in Galveston on May 17–19, 1931, with some three thousand people attending. *Caldwell News*, April 10. 1931. The national *Saengerfest*, which was held in Dallas on October 4–6, 1936 (a date coinciding with German-American Day), in conjunction with the Texas Centennial Exhibition in Dallas, was apparently already in planning when Trenckmann wrote in 1933. *Denison Press*, September 17, 1936.

15. Trenckmann was somewhat too pessimistic; Texas was the only state in the Union where third-generation speakers of German outnumbered those of the second generation in the 1940 census. At that time the counties dominated by Fredericksburg, New Braunfels, and Giddings still supported German weeklies with circulations that were at least quadruple, or in the latter two cases about ten times their German-born populations. German newspapers were still hanging on in all three of these locations when World War II ended. According to the 1970 census, a majority of the population in Gillespie County (Fredericksburg) claimed German mother tongue, as did 22 percent in Austin County, more than one-fourth of the inhabitants of neighboring Fayette and Washington Counties, and more than one-third in Lee County. If rates are calculated on the basis of white population only, 41 percent of Lee County whites and more than one-third of those in Washington County still claimed German as their mother tongue. Kamphoefner, "The Klan, Language Issues, and Prohibition," 66.

Appendixes

Christmas in Troubled Times

It's strange how human memory works! Many experiences that at one time made our hearts beat more joyfully or tremble in pain— experiences we thought would be stamped on our minds forever— become indistinct and are finally altogether erased by the multitude of impressions produced by every single day; whereas other experiences, which we may anxiously endeavor to forget, seem ineradicable, as if carved in stone, and appear before our mind's eye in the sleepless hours of the night or the hustle and bustle of the day. Events significant and worthy of note are often quickly forgotten, while those insignificant and objectionable are faithfully preserved. I have been told by people who are well on in years that in advanced age the happenings of earliest childhood are recalled all the more vividly, though the occurrences of the present are already covered by the veil of oblivion in a matter of hours and days.

In my case, as probably in the case of many another of my readers, the earliest distinct memory is associated with Christmas. If I now intend to try to evoke this memory and dress it in words as vividly as possible, then I do so chiefly with the intention of making possible a comparison between the much-praised "good old days" and the frequently scorned present. In recent weeks, in conversation with heads of families, I have quite often heard the statement, "Times

Originally published in the Wochenblatt Kalender fuer 1894/Beilage zu No. 11 des Bellville Wochenblatt 3 (December 1893): 8–13. Translated by Anders Saustrup and published in booklet form by the Friends of Winedale, Christmas 1976. Used with permission.

are too bad and money is too scarce; there is no way we can think of having a merry Christmas." As if the joy of celebration depended on the quantity and the monetary value of the gifts, rather than on the spirit of love with which they are chosen and given to our little ones.

Nowadays it is made so easy even for people without means (fortunately we don't as yet have real poverty out here in the country) to make their children happy at Christmas. In all districts of Germany, in France and Switzerland, in far-off Japan and the United States, thousands of wise minds are thinking, hundreds of thousands of diligent hands are stirring, year in and year out, in order to produce a thousand different kinds of more or less valuable objects, which are intended for the sole purpose of delighting the little ones of all nations.

Things were different thirty years ago, at the time into which I would like to project my readers in spirit. Back then there truly was "no money" in circulation, with the exception of worthless paper money, which no one wanted to accept; and even those few who still were in possession of good money were not even able to use it to purchase those things that we today consider to be necessities of life, and much less articles of luxury or even toys. In such a situation it was only the all-conquering, sacrificing love on the part of fathers and mothers that, even in the days of severe distress, managed to preserve the beautiful customs of the old German homeland; that made them forget distress and misery and brightened the gloomy days for their children with the glimmering of the Christmas tree.[1]

Christmas of 1863!—that was perhaps the very most troubled point in time of that terrible period in which the disastrous fraternal war was raging, transforming one part of the sunny South into a wilderness and the rest into a great house of mourning. After the battles

---

1. In that era the Christmas tree was largely a German American custom except for a few Anglo-Americans in the Northeast. The Texas legislature was in session on December 25, 1861, and passed an act placing state troops on a war footing. In the newspapers digitized on the Portal to Texas History website as of September 2016, there were only two mentions of a Christmas tree in the 1840s, just four in the 1850s, and only ten in the 1860s, nearly all from literature or reports from afar, compared to nearly five hundred in the 1870s. The first mention of a Texas tree was in the Indianola Courier, January 5, 1861; the next was from Austin in 1867, plus an 1865 ornament ad from Houston.

of Gettysburg and Vicksburg, not only the expectation of a victory for their cause, but also the hope of an acceptable settlement had vanished even on the part of the most zealous Southern Bourbons. The flower of Southern manhood had fallen on the blooddrenched fields of Virginia and at Gettysburg or ended up imprisoned in the North, and whoever did not deliberately keep his eyes closed had to recognize clearly that all martial art of the Southern military leaders, all the heroic courage of the Southern soldiers, were [*sic*] futile in the face of the inexhaustible resources of the North and would prolong a struggle that had no prospects. But even in the hearts of those who cherished no sympathy for Secession, no cheerful feelings could be aroused. Persecuted by the hate of the zealous secessionists and described as traitors, they were hovering in constant danger and saw ruination before their eyes, however the fortunes of war might turn.

The situation was saddest of all in the German settlements of our state. In most cases the settlers had been in the country for only a few years and had but limited means; for that reason they could not pay for a substitute, as did the rich slaveowners. At the very beginning of the war a few had fled across the Mexican border or to the North so that they would not have to join the Southern army; still others had gone to war, either of their own free will or under duress, leaving wife and child helpless and without protection. Others instead were hiding out in the bushes and ventured home only at night by devious routes in order not to fall into the hands of the zealous conscriptors, who were hunting draft evaders everywhere. As a result of the iron belt of the blockade, the South was now entirely cut off from the world. Food supplies, items of clothing, even drugs were either not to be had at all or at best only at prices that were almost impossible. The fields had been tilled in a makeshift manner by women and children or were lying completely fallow. Mourning, worry, fear, or dire need—these had made themselves at home in every house.

Nor was the house of my parents spared by these ugly guests. My father, to be sure, was too old to be drafted, but since all his sons were in the field, he had been forced to lease his gin, mill, and farmland as well. My oldest brother, who already had a family of his own, had been taken prisoner at Vicksburg and was now waiting somewhere in Ohio to be released. My brother Otto was in winter quarters with Sibley's brigade in Louisiana and did not seem to have lost his good spirits. Brother Hugo was in a swampy camp on the Texas coast, and for months already our brother Adolph, dashing and always cheerful, had been sleeping the sleep of the dead on a Virginia battlefield. All that was known at the time was that the larger part of his regiment had been mowed down while storming the enemy position. His name was, however, not on the list of the fallen, and thus in their hearts our parents could still nourish the hope that he might have been captured, and they continued to hope for news of him. It never came, this news so eagerly awaited.[2] That was the darkest shadow hovering over my parents' house at the time. Our queer daredevil cousin—or rather Uncle Hermann—who, being a German subject, had joined the great war just for the fun of it, was at home recovering from a bullet through his cheek, a wound in his leg, and the hospital fare. He was already hobbling around rather nimbly on a crutch, entertaining everybody within reach with his war experiences, and when every once in a while a battle report arrived, he would complain loudly about not having been there.[3]

Whether joy or sorrow prevails in the hearts of men, whether tranquil peace or war and pestilence rule on earth—still, time moves uniformly and indifferently along its inexorable course. In the bloody war year of 1863, Christmas was drawing near, with its tidings of love and joy.

I first heard of the coming of Christmas on a rainy October day. I was at that time a towheaded little fellow of four, the pampered youngest child of the family. I was watching the passageway with curiosity as hams, sausages, and bacon, woolen stockings, shirts and underclothes, and—most welcome of all—enormous rolls of

2. Greater details on the brothers' war experiences are presented in the chapter above, "Childhood and Youth."

3. Hermann had traveled from Hamburg on the steamship Hammonia to New York, arriving in New York on August 9, 1859, so in 1863 he would not yet have been eligible for naturalization. At age twenty-eight he had enlisted together with Otto in the heavily German Company G, Fourth Texas Cavalry, in Sibley's brigade. Hermann was wounded at the battle of Val Verde, hospitalized, left behind, and taken prisoner before being exchanged in August 1862, and he was wounded again on June 28, 1863, at Donaldsonville, Louisiana. He never advanced beyond the rank of private.

tobacco were being carefully sewn into packages and labeled. "For Christmas for your brothers in the war!" was the answer to my question about the destination of all these fine things. "For Christmas!" These words were enough to awaken in my little head the slumbering memory of the splendors of the past Christmas. From now on I did nothing but pester my mother to tell me about Santa Claus and Christmas, and Little Red Riding Hood and Tom Thumb had lost all their attraction for me. My two sisters, who were then nine and eleven, exploited this opportunity for educational purposes by threatening their little brother, on occasions when he was misbehaving too much even for the youngest of the family, that he would be completely ignored by Santa Claus; or, when he was good, whispering to him about the wonderful things that Santa Claus carries in his sack for well-behaved children. Nor were their efforts entirely in vain, for I still remember how at this time I dedicated myself with great zeal and much success to my "chores," which, to be sure, consisting merely of hunting for pins and nails as well as pulling nails out of all old shingles and boards. Even Sally, the old black woman whom my father had bought less for the work she could perform than out of pity, stopped terrifying us with stories about witches and instead told us about the splendors of "Kismus" week, during which the slaves on most plantations were completely at liberty and all week long were allowed to live as if in a veritable fool's paradise.[4] Father and Mother, to be sure, looked forward to Christmas with apprehension and were racking their brains about how to manage, in such troubled times, not to deprive the children of the eagerly awaited Christmas celebration. Often my mother would stay up until long after midnight, ripping up old clothes in order to turn them into new ones.

During the week before the celebration all kinds of strange experiments were carried out in the kitchen; since I could not very well be banished from the kitchen, because of the prevailing wet weather, I

---

4. As noted elsewhere, there is no record that Trenckmanns ever owned any slaves, though they may have rented Sally. These "Christmas revels" were apparently ubiquitous across slaveholding America, and as Frederick Douglass acutely observed at a distance of several decades and hundreds of miles in 1833 Maryland, they were an effective tool of psychological manipulation. Michael Meyer, Frederick Douglass: The Narrative and Selected Writings (New York: Modern Library, 1984), 82–85.

was allowed to watch most of them. The problem was how to bake cookies for the Christmas tree without wheat flour, without raisins and almonds and all of the usual ingredients. And indeed, the baking was successfully accomplished with finely ground cornmeal and honey; instead of almonds and raisins, scalded peach kernels and shelled pecans were used for decoration. To us the cookies tasted splendid, but they had the disadvantage of being very brittle, and these little stars and animal figures soon fell from the tree. Concerning the candles for the tree, however, we were better off than we are today, for they were carefully molded of beeswax, and although they were not beautifully colored, like those we have now, they were all the more fragrant.

The day before Christmas brought a serious disturbance of our anticipation. Before daybreak my father was aroused from his sleep by the barking of dogs and anxious hallos. A boy brought him a message of such a serious nature that he rode off even before sunrise on his big trotting horse to Camp Groce near Hempstead.[5] My recollection is that it had something to do with getting a fellow countryman out of trouble—a man who had been captured by the conscriptors and was to be court-martialed. I don't know this for sure, and I can no longer find out anything about it, for of all those who were at my parents' house at the time, only old Sally is still alive, and she lost her memory years ago.

That evening my mother said, "If Father isn't back by tomorrow evening, then Santa Claus won't be coming either"—a terrible piece of news for us children.

The following morning rain was pouring down, and the dual concern about the arrival of my father and of Santa Claus increased from hour to hour. Whenever the rain stopped for a few minutes, I was certain to be found sitting on the tall gatepost keeping watch. Towards noon a norther came sweeping in, and the rain turned into sleet and snow; now I could stay at my post, where, to be sure, it soon became uncomfortably cool. It was probably three or four o'clock in the afternoon when my father finally came trotting along,

---

5. Camp Groce, more than twenty miles distant on the opposite side of the Brazos, was the site of a Confederate prisoner of war camp.

thoroughly frozen but in an extremely good mood, so his mission must have been successful. In his saddlebags he brought along a precious treasure: four pounds of real genuine coffee, which he had been able to buy in Hempstead for two shiny silver dollars a pound. These saddlebags also concealed something else, which we children were not permitted to see. Now everything was fine again, and two ragged, miserable-looking soldiers on leave, who shortly afterwards asked for something to eat, probably had not had such a hearty welcome for a long time or been shown such sumptuous hospitality.

Hardly had dusk arrived when the supper bell rang. I don't have much to report about the evening meal, since of course I was so excited that I couldn't get a bite down. This much I still recall, that on that evening, in honor of the event, instead of the usual prairie tea, coffee was drunk—not acorn, grain, or sweet-potato coffee, but coffee made from genuine, freshly roasted beans that had just been shipped in. The main attraction of the meal, however, was an enormous wild tom turkey, which our cousin had killed the day before from his bedroom window.

And now we still had to wait for a little while in the kitchen. Normally it was pleasant there by the flickering fire, the most beautiful place to listen to tales being told. But our impatience was too great for anything like that, and soon the three of us, my sisters and I, were standing on tiptoe at the planked door, trying hard to peek through the cracks, while old Sally, to no avail, warned us of the sin of improper curiosity. Finally, finally: the longed-for ringing of the bell from the main house! In the greatest hurry we dashed through the dark passageway; on the porch, which was slicked over with ice, all three of us lost our footing, and I hit my head against a post so hard that at any other time it would probably have produced a cry of pain. Alarmed by the enormous commotion, our parents quickly opened the door, helped us safely back onto our feet, and now we plunged breathlessly into the room. I for my part had eyes only for the Christmas tree for quite some time. It was a beautiful, slender young wild peach tree that reached to the ceiling. For decorations they had used red berries from the woods, the Christmas cookies that had been so laboriously produced, and nuts in little baskets of colored paper. There were also candy sticks on the tree, but they had been made of brown Louisiana sugar and were not much to look at, although they had a marvelous taste. But two gigantic golden-yellow oranges, which my father had brought back from his trip, were the most marvelous thing on the whole tree. All these splendors stood out all the more strikingly against the dark, shiny deep green of the wild peach tree in which the numerous candles were reflected. In the doorway to the room old Sally was standing, and by the windows Colonel Bouldin's slaves, staring goggle-eyed, their mouths wide open, at the tree and the German Christmas celebration.[6]

After my father, mother, and sisters had sung a Christmas song, everyone set out to inspect his share of gifts. My presents were stacked on a footstool under the tree, and I still see everything before me as if it were happening today. A straw hat, carefully woven of palmetto leaves by Grandmother Buntzel and with a wonderful red lining, as well as a new smock (back then boys were often still running around in little dresses until the age of eight) made of brown velvet with red dots—probably originating from someone's best dress—received no attention, although I later enjoyed them all the more.[7] But there were also real toys: a fence that could be taken apart and put together at will, which had been whittled from an old box with a pocket knife by black Henry—a big good-for-nothing, but the smartest of Bouldin's Negroes—and inside the enclosure there was a little sheep, which probably was left over from an old Noah's Ark, but which had been given a coat of real wool and decorated with a little ribbon around its neck.—If my boys get as much pleasure from the beautiful toys that Baby Jesus will bring them as I did from the little sheep, then I shall be well content.[8]

6. The reference is unclear. Colonel William Graves Bouldin died in 1857 at Chapel Hill, Washington County, and two of his sons were slaveowning farmers in the Travis community of Austin County in 1860. There were thirty black Bouldins in the 1870 census, all but one in the Industry–Cat Spring precinct, but none named Henry.

7. "Grandmother" Buntzel was only forty years old in the 1860 census, living a dozen families away from Trenckmanns.

8. In the German tradition it is the Christ Child rather than Santa Claus who brings Christmas presents. It is interesting to see this custom passed on into the second and third generations in America by a freethinker.

Of the presents to others I still remember that everybody got a new pair of shoes made by shoemaker Necker of leather tanned in Frelsburg.[9] Out of consideration I had been spared any such gift—indeed, even ten years later any kind of footwear was still an object of my profoundest scorn. My father found at his place a pair of leggings made of the indestructible cloth woven by our neighbor and a velvet nightcap; my sisters found earrings and new clothes. For the grownups, meanwhile, a punch had been prepared, about which I have nothing to report except that it made our cousin so jolly that he started dancing on his crutch and missed by a hair toppling over the tree that had been set up so carefully. When the wax candles had all gone out, the room was almost dark, for the lard-oil lamps and tallow candles produced only poor light, even though the latter had been placed in silver candlesticks in honor of the event. The grownups sat down around the table and told stories of times past in order to banish as much as possible any memory of the troubled present, and I fell asleep over my toys and lapsed blissfully into the golden sleep of childhood, waking up the next morning with the little sheep clutched firmly in my hand.

This is how Christmas was celebrated in my parents' house in the terrible year of 1863. I would not be without this memory for any price; if I should ever be tempted to deprive my children of some joy, this memory would be the most effective admonition to provide for them what my parents granted me and what nothing else in life can replace—a happy childhood.

9. Carl or Charles Neckar had been a shoemaker in Germany but a farmer in Texas. *Cat Spring Story*, 65–66. He was a neighbor of the Buengers in Industry. Frelsburg was twenty miles distant; having to obtain shoes from such a distance is an indication of wartime scarcity.

Trenckmann's 1907 A&M
Reminiscence

In comparison with the Paleozoic age and the time taken up in waiting for connections at Milano Junction, thirty years isn't so very long, but long enough to acquire considerable experience and an interesting family in passing through them. If the devoted student of the A. and M. of this day wishes to realize how far 1876 lies back, he has only to recall that when the doors of this, the first of all the state schools for higher education, were thrown open, deer in numbers still ran unmolested over the College prairies; that in the fall of 1876 the scream of the puma or Mexican lion frequently startled the sentries on the lower floor of the Main Building from their dreams "of pleasures that waited on life's merry morn," and an unlimited supply of "cush"; that baseball was then in its infancy in Texas, football had never been heard of, and no college yell had yet been composed.[1] Then will he realize that one who can talk of the early days from personal experience must be old enough to be a grandfather. If the mists of thirty years obscure the dark shadows and help to give a rosy hue to events that had a deeper tinge at their occurrence, so much the better, for, as I understand it, the *Long Horn* wants "reminiscences," and not a chronicle.

I am not sure whether it was on the last Saturday in September 1876, or the first Saturday in October, when, from a window of a

Originally published in the 1907 *Long Horn* (Texas A&M College yearbook), 112–13.
  1. "Cush" was Aggie argot for dessert.

Central passenger coach, the Main Building, the old Mess Hall, and a row of two-story brick houses erected to accommodate the professors and their families first loomed up before my expectant gaze. Passenger trains moved more slowly then, and the trip from Hempstead had seemed an age to my youthful imagination. No devoted crusader ever hailed the sight of the Holy City with greater joy than I felt when those buildings on the bald College prairie arose before me. Just then the vision was partly obscured by a phenomenon that, as far as my memory reaches back, had not been seen before in Texas. Great clouds of grasshoppers that had devoured the grain of Kansas, in their flight southward hid the bright autumn sun; they covered the track, the wheels were slipping, and the engineer had to throw wide open the throttle to keep the train in motion, and in a few minutes the College was left far behind and I had to disembark in Bryan. There I was told that the College wagon would probably come in soon.[2] But that wagon, drawn by a span of big mules, did not show up in Bryan till late on Sunday—it was the longest Sunday of all my life—to carry me and a load of groceries to the College. I got there all right, and half an hour later I was profoundly sorry for it and longed for nothing so much as for the old farm in Millheim and a stout hoe handle. Supper over, I found myself the center of attraction for some twenty young Texans, between fifteen and twenty-five, who had arrived during the preceding week, had witnessed the opening exercises, listened to noble oratorical effort by the great men of Texas, and then, to pass the time, set out to do a little hazing that would have made a West Pointer green with envy. That the long, lank, raw-boned youth from Austin County, who hadn't had a chance to speak English for months and years, formed an inviting subject for their efforts is easily understood. What happened that night in the Main Building to the latest arrival has, as I have been informed, furnished the theme for some excellent banquet stories, and I am not going to spoil them by giving my own recollections. Suffice it to say that I was "initiated" to the "queen's taste," and that, when I finally fell into a troubled sleep, my opinion of those fine young fellows who

2. There were numerous newspaper reports of grasshopper swarms in those weeks; for example, the *Victoria Advocate*, October 5, 1876, reported their arrival in Austin on September 29. College Station, about six miles south of downtown Bryan, did not have a railroad depot until 1883.

had greeted me so cordially had fallen to a zero point, and I had made up my mind to use the muscle acquired in exercises with maul and axe on anybody who might try to put me on guard duty again. But that never became necessary; it seems that I had not stood the test so badly, and next morning I was well acquainted and at home at the A. and M. College of Texas.

Monday morning, bright and early, we took possession of the Main Building, which was to be our dormitory. Matriculation over, roommates were selected, quarters chosen, an attempt at classification made, and "rules and regulations" read that sounded as severe as the code of Draco. In the afternoon Major Morrill [Morris], the commandant, gave us an insight into the military feature by drilling the awkward squad. The Major was martial from the word go. Although rather small in stature, his voice sounded clear across the campus, which at that time extended to the railroad tracks. The Major had evidently made up his mind that A. and M. cadets should soon set an example to those of his Alma Mater, the Virginia Military Institute. Setting-up exercises, marching single file with raw recruits who tread on each others' heels, etc., are not so very funny, as "Fish" of modern times will testify, but we had a good drillmaster, who soon brought order out of chaos.[3] My military career was destined to be brief, for the Major soon discovered in which direction my talents did not lie, and after I succeeded in leading the left wing of the battalion into a ditch at the Volkfest [*sic*] at Houston, in May 1877, I was made quartermaster and could watch the beautiful wheels and the soul-stirring bayonet exercises and artillery drills in which the Major delighted or go botanizing in the dewberry patches—side-tracked on the road to martial fame, and yet the envy of many.[4]

3. Robert Page Walter Morris (1853–1924), age twenty-three and only recently graduated, was the first commandant of the Corps of Cadets and designed its first set of regulations, of which there were 157 under the category of "Discipline." Draco was an Athenian lawgiver whose severe code inspired the term *draconian*. "Major" was an honorary rank that did not necessarily indicate military experience; "Fish" is the Aggie designation for freshman. John A. Adams, *Keeper of the Spirit: The Corps of Cadets at Texas A&M University, 1876–2001* (College Station: Texas A&M University Press, 2001), 11, 16–18.

4. This was a German Volksfest, further evidence of the general acceptance of German Texans. The *Galveston Daily News*, May 6, 1877, advertised the event on May 7–8 at the Houston Fairgrounds with a military parade.

The teachers make the school, so we must take a glance at the faculty which, however, deserves more than a glance, for it consisted of men not easily to be forgotten. At the head President Gathright, an intimate of the great leader of the "Lost Cause," a college man, and yet a soldier in his bearing, whose mien and voice called for unquestioning obedience.[5] Though past middle age, his temper was fiery, but he possessed, withal, a kind heart. In addition to these qualities he had a rich store of knowledge and a scorn of everything mean, untruthful, or ungentlemanly. Sometimes [he] erred, but when he did he made amends lavishly. Many of the lectures he delivered to the students in the old chapel (now Professor Giesecke's realm) have proven an inspiration to us all.[6] Their burden always was: "Whatever you be, whatever you do, be a man, be a gentleman." Dr. Martin, Doctor of Theology, and deeply versed in Latin and Greek, was chaplain and teacher of Science. His hair was gray, his honors and his years many, and he labored faithfully for our spiritual welfare. He tried his best to harmonize the views of a strict Presbyterian of the older days with the teaching of modern science; and if his instruction was mostly theory and no practice, it is to be remembered that such was the rule then, and that practically there were no appliances, no apparatus to work with. Some of his students in Chemistry, however, succeeded in making the section room, and even the entire Main Building, uninhabitable with sulphuretted hydrogen and chlorine gas on several occasions.

The chair of Modern Languages was held by Major Banks, big in body, big of heart, gentle and kindly, and ready to give help and fatherly advice to all.[7] It was a pleasure to know Major Banks, and

5. The reference is to Jefferson Davis, who was offered the college presidency and recommended fellow Mississippian Thomas Gathright instead.

6. Professor Frederick Ernest Giesecke (1869–1953), a Texas German with many parallels to Trenckmann, graduated first in his class and was immediately hired as an instructor at Texas A&M, where he had a distinguished career in engineering and architecture, designing and supervising the construction of a number of buildings on campus. *Handbook of Texas Online*, Linda Geren Nichols, "Giesecke, Frederick Ernest," accessed September 10, 2016, http://www.tshaonline.org/handbook/online/articles/fgi10, uploaded on June 15, 2010, modified on May 16, 2016, published by the Texas State Historical Association.

7. William A. Banks (1823–1902), a Virginia native, was a Confederate veteran and earned an A&M degree at Washington and Lee College. He had previously taught five

his memory will live until all the pioneer A. and M. cadets have answered the last roll call. If the younger generation of Texans in those days were considered rather uncouth, "wild and woolly," by the outside world, no better model could have been selected for us than Professor Hand, who occupied the chair of Ancient Languages, beside whom even Lord Chesterfield would have appeared a veritable boor. His politeness, however, was not only an outward gloss, but it came from a kind and generous soul.[8] Professor Alexander Hogg and Major R. P. W. Morris, whose spheres were Pure Mathematics and Applied Mathematics, respectively, alone of this first faculty are still in the land of the living, and I will spare their modesty by omitting the encomiums which they well deserve. Both are well known to the world; Professor Hogg as an ardent advocate of industrial progress, Major Morris by his participation in the political affairs of his native state.[9]

All were men of high standing in their chosen profession, perhaps the strongest and best informed that could have been selected in the Southland. The fact, however, that most of them before they came to Texas had been at the head of educational institutions, bore within it the seed of discord which, fortunately, did not germinate until after my time. Today a professor or an instructor at the A. and M. College must be a specialist in some particular line, always striving to excel in that line. Then it was different; for the school was an agricultural and technical training school in name only; it was a

---

languages at Saint John's College in Little Rock, Arkansas, before his first stint at Texas A&M. Thereafter he served ten years as Bryan school superintendent, returning to A&M in 1894. *Bryan Morning Eagle*, September 16, 1902.

8. Georgia native John T. Hand (1835–1907) was a graduate of Mercer University and taught for seventeen years in Tyler schools before his employment at Texas A&M, and he served as superintendent of the Brenham, Corsicana, and Dallas public schools thereafter.

9. Alexander Hogg (1830–1911), a Virginia native, later became superintendent of schools in Fort Worth. Besides teaching mathematics, Robert Page Walter Morris (1853–1924) was the first commandant of the Corps of Cadets. Although he returned to his native Virginia and ran unsuccessfully for Congress, his "participation in political affairs" was more successful in Duluth, Minnesota, where he moved in 1886 and which he represented in Congress for three terms as a Republican (1897–1903). "Morris, Robert Page Walter, (1853–1924)," Biographical Directory of the United States Congress, http://bioguide.congress.gov/scripts/biodisplay.pl?index=M000986.

literary institution mainly, and as such it soon took high rank, for certainly it could not have been the good looks and brass buttons of its students alone which within a single year made it the most popular school in Texas.

And now, as to the students. They had come from the farthest confines of Texas, east and west, north and south, and from many different walks of life. Some were the sons of lawyers, merchants, ministers, and teachers and had enjoyed the best training that our higher schools then afforded. Some were sons of farmers and ranchmen and more at home in the saddle than in a section room. Some were mere striplings, others well advanced in years and tried and tested in the storms of life. Take them all in all (pardon me if this sounds boastful), they were as fine an aggregation of young Texans as one might wish to see, though by no means inclined to grow pale and haggard with overmuch study. From week to week their number increased. Perhaps fifty went home on furlough in the first Christmas vacation. Seventy came back. At the beginning of the second term in February the number had increased to one hundred and thirty, and the upper stories of the Old Mess Hall had to be used as a dormitory. When the second session opened, we were literally "as thick as three in a bed," and in the crush and jam at the beginning of that session, trying to find a bunk for everyone, fitting two hundred and sixty cadets of all sizes and proportions into as many uniforms ordered without measurement. I learned that even a quartermaster's occupation wasn't altogether a sinecure. Wooden barracks were hastily erected, a big two-story box house, and in the upper story of this makeshift structure I roomed for a year with Captain Sleeper, whom I followed as a shadow.[10]

Early in the first session the Stephen F. Austin Literary Society was organized, and the debates and oratory made the "welkin ring" with the recital of patriotism and glory of Spartacus, Mark Anthony, and Patrick Henry. The Society grew and prospered, until out of prosperity arose jealousy, and finally secession. The Calliopean Society came

10. William M. Sleeper of Waco was elected president, and Trenckmann a vice president, when the Association of Ex-Cadets was organized in 1880. Sleeper was also the one friend Trenckmann mentions visiting before his intended departure for Australia in 1883.

into being, rivalry between the two societies was keen, and great were the joint debates at Commencement.[11]

The rapid increase in attendance brought with it other troubles than lack of room and overwork for the teachers. Many parents imagined that military discipline at the A. and M. would prove a cure-all for wayward sons, and many of the latter came with their minds set on getting just as much fun as possible out of their banishment. Major Morris and his successor, Captain Olmstead, of the United States Army, had their hands full in trying to control these young rebels.[12] Strict regulations only added zest to their violation, and stolen excursions at night were all the more delightful when all the floors were guarded by sentries with fixed bayonets. A lightning rod furnished the means of escape from the fourth stoop. Gambling and drinking cropped out, and it was only by the united efforts of the faculty and the more thoughtful students that a better spirit got the upper hand. The student officers, especially, were in a trying position, for young men who had not learned to respect parents or teachers at home were reluctant to obey orders from fellow students wearing the stripes of corporal, sergeant, or other officer. Finally, the precedent was set and the rule established that certain differences between officers and privates were not to be taken before the commandant, but must be settled according to the primitive method in an honest fistfight, and while this was not strictly military, results were quite satisfactory.

The "grub" question is likely to be an interesting one to students at all times, and I must say a few words about the Mess Hall. General H. P. Bee, the gallant soldier and dignified Southern gentleman, was in charge, and, if I mistake not, our young appetites came near bankrupting this generous man, who gave the best he had without carefully figuring out the profits. His noble wife appeared as an angel of mercy by her motherly visits to many a poor, lonesome cadet who

11. The second society was named after Calliope, the Greek muse of eloquence and epic poetry. Both societies were "exclusive and secretive," according to Adams, *Keepers of the Spirit*, 27.

12. New Jersey native George T. Olmstead Jr. (1841–1903) was an 1865 graduate of West Point and was assigned to serve as commandant of the Corps of Cadets and teach military science at Texas A&M from 1877 to 1881. He was working as a civil engineer in Saint Louis when he died.

lay in his room ill and homesick at the same time. After General Bee came Mr. Sbisa, and Sbisa it has been to this day.[13] That neither Bee nor Sbisa ever succeeded in satisfying all demands I need hardly tell, for college boys have always been "kickers," and probably will continue so to the end of time. Many were the mess hall rebellions and numerous squibs and innuendos directed at the mess hall fare in the *Collegian*.

In the line of amusements there was a little baseball, foraging expeditions into rural districts and surroundings on Saturdays, stag dances and debates on Saturday nights, now and then a concert or circus in Bryan, a fire alarm at night, the Commencement ball, and the never-to-be-forgotten April Fool's day. The long excursions on foot into the wildwoods of Brazos County, with a possum hunt and a chicken dinner as crowning the event, and the glorious comradeship which the very isolation of the school helped to develop, are to me cherished remembrances.

A thousand happenings, amusing or sad, and often a blending of fun and sadness, I can recall and might relate, and I believe that General Rogan wouldn't mind now if I told about that "kangaroo court," or about good old Dr. Martin granting full pardon to those who turned his shed bottom side up, long before he went to his last reward.[14] But I have already taken up too much space in telling of these old times to those who live in the new. May the dear old A. and M. prosper and expand in its great work for Texas!

W. A. Trenckmann, Class of 1879

13. Confederate General Hamilton P. Bee served the entire war in Texas and Louisiana and fled to Mexico for some years thereafter. He was succeeded in 1878 as mess hall steward by Czech immigrant Bernard Sbisa, who served until 1929 and gave his name to the campus dining hall in 1913. *Handbook of Texas Online*, Thomas W. Cutrer, "Bee, Hamilton Prioleau," accessed September 9, 2016, http://www.tshaonline.org/handbook/online/articles/fbe24, uploaded on June 12, 2010, modified on July 25, 2016, published by the Texas State Historical Association.

14. This is probably classmate Charles Rogan; why he is designated "General" is unclear, though he was heading the Texas General Land Office at the time. *Handbook of Texas Online*, William N. Todd IV and Gerald Knape, "Rogan, Charles," accessed July 24, 2016, http://www.tshaonline.org/handbook/online/articles/fr057, uploaded on June 15, 2010, published by the Texas State Historical Association.

Suggested Readings

Primary Sources

Bracht, Viktor. *Texas in 1848*. Translated by Charles Frank Schmidt. Introduction by Theodore G. Gish. Manchaca, Texas: German-Texan Heritage Society, 1991.

Cat Spring Agricultural Society. *A Century of Agricultural Progress, 1856–1956: Minutes of the Cat Spring Agricultural Society*. Cat Spring, Texas: Cat Spring Agricultural Society, 1956.

Dunt, Detlef. *Journey to Texas, 1833*. Translated by Anders Saustrop. Edited by James C. Kearney and Geier Bentzen. Austin: University of Texas Press, 2015.

Foster, L. L. *Forgotten Texas Census: First Annual Report of the Agricultural Bureau of the Department of Agriculture, Insurance, Statistics, and History, 1887–88*. Introduction by Barbara J. Rozek. Austin; Texas State Historical Association Press, 2001.

Goeth, Ottilie Fuchs. *Memoirs of a Texas Pioneer Grandmother (Was Grossmutter erzaehlt), 1805–1915*. Translation, research and additions by Irma Goeth Guenther. Burnet, Texas: Eakin Press, 1982.

Jordan, Gilbert John. *Yesterday in the Texas Hill Country*. College Station: Texas A&M University Press, 1979.

Olmsted, Frederick Law. *A Journey through Texas; or, A Saddle-Trip on the Southwestern Frontier*. Edited by Randolph B. Campbell. Dallas: DeGolyer Library and William P. Clements Center for Southwest Studies, Southern Methodist University, 2004.

Regenbrecht, Adalbert. "The German Settlers of Millheim (Texas) before the Civil War." *Southwestern Historical Quarterly* 20 (July 1916): 28–34.

Seele, Hermann. *The Diary of Hermann Seele and Seele's Sketches from Texas: Pioneer, Civic and Cultural Leader, German-Texan Writer*. Translation, introduction, and notes by Theodore Gish. Austin: German-Texan Heritage Society, 1995.

Secondary Sources

Barr, Alwyn. *Reconstruction to Reform: Texas Politics, 1876–1906*. Austin: University of Texas Press, 1971.

Biesele, Rudolph Leopold. *The History of German Settlements in Texas, 1831–1861*. Austin, Von Boeckmann-Jones, 1930.

Brown, Norman D. *Hood, Bonnet, and Little Brown Jug: Texas Politics, 1921–1928*. College Station: Texas A&M University Press, 1984.

Buenger, Walter L. *The Path to a Modern South: Northeast Texas between Reconstruction and the Great Depression*. Austin: University of Texas Press, 2001.

———. *Secession and the Union in Texas*. Austin: University of Texas Press, 1984.

Cat Spring Agricultural Society. *The Cat Spring Story*. San Antonio: Lone Star Printing, 1956.

Eby, Frederick. *The Development of Education in Texas*. New York: MacMillan, 1925.

Gould, Lewis L. *Progressives and Prohibitionists: Texas Democrats in the Wilson Era*. Austin: University of Texas Press, 1973.

Jordan, Terry G. *German Seed in Texas Soil: Immigrant Farmers in Nineteenth-Century Texas*. Austin: University of Texas Press, 1966.

———. "The German Settlement of Texas after 1865." *Southwestern Historical Quarterly* 73 (October 1969): 193–212.

Kamphoefner, Walter D. "The Handwriting on the Wall: The Klan, Language Issues, and Prohibition in the German Settlements of Eastern Texas." *Southwestern Historical Quarterly* 112 (2008): 52–66.

———. "New Americans or New Southerners? Unionist German Texans." In *Lone Star Unionism, Dissent, and Resistance: Other Sides of Civil War Texas*. Edited by J. F. de la Teja, 101–22. Norman: University of Oklahoma Press, 2016.

Kearney, James C. *Nassau Plantation: The Evolution of a Texas German Slave Plantation*. Denton: University of North Texas Press, 2010.

———. "European Immigrant History in the Nineteenth Century." In *Discovering Texas History*. Edited by Bruce A. Glasrud, Light Townsend Cummins, and Cary D. Wintz, 94–106. Norman: University of Oklahoma Press, 2014.

Kelley, Sean M. *Los Brazos de Dios: A Plantation Society in the Texas Borderlands, 1821–1865*. Baton Rouge: LSU Press, 2010.

McKay, Seth Shepard. *Texas Politics, 1906–1944: With Special Reference to the German Counties*. Lubbock: Texas Tech Press, 1952.

Sitton, Thad, and Dan K. Utley. *From Can See to Can't: Texas Cotton Farms on the Southern Prairie*. Austin: University of Texas Press, 1997.

Tippens, Matthew D. *Turning Germans into Texans: World War I and the Assimilation and Survival of German Culture in Texas*. Austin: Kleingarten Press, 2010.

Index

www.ingramcontent.com/pod-product-compliance
Lightning Source LLC
Chambersburg PA
CBHW072001260326
41914CB00004B/880